HISTORY OF THE CONFLICT BETWEEN RELIGION AND SCIENCE

By John William Draper

Table of Contents

PREFACE.

WHOEVER has had an opportunity of becoming acquainted with the mental condition of the intelligent classes in Europe and America, must have perceived that there is a great and rapidly-increasing departure from the public religious faith, and that, while among the more frank this divergence is not concealed, there is a far more extensive and far more dangerous secession, private and unacknowledged.

So wide-spread and so powerful is this secession, that it can neither be treated with contempt nor with punishment. It cannot be extinguished by derision, by vituperation, or by force. The time is rapidly approaching when it will give rise to serious political results.

Ecclesiastical spirit no longer inspires the policy of the world. Military fervor in behalf of faith has disappeared. Its only souvenirs are the marble effigies of crusading knights, reposing in the silent crypts of churches on their tombs.

That a crisis is impending is shown by the attitude of the great powers toward the papacy. The papacy represents the ideas and aspirations of two-thirds of the population of Europe. It insists on a political supremacy in accordance with its claims to a divine origin and mission, and a restoration of the mediaeval order of things, loudly declaring that it will accept no reconciliation with modern civilization.

The antagonism we thus witness between Religion and Science is the continuation of a struggle that commenced when Christianity began to attain political power. A divine revelation must necessarily be intolerant of contradiction; it must repudiate all improvement in itself, and view with disdain that arising from the progressive intellectual development of man. But our opinions on every subject are continually liable to modification, from the irresistible advance of human knowledge.

Can we exaggerate the importance of a contention in which every thoughtful person must take part whether he will or not? In a matter so solemn as that of religion, all men, whose temporal interests are not involved in existing institutions, earnestly desire to find the truth. They seek information as to the subjects in dispute, and as to the conduct of the disputants.

The history of Science is not a mere record of isolated discoveries; it is a narrative of the conflict of two contending powers, the expansive force of the human intellect on one side, and the compression arising from traditionary faith and human interests on the other.

No one has hitherto treated the subject from this point of view. Yet from this point it presents itself to us as a living issue—in fact, as the most important of all living issues.

A few years ago, it was the politic and therefore the proper course to abstain from all allusion to this controversy, and to keep it as far as possible in the background. The tranquillity of society depends so much on the stability of its religious convictions, that no one can be justified in wantonly disturbing them. But faith is in its nature unchangeable, stationary; Science is in its nature progressive; and eventually a divergence between them, impossible to conceal, must take place. It then becomes the duty of those whose lives have made them familiar with both modes of thought, to present modestly, but firmly, their views; to compare the antagonistic pretensions calmly, impartially, philosophically. History shows that, if this be not done, social misfortunes, disastrous and enduring, will ensue. When the old mythological religion of Europe broke down under the weight of its own inconsistencies, neither the Roman emperors nor the philosophers of those times did any thing adequate for the guidance of public opinion. They left religious affairs to take their chance, and accordingly those affairs fell into the hands of ignorant and infuriated ecclesiastics, parasites, eunuchs, and slaves.

The intellectual night which settled on Europe, in consequence of that great neglect of duty, is passing away; we live in the daybreak of better things. Society is anxiously expecting light, to see in what direction it is drifting. It plainly discerns that the track along which the voyage of civilization has thus far been made, has been left; and that a new departure, on all unknown sea, has been taken.

Though deeply impressed with such thoughts, I should not have presumed to write this book, or to intrude on the public the ideas it presents, had I not made the facts with which it deals a subject of long and earnest meditation. And I have gathered a strong incentive to undertake this duty from the circumstance that a "History of the Intellectual Development of Europe," published by me several years ago, which has passed through many editions in America, and has been reprinted in numerous European languages, English, French, German, Russian, Polish, Servian, etc., is everywhere received with favor.

In collecting and arranging the materials for the volumes I published under the title of "A History of the American Civil War," a work of very great labor, I had become accustomed to the comparison of conflicting statements, the adjustment of conflicting claims. The approval with which that book has been received by the American public, a critical judge of the events considered, has inspired me with additional confidence. I had also devoted much attention to the experimental investigation of natural phenomena, and had published many well-known memoirs on such subjects. And perhaps no one can give himself to these pursuits, and spend a large part of his life in the public teaching of science, without partaking of that love of impartiality and truth which Philosophy incites. She inspires us with a desire to dedicate our days to the good of our race, so that in the fading light of life's evening we may not, on looking back, be forced to acknowledge how unsubstantial and useless are the objects that we have pursued.

Though I have spared no pains in the composition of this book, I am very sensible how unequal it is to the subject, to do justice to which a knowledge of science, history, theology, politics, is required; every page should be alive with intelligence and glistening with facts. But then I have remembered that this is only as it were the preface, or forerunner, of a body of literature, which the events and wants of our times will call forth. We have come to the brink of a great intellectual change. Much of the frivolous reading of the present will be supplanted by a thoughtful and austere literature, vivified by endangered interests, and made fervid by ecclesiastical passion.

What I have sought to do is, to present a clear and impartial statement of the views and acts of the two contending parties. In one sense I have tried to identify myself with each, so as to comprehend thoroughly their motives; but in another and higher sense I have endeavored to stand aloof, and relate with impartiality their actions.

I therefore trust that those, who may be disposed to criticise this book, will bear in mind that its object is not to advocate the views and pretensions of either party, but to explain clearly, and without shrinking those of both. In the management of each chapter I have usually set forth the orthodox view first, and then followed it with that of its opponents.

In thus treating the subject it has not been necessary to pay much regard to more moderate or intermediate opinions, for, though they may be intrinsically of great value, in conflicts of this kind it is not with the moderates but with the extremists that the impartial reader is mainly concerned. Their movements determine the issue.

For this reason I have had little to say respecting the two great Christian confessions, the

Protestant and Greek Churches. As to the latter, it has never, since the restoration of science, arrayed itself in opposition to the advancement of knowledge. On the contrary, it has always met it with welcome. It has observed a reverential attitude to truth, from whatever quarter it might come. Recognizing the apparent discrepancies between its interpretations of revealed truth and the discoveries of science, it has always expected that satisfactory explanations and reconciliations would ensue, and in this it has not been disappointed. It would have been well for modern civilization if the Roman Church had done the same.

In speaking of Christianity, reference is generally made to the Roman Church, partly because its adherents compose the majority of Christendom, partly because its demands are the most pretentious, and partly because it has commonly sought to enforce those demands by the civil power. None of the Protestant Churches has ever occupied a position so imperious—none has ever had such wide-spread political influence. For the most part they have been averse to constraint, and except in very few instances their opposition has not passed beyond the exciting of theological odium.

As to Science, she has never sought to ally herself to civil power. She has never attempted to throw odium or inflict social ruin on any human being. She has never subjected any one to mental torment, physical torture, least of all to death, for the purpose of upholding or promoting her ideas. She presents herself unstained by cruelties and crimes. But in the Vatican —we have only to recall the Inquisition—the hands that are now raised in appeals to the Most Merciful are crimsoned. They have been steeped in blood!

There are two modes of historical composition, the artistic and the scientific. The former implies that men give origin to events; it therefore selects some prominent individual, pictures him under a fanciful form, and makes him the hero of a romance. The latter, insisting that human affairs present an unbroken chain, in which each fact is the offspring of some preceding fact, and the parent of some subsequent fact, declares that men do not control events, but that events control men. The former gives origin to compositions, which, however much they may interest or delight us, are but a grade above novels; the latter is austere, perhaps even repulsive, for it sternly impresses us with a conviction of the irresistible dominion of law, and the insignificance of human exertions. In a subject so solemn as that to which this book is devoted, the romantic and the popular are altogether out of place. He who presumes to treat of it must fix his eyes steadfastly on that chain of destiny which universal history displays; he must turn with disdain from the phantom impostures of pontiffs and statesmen and kings.

If any thing were needed to show us the untrustworthiness of artistic historical compositions, our personal experience would furnish it. How often do our most intimate friends fail to perceive the real motives of our every-day actions; how frequently they misinterpret our intentions! If this be the case in what is passing before our eyes, may we not be satisfied that it is impossible to comprehend justly the doings of persons who lived many years ago, and whom we have never seen.

In selecting and arranging the topics now to be presented, I have been guided in part by "the Confession" of the late Vatican Council, and in part by the order of events in history. Not without interest will the reader remark that the subjects offer themselves to us now as they did to the old philosophers of Greece. We still deal with the same questions about which they disputed. What is God? What is the soul? What is the world? How is it governed? Have we any standard or criterion of truth? And the thoughtful reader will earnestly ask, "Are our solutions of these problems any better than theirs?"

The general argument of this book, then, is as follows:

I first direct attention to the origin of modern science as distinguished from ancient, by depending on observation, experiment, and mathematical discussion, instead of mere speculation, and shall show that it was a consequence of the Macedonian campaigns, which brought Asia and Europe into contact. A brief sketch of those campaigns, and of the Museum of Alexandria, illustrates its character.

Then with brevity I recall the well-known origin of Christianity, and show its advance to the attainment of imperial power, the transformation it underwent by its incorporation with paganism, the existing religion of the Roman Empire. A clear conception of its incompatibility with science caused it to suppress forcibly the Schools of Alexandria. It was constrained to this by the political necessities of its position.

The parties to the conflict thus placed, I next relate the story of their first open struggle; it is the first or Southern Reformation. The point in dispute had respect to the nature of God. It involved the rise of Mohammedanism. Its result was, that much of Asia and Africa, with the historic cities Jerusalem, Alexandria, and Carthage, were wrenched from Christendom, and the doctrine of the Unity of God established in the larger portion of what had been the Roman Empire.

This political event was followed by the restoration of science, the establishment of colleges, schools, libraries, throughout the dominions of the Arabians. Those conquerors, pressing forward rapidly in their intellectual development, rejected the anthropomorphic ideas of the nature of God remaining in their popular belief, and accepted other more philosophical ones, akin to those that had long previously been attained to in India. The result of this was a second conflict, that respecting the nature of the soul. Under the designation of Averroism, there came into prominence the theories of Emanation and Absorption. At the close of the middle ages the Inquisition succeeded in excluding those doctrines from Europe, and now the Vatican Council has formally and solemnly anathematized them.

Meantime, through the cultivation of astronomy, geography, and other sciences, correct views had been gained as to the position and relations of the earth, and as to the structure of the world; and since Religion, resting itself on what was assumed to be the proper interpretation of the Scriptures, insisted that the earth is the central and most important part of the universe, a third conflict broke out. In this Galileo led the way on the part of Science. Its issue was the overthrow of the Church on the question in dispute. Subsequently a subordinate controversy arose respecting the age of the world, the Church insisting that it is only about six thousand years old. In this she was again overthrown The light of history and of science had been gradually spreading over Europe. In the sixteenth century the prestige of Roman Christianity was greatly diminished by the intellectual reverses it had experienced, and also by its political and moral condition. It was clearly seen by many pious men that Religion was not accountable for the false position in which she was found, but that the misfortune was directly traceable to the alliance she had of old contracted with Roman paganism. The obvious remedy, therefore, was a return to primitive purity. Thus arose the fourth conflict, known to us as the Reformation —the second or Northern Reformation. The special form it assumed was a contest respecting the standard or criterion of truth, whether it is to be found in the Church or in the Bible. The determination of this involved a settlement of the rights of reason, or intellectual freedom. Luther, who is the conspicuous man of the epoch, carried into effect his intention with no inconsiderable success; and at the close of the struggle it was found that Northern Europe was lost to Roman Christianity.

We are now in the midst of a controversy respecting the mode of government of the world, whether it be by incessant divine intervention, or by the operation of primordial and unchangeable law. The intellectual movement of Christendom has reached that point which Arabism had attained to in the tenth and eleventh centuries; and doctrines which were then discussed are presenting themselves again for review; such are those of Evolution, Creation, Development.

Offered under these general titles, I think it will be found that all the essential points of this great controversy are included. By grouping under these comprehensive heads the facts to be considered, and dealing with each group separately, we shall doubtless acquire clear views of their inter-connection and their historical succession.

I have treated of these conflicts as nearly as I conveniently could in their proper chronological order, and, for the sake of completeness, have added chapters on—

An examination of what Latin Christianity has done for modern civilization.

A corresponding examination of what Science has done.

The attitude of Roman Christianity in the impending conflict, as defined by the Vatican Council.

The attention of many truth-seeking persons has been so exclusively given to the details of sectarian dissensions, that the long strife, to the history of which these pages are devoted, is popularly but little known. Having tried to keep steadfastly in view the determination to write this work in an impartial spirit, to speak with respect of the contending parties, but never to conceal the truth, I commit it to the considerate judgment of the thoughtful reader.

JOHN WILLIAM DRAPER

UNIVERSITY, NEW YORK, December, 1873.

HISTORY OF THE CONFLICT BETWEEN RELIGION AND SCIENCE.

CHAPTER I.

THE ORIGIN OF SCIENCE.

Religious condition of the Greeks in the fourth century before Christ.—Their invasion of the Persian Empire brings them in contact with new aspects of Nature, and familiarizes them with new religious systems.—The military, engineering, and scientific activity, stimulated by the Macedonian campaigns, leads to the establishment in Alexandria of an institute, the Museum, for the cultivation of knowledge by experiment, observation, and mathematical discussion.—It is the origin of Science.

GREEK MYTHOLOGY. No spectacle can be presented to the thoughtful mind more solemn, more mournful, than that of the dying of an ancient religion, which in its day has given consolation to many generations of men.

Four centuries before the birth of Christ, Greece was fast outgrowing her ancient faith. Her philosophers, in their studies of the world, had been profoundly impressed with the contrast between the majesty of the operations of Nature and the worthlessness of the divinities of Olympus. Her historians, considering the orderly course of political affairs, the manifest uniformity in the acts of men, and that there was no event occurring before their eyes for which they could not find an obvious cause in some preceding event, began to suspect that the miracles and celestial interventions, with which the old annals were filled, were only fictions. They demanded, when the age of the supernatural had ceased, why oracles had become mute, and why there were now no more prodigies in the world.

Traditions, descending from immemorial antiquity, and formerly accepted by pious men as unquestionable truths, had filled the islands of the Mediterranean and the conterminous countries with supernatural wonders—enchantresses, sorcerers, giants, ogres, harpies, gorgons, centaurs, cyclops. The azure vault was the floor of heaven; there Zeus, surrounded by the gods with their wives and mistresses, held his court, engaged in pursuits like those of men, and not refraining from acts of human passion and crime.

A sea-coast broken by numerous indentations, an archipelago with some of the most lovely islands in the world, inspired the Greeks with a taste for maritime life, for geographical discovery, and colonization. Their ships wandered all over the Black and Mediterranean Seas. The time-honored wonders that had been glorified in the "Odyssey," and sacred in public faith, were found to have no existence. As a better knowledge of Nature was obtained, the sky was shown to be an illusion; it was discovered that there is no Olympus, nothing above but space and stars. With the vanishing of their habitation, the gods disappeared, both those of the Ionian type of Homer and those of the Doric of Hesiod.

EFFECTS OF DISCOVERY AND CRITICISM. But this did not take place without resistance. At first, the public, and particularly its religious portion, denounced the rising doubts as atheism. They despoiled some of the offenders of their goods, exiled others; some they put to death. They asserted that what had been believed by pious men in the old times, and had stood the test of ages, must necessarily be true. Then, as the opposing evidence became irresistible, they were content to admit that these marvels were allegories under which the wisdom of the ancients had concealed many sacred and mysterious things. They tried to reconcile, what now in their misgivings they feared might be myths, with their advancing intellectual state. But their efforts were in vain, for there are predestined phases through which on such an occasion public opinion must pass. What it has received with veneration it begins to doubt, then it offers new interpretations, then subsides into dissent, and ends with a rejection of the whole as a mere fable.

In their secession the philosophers and historians were followed by the poets. Euripides incurred the odium of heresy. Aeschylus narrowly escaped being stoned to death for blasphemy. But the frantic efforts of those who are interested in supporting delusions must always end in defeat. The demoralization resistlessly extended through every branch of literature, until at length it reached the common people.

THE PERSIAN EMPIRE. Greek philosophical criticism had lent its aid to Greek philosophical discovery in this destruction of the national faith. It sustained by many arguments the wide-spreading unbelief. It compared the doctrines of the different schools with each other, and showed from their contradictions that man has no criterion of truth; that, since his ideas of what is good and what is evil differ according to the country in which he lives, they can have no foundation in Nature, but must be altogether the result of education; that right and wrong are nothing more than fictions created by society for its own purposes. In Athens, some of the more advanced classes had reached such a pass that they not only denied the unseen, the supernatural, they even affirmed that the world is only a day-dream, a phantasm, and that nothing at all exists.

The topographical configuration of Greece gave an impress to her political condition. It divided her people into distinct communities having conflicting interests, and made them incapable of centralization. Incessant domestic wars between the rival states checked her advancement. She was poor, her leading men had become corrupt. They were ever ready to barter patriotic considerations for foreign gold, to sell themselves for Persian bribes. Possessing a perception of the beautiful as manifested in sculpture and architecture to a degree never attained elsewhere either before or since, Greece had lost a practical appreciation of the Good and the True.

While European Greece, full of ideas of liberty and independence, rejected the sovereignty of Persia, Asiatic Greece acknowledged it without reluctance. At that time the Persian Empire in territorial extent was equal to half of modern Europe. It touched the waters of the Mediterranean, the Aegean, the Black, the Caspian, the Indian, the Persian, the Red Seas. Through its territories there flowed six of the grandest rivers in the world—the Euphrates, the Tigris, the Indus, the Jaxartes, the Oxus, the Nile, each more than a thousand miles in length. Its surface reached from thirteen hundred feet below the sea-level to twenty thousand feet above. It yielded, therefore, every agricultural product. Its mineral wealth was boundless. It inherited the prestige of the Median, the Babylonian, the Assyrian, the Chaldean Empires, whose annals reached back through more than twenty centuries.

THE PERSIAN EMPIRE. Persia had always looked upon European Greece as politically insignificant, for it had scarcely half the territorial extent of one of her satrapies. Her expeditions for compelling its obedience had, however, taught her the military qualities of its people. In her forces were incorporated Greek mercenaries, esteemed the very best of her troops. She did not hesitate sometimes to give the command of her armies to Greek generals, of her fleets to Greek captains. In the political convulsions through which she had passed, Greek soldiers had often been used by her contending chiefs. These military operations were attended by a momentous result. They revealed, to the quick eye of these warlike mercenaries, the political weakness of the empire and the possibility of reaching its centre. After the death of Cyrus on the battle-field of Cunaxa, it was demonstrated, by the immortal retreat of the ten thousand under Xenophon, that a Greek army could force its way to and from the heart of Persia.

That reverence for the military abilities of Asiatic generals, so profoundly impressed on the Greeks by such engineering exploits as the bridging of the Hellespont, and the cutting of the isthmus at Mount Athos by Xerxes, had been obliterated at Salamis, Platea, Mycale. To plunder rich Persian provinces had become an irresistible temptation. Such was the expedition of Agesilaus, the Spartan king, whose brilliant successes were, however, checked by the Persian government resorting to its time-proved policy of bribing the neighbors of Sparta to attack her. "I have been conquered by thirty thousand Persian archers," bitterly exclaimed Agesilaus, as he re-embarked, alluding to the Persian coin, the Daric, which was stamped with the image of an archer.

THE INVASION OF PERSIA BY GREECE. At length Philip, the King of Macedon, projected a renewal of these attempts, under a far more formidable organization, and with a grander object. He managed to have himself appointed captain-general of all Greece not for the purpose of a mere foray into the Asiatic satrapies, but for the overthrow of the Persian dynasty in the very centre of its power. Assassinated while his preparations were incomplete, he was succeeded by his son Alexander, then a youth. A general assembly of Greeks at Corinth had unanimously elected him in his father's stead. There were some disturbances in Illyria; Alexander had to march his army as far north as the Danube to quell them. During his absence the Thebans with some others conspired against him. On his return he took Thebes by assault. He massacred six thousand of its inhabitants, sold thirty thousand for slaves, and utterly demolished the city. The military wisdom of this severity was apparent in his Asiatic campaign. He was not troubled by any revolt in his rear.

THE MACEDONIAN CAMPAIGN. In the spring B.C. 334 Alexander crossed the Hellespont into Asia. His army consisted of thirty-four thousand foot and four thousand horse. He had with him only seventy talents in money. He marched directly on the Persian army, which, vastly exceeding him in strength, was holding the line of the Granicus. He forced the passage of the river, routed the enemy, and the possession of all Asia Minor, with its treasures, was the fruit of the victory. The remainder of that year he spent in the military organization of the conquered provinces. Meantime Darius, the Persian king, had advanced an army of six hundred thousand men to prevent the passage of the Macedonians into Syria. In a battle that ensued among the mountain-defiles at Issus, the Persians were again overthrown. So great was the slaughter that Alexander, and Ptolemy, one of his generals, crossed over a ravine choked with dead bodies. It was estimated that the Persian loss was not less than ninety thousand foot and ten thousand horse. The royal pavilion fell into the conqueror's hands, and with it the wife and several of the children of Darius. Syria was thus added to the Greek conquests. In Damascus were found many of the concubines of Darius and his chief officers, together with a vast treasure.

Before venturing into the plains of Mesopotamia for the final struggle, Alexander, to secure his rear and preserve his communications with the sea, marched southward down the Mediterranean coast, reducing the cities in his way. In his speech before the council of war after Issus, he told his generals that they must not pursue Darius with Tyre unsubdued, and Persia in possession of Egypt and Cyprus, for, if Persia should regain her seaports, she would transfer the war into Greece, and that it was absolutely necessary for him to be sovereign at sea. With Cyprus and Egypt in his possession he felt no solicitude about Greece. The siege of Tyre cost him more than half a year. In revenge for this delay, he crucified, it is said, two thousand of his prisoners. Jerusalem voluntarily surrendered, and therefore was treated leniently: but the passage of the Macedonian army into Egypt being obstructed at Gaza, the Persian governor of which, Betis, made a most obstinate defense, that place, after a siege of two months, was carried by assault, ten thousand of its men were massacred, and the rest, with their wives and children, sold into slavery. Betis himself was dragged alive round the city at the chariot-wheels of the conqueror. There was now no further obstacle. The Egyptians, who detested the Persian rule, received their invader with open arms. He organized the country in his own interest, intrusting all its military commands to Macedonian officers, and leaving the civil government in the hands of native Egyptians.

CONQUEST OF EGYPT. While preparations for the final campaign were being made, he undertook a journey to the temple of Jupiter Ammon, which was situated in an oasis of the Libyan Desert, at a distance of two hundred miles. The oracle declared him to be a son of that god who, under the form of a serpent, had beguiled Olympias, his mother. Immaculate conceptions and celestial descents were so currently received in those days, that whoever had greatly distinguished himself in the affairs of men was thought to be of supernatural lineage. Even in Rome, centuries later, no one could with safety have denied that the city owed its founder, Romulus, to an accidental meeting of the god Mars with the virgin Rhea Sylvia, as she went with her pitcher for water to the spring. The Egyptian disciples of Plato would have looked with anger on those who rejected the legend that Perictione, the mother of that great philosopher, a pure virgin, had suffered an immaculate conception through the influences of Apollo, and that the god had declared to Ariston, to whom she was betrothed, the parentage of the child. When Alexander issued his letters, orders, and decrees, styling himself "King Alexander, the son of Jupiter Ammon," they came to the inhabitants of Egypt and Syria with an authority that now can hardly be realized. The free-thinking Greeks, however, put on such a supernatural pedigree its proper value. Olympias, who, of course, better than all others knew the facts of the case, used jestingly to say, that "she wished Alexander would cease from incessantly embroiling her with Jupiter's wife." Arrian, the historian of the Macedonian expedition, observes, "I cannot condemn him for endeavoring to draw his subjects into the belief of his divine origin, nor can I be induced to think it any great crime, for it is very reasonable to imagine that he intended no more by it than merely to procure the greater authority among his soldiers."

GREEK CONQUEST OF PERSIA. All things being thus secured in his rear, Alexander, having returned into Syria, directed the march of his army, now consisting of fifty thousand veterans, eastward. After crossing the Euphrates, he kept close to the Masian hills, to avoid the intense heat of the more southerly Mesopotamian plains; more abundant forage could also thus be procured for the cavalry. On the left bank of the Tigris, near Arbela, he encountered the great army of eleven hundred thousand men brought up by Darius from Babylon. The death of the Persian monarch, which soon followed the defeat he suffered, left the Macedonian general master of all the countries from the Danube to the Indus. Eventually he extended his conquest to the Ganges. The treasures he seized are almost beyond belief. At Susa alone he found—so Arrian says—fifty thousand talents in money.

EVENTS OF THE CAMPAIGNS. The modern military student cannot look upon these wonderful campaigns without admiration. The passage of the Hellespont; the forcing of the Granicus; the winter spent in a political organization of conquered Asia Minor; the march of the right wing and centre of the army along the Syrian Mediterranean coast; the engineering difficulties overcome at the siege of Tyre; the storming of Gaza; the isolation of Persia from Greece; the absolute exclusion of her navy from the Mediterranean; the check on all her attempts at intriguing with or bribing Athenians or Spartans, heretofore so often resorted to with success; the submission of Egypt; another winter spent in the political organization of that venerable country; the convergence of the whole army from the Black and Red Seas toward the nitre-covered plains of Mesopotamia in the ensuing spring; the passage of the Euphrates fringed with its weeping-willows at the broken bridge of Thapsacus; the crossing of the Tigris; the nocturnal reconnaissance before the great and memorable battle of Arbela; the oblique movement on the field; the piercing of the enemy's centre—a manoeuvre destined to be repeated many centuries subsequently at Austerlitz; the energetic pursuit of the Persian monarch; these are exploits not surpassed by any soldier of later times.

A prodigious stimulus was thus given to Greek intellectual activity. There were men who had marched with the Macedonian army from the Danube to the Nile, from the Nile to the Ganges. They had felt the hyperborean blasts of the countries beyond the Black Sea, the simooms and sand-tempests of the Egyptian deserts. They had seen the Pyramids which had already stood for twenty centuries, the hieroglyph-covered obelisks of Luxor, avenues of silent and mysterious sphinxes, colossi of monarchs who reigned in the morning of the world. In the halls of Esar-haddon they had stood before the thrones of grim old Assyrian kings, guarded by winged bulls. In Babylon there still remained its walls, once more than sixty miles in compass, and, after the ravages of three centuries and three conquerors, still more than eighty feet in height; there were still the ruins of the temple of cloud encompassed Bel, on its top was planted the observatory wherein the weird Chaldean astronomers had held nocturnal communion with the stars; still there were vestiges of the two palaces with their hanging gardens in which were great trees growing in mid-air, and the wreck of the hydraulic machinery that had supplied them with water from the river. Into the artificial lake with its vast apparatus of aqueducts and sluices the melted snows of the Armenian mountains found their way, and were confined in their course through the city by the embankments of the Euphrates. Most wonderful of all, perhaps, was the tunnel under the river-bed.

EFFECT ON THE GREEK ARMY. If Chaldea, Assyria, Babylon, presented stupendous and venerable antiquities reaching far back into the night of time, Persia was not without her wonders of a later date. The pillared halls of Persepolis were filled with miracles of art—carvings, sculptures, enamels, alabaster libraries, obelisks, sphinxes, colossal bulls. Ecbatana, the cool summer retreat of the Persian kings, was defended by seven encircling walls of hewn and polished blocks, the interior ones in succession of increasing height, and of different colors, in astrological accordance with the seven planets. The palace was roofed with silver tiles, its beams were plated with gold. At midnight, in its halls the sunlight was rivaled by many a row of naphtha cressets. A paradise—that luxury of the monarchs of the East—was planted in the midst of the city. The Persian Empire, from the Hellespont to the Indus, was truly the garden of the world.

EFFECTS ON THE GREEK ARMY. I have devoted a few pages to the story of these marvelous campaigns, for the military talent they fostered led to the establishment of the mathematical and practical schools of Alexandria, the true origin of science. We trace back all our exact knowledge to the Macedonian campaigns. Humboldt has well observed that an introduction to new and grand objects of Nature enlarges the human mind. The soldiers of Alexander and the hosts of his camp-followers encountered at every march unexpected and picturesque scenery. Of all men, the Greeks were the most observant, the most readily and profoundly impressed. Here there were interminable sandy plains, there mountains whose peaks were lost above the clouds. In the deserts were mirages, on the hill-sides shadows of fleeting clouds sweeping over the forests. They were in a land of amber-colored date-palms and cypresses, of tamarisks, green myrtles, and oleanders. At Arbela they had fought against Indian elephants; in the thickets of the Caspian they had roused from his lair the lurking royal tiger. They had seen animals which, compared with those of Europe, were not only strange, but colossal—the rhinoceros, the hippopotamus, the camel, the crocodiles of the Nile and the Ganges. They had encountered men of many complexions and many costumes: the swarthy Syrian, the olive-colored Persian, the black African. Even of Alexander himself it is related that on his death-bed he caused his admiral, Nearchus, to sit by his side, and found consolation in listening to the adventures of that sailor—the story of his voyage from the Indus up the Persian Gulf. The conqueror had seen with astonishment the ebbing and flowing of the tides. He had built ships for the exploration of the Caspian, supposing that it and the Black Sea might be gulfs of a great ocean, such as Nearchus had discovered the Persian and Red Seas to be. He had formed a resolution that his fleet should attempt the circumnavigation of Africa, and come into the Mediterranean through the Pillars of Hercules—a feat which, it was affirmed, had once been accomplished by the Pharaohs.

INTELLECTUAL CONDITION OF PERSIA. Not only her greatest soldiers, but also her greatest philosophers, found in the conquered empire much that might excite the admiration of Greece. Callisthenes obtained in Babylon a series of Chaldean astronomical observations ranging back through 1,903 years; these he sent to Aristotle. Perhaps, since they were on burnt bricks, duplicates of them may be recovered by modern research in the clay libraries of the Assyrian kings. Ptolemy, the Egyptian astronomer, possessed a Babylonian record of eclipses, going back 747 years before our era. Long-continued and close observations were necessary, before some of these astronomical results that have reached our times could have been ascertained. Thus the Babylonians had fixed the length of a tropical year within twenty-five seconds of the truth; their estimate of the sidereal year was barely two minutes in excess. They had detected the precession of the equinoxes. They knew the causes of eclipses, and, by the aid of their cycle called Saros, could predict them. Their estimate of the value of that cycle, which is more than 6,585 days, was within nineteen and a half minutes of the truth.

INTELLECTUAL CONDITION OF PERSIA. Such facts furnish incontrovertible proof of the patience and skill with which astronomy had been cultivated in Mesopotamia, and that, with very inadequate instrumental means, it had reached no inconsiderable perfection. These old observers had made a catalogue of the stars, had divided the zodiac into twelve signs; they had parted the day into twelve hours, the night into twelve. They had, as Aristotle says, for a long time devoted themselves to observations of star-occultations by the moon. They had correct views of the structure of the solar system, and knew the order of the emplacement of the planets. They constructed sundials, clepsydras, astrolabes, gnomons.

Not without interest do we still look on specimens of their method of printing. Upon a revolving roller they engraved, in cuneiform letters, their records, and, running this over plastic clay formed into blocks, produced ineffaceable proofs. From their tile-libraries we are still to reap a literary and historical harvest. They were not without some knowledge of optics. The convex lens found at Nimroud shows that they were not unacquainted with magnifying instruments. In arithmetic they had detected the value of position in the digits, though they missed the grand Indian invention of the cipher.

What a spectacle for the conquering Greeks, who, up to this time, had neither experimented nor observed! They had contented themselves with mere meditation and useless speculation.

ITS RELIGIOUS CONDITION. But Greek intellectual development, due thus in part to a more extended view of Nature, was powerfully aided by the knowledge then acquired of the religion of the conquered country. The idolatry of Greece had always been a horror to Persia, who, in her invasions, had never failed to destroy the temples and insult the fanes of the bestial gods. The impunity with which these sacrileges had been perpetrated had made a profound impression, and did no little to undermine Hellenic faith. But now the worshiper of the vile Olympian divinities, whose obscene lives must have been shocking to every pious man, was brought in contact with a grand, a solemn, a consistent religious system having its foundation on a philosophical basis. Persia, as is the case with all empires of long duration, had passed through many changes of religion. She had followed the Monotheism of Zoroaster; had then accepted Dualism, and exchanged that for Magianism. At the time of the Macedonian expedition, she recognized one universal Intelligence, the Creator, Preserver, and Governor of all things, the most holy essence of truth, the giver of all good. He was not to be represented by any image, or any graven form. And, since, in every thing here below, we see the resultant of two opposing forces, under him were two coequal and coeternal principles, represented by the imagery of Light and Darkness. These principles are in never-ending conflict. The world is their battle-ground, man is their prize.

In the old legends of Dualism, the Evil Spirit was said to have sent a serpent to ruin the paradise which the Good Spirit had made. These legends became known to the Jews during their Babylonian captivity.

The existence of a principle of evil is the necessary incident of the existence of a principle of good, as a shadow is the necessary incident of the presence of light. In this manner could be explained the occurrence of evil in a world, the maker and ruler of which is supremely good. Each of the personified principles of light and darkness, Ormuzd and Ahriman, had his subordinate angels, his counselors, his armies. It is the duty of a good man to cultivate truth, purity, and industry. He may look forward, when this life is over, to a life in another world, and trust to a resurrection of the body, the immortality of the soul, and a conscious future existence.

In the later years of the empire, the principles of Magianism had gradually prevailed more and more over those of Zoroaster. Magianism was essentially a worship of the elements. Of these, fire was considered as the most worthy representative of the Supreme Being. On altars erected, not in temples, but under the blue canopy of the sky, perpetual fires were kept burning, and the rising sun was regarded as the noblest object of human adoration. In the society of Asia, nothing is visible but the monarch; in the expanse of heaven, all objects vanish in presence of the sun.

DEATH OF ALEXANDER. Prematurely cut off in the midst of many great projects Alexander died at Babylon before he had completed his thirty-third year (B.C. 323). There was a suspicion that he had been poisoned. His temper had become so unbridled, his passion so ferocious, that his generals and even his intimate friends lived in continual dread. Clitus, one of the latter, he in a moment of fury had stabbed to the heart. Callisthenes, the intermedium between himself and Aristotle, he had caused to be hanged, or, as was positively asserted by some who knew the facts, had had him put upon the rack and then crucified. It may have been in self-defense that the conspirators resolved on his assassination. But surely it was a calumny to associate the name of Aristotle with this transaction. He would have rather borne the worst that Alexander could inflict, than have joined in the perpetration of so great a crime.

A scene of confusion and bloodshed lasting many years ensued, nor did it cease even after the Macedonian generals had divided the empire. Among its vicissitudes one incident mainly claims our attention. Ptolemy, who was a son of King Philip by Arsinoe, a beautiful concubine, and who in his boyhood had been driven into exile with Alexander, when they incurred their father's displeasure, who had been Alexander's comrade in many of his battles and all his campaigns, became governor and eventually king of Egypt.

FOUNDATION OF ALEXANDER. At the siege of Rhodes, Ptolemy had been of such signal service to its citizens that in gratitude they paid divine honors to him, and saluted him with the title of Soter (the Savior). By that designation—Ptolemy Soter—he is distinguished from succeeding kings of the Macedonian dynasty in Egypt.

He established his seat of government not in any of the old capitals of the country, but in Alexandria. At the time of the expedition to the temple of Jupiter Ammon, the Macedonian conqueror had caused the foundations of that city to be laid, foreseeing that it might be made the commercial entrepot between Asia and Europe. It is to be particularly remarked that not only did Alexander himself deport many Jews from Palestine to people the city, and not only did Ptolemy Soter bring one hundred thousand more after his siege of Jerusalem, but Philadelphus, his successor, redeemed from slavery one hundred and ninety-eight thousand of that people, paying their Egyptian owners a just money equivalent for each. To all these Jews the same privileges were accorded as to the Macedonians. In consequence of this considerate treatment, vast numbers of their compatriots and many Syrians voluntarily came into Egypt. To them the designation of Hellenistical Jews was given. In like manner, tempted by the benign government of Soter, multitudes of Greeks sought refuge in the country, and the invasions of Perdiccas and Antigonus showed that Greek soldiers would desert from other Macedonian generals to join is armies.

The population of Alexandria was therefore of three distinct nationalities: 1. Native Egyptians 2. Greeks; 3. Jews—a fact that has left an impress on the religious faith of modern Europe.

Greek architects and Greek engineers had made Alexandria the most beautiful city of the ancient world. They had filled it with magnificent palaces, temples, theatres. In its centre, at the intersection of its two grand avenues, which crossed each other at right angles, and in the midst of gardens, fountains, obelisks, stood the mausoleum, in which, embalmed after the manner of the Egyptians, rested the body of Alexander. In a funereal journey of two years it had been brought with great pomp from Babylon. At first the coffin was of pure gold, but this having led to a violation of the tomb, it was replaced by one of alabaster. But not these, not even the great light-house, Pharos, built of blocks of white marble and so high that the fire continually burning on its top could be seen many miles off at sea—the Pharos counted as one of the seven wonders of the world—it is not these magnificent achievements of architecture that arrest our attention; the true, the most glorious monument of the Macedonian kings of Egypt is the Museum. Its influences will last when even the Pyramids have passed away.

THE ALEXANDRIAN MUSEUM. The Alexandrian Museum was commenced by Ptolemy Soter, and was completed by his son Ptolemy Philadelphus. It was situated in the Bruchion, the aristocratic quarter of the city, adjoining the king's palace. Built of marble, it was surrounded with a piazza, in which the residents might walk and converse together. Its sculptured apartments contained the Philadelphian library, and were crowded with the choicest statues and pictures. This library eventually comprised four hundred thousand volumes. In the course of time, probably on account of inadequate accommodation for so many books, an additional library was established in the adjacent quarter Rhacotis, and placed in the Serapion or temple of Serapis. The number of volumes in this library, which was called the Daughter of that in the Museum, was eventually three hundred thousand. There were, therefore, seven hundred thousand volumes in these royal collections.

Alexandria was not merely the capital of Egypt, it was the intellectual metropolis of the world. Here it was truly said the Genius of the East met the Genius of the West, and this Paris of antiquity became a focus of fashionable dissipation and universal skepticism. In the allurements of its bewitching society even the Jews forgot their patriotism. They abandoned the language of their forefathers, and adopted Greek.

In the establishment of the Museum, Ptolemy Soter and his son Philadelphus had three objects in view: 1. The perpetuation of such knowledge as was then in the world; 2. Its increase; 3. Its diffusion.

1. For the perpetuation of knowledge. Orders were given to the chief librarian to buy at the king's expense whatever books he could. A body of transcribers was maintained in the Museum, whose duty it was to make correct copies of such works as their owners were not disposed to sell. Any books brought by foreigners into Egypt were taken at once to the Museum, and, when correct copies had been made, the transcript was given to the owner, and the original placed in the library. Often a very large pecuniary indemnity was paid. Thus it is said of Ptolemy Euergetes that, having obtained from Athens the works of Euripides, Sophocles, and Aeschylus, he sent to their owners transcripts, together with about fifteen thousand dollars, as an indemnity. On his return from the Syrian expedition he carried back in triumph all the Egyptian monuments from Ecbatana and Susa, which Cambyses and other invaders had removed from Egypt. These he replaced in their original seats, or added as adornments to his museums. When works were translated as well as transcribed, sums which we should consider as almost incredible were paid, as was the case with the Septuagint translation of the Bible, ordered by Ptolemy Philadelphus.

2. For the increase of knowledge. One of the chief objects of the Museum was that of serving as the home of a body of men who devoted themselves to study, and were lodged and maintained at the king's expense. Occasionally he himself sat at their table. Anecdotes connected with those festive occasions have descended to our times. In the original organization of the Museum the residents were divided into four faculties—literature; mathematics, astronomy, medicine. Minor branches were appropriately classified under one of these general heads; thus natural history was considered to be a branch of medicine. An officer of very great distinction presided over the establishment, and had general charge of its interests. Demetrius Phalareus, perhaps the most learned man of his age, who had been governor of Athens for many years, was the first so appointed. Under him was the librarian, an office sometimes held by men whose names have descended to our times, as Eratosthenes, and Apollonius Rhodius.

ORGANIZATION OF THE MUSEUM. In connection with the Museum were a botanical and a zoological garden. These gardens, as their names import, were for the purpose of facilitating the study of plants and animals. There was also an astronomical observatory containing armillary spheres, globes, solstitial and equatorial armils, astrolabes, parallactic rules, and other apparatus then in use, the graduation on the divided instruments being into degrees and sixths. On the floor of this observatory a meridian line was drawn. The want of correct means of measuring time and temperature was severely felt; the clepsydra of Ctesibius answered very imperfectly for the former, the hydrometer floating in a cup of water for the latter; it measured variations of temperature by variations of density. Philadelphus, who toward the close of his life was haunted with an intolerable dread of death, devoted much of his time to the discovery of an elixir. For such pursuits the Museum was provided with a chemical laboratory. In spite of the prejudices of the age, and especially in spite of Egyptian prejudices, there was in connection with the medical department an anatomical room for the dissection, not only of the dead, but actually of the living, who for crimes had been condemned.

3. For the diffusion of knowledge. In the Museum was given, by lectures, conversation, or other appropriate methods instruction in all the various departments of human knowledge. There flocked to this great intellectual centre, students from all countries. It is said that at one time not fewer than fourteen thousand were in attendance. Subsequently even the Christian church received from it some of the most eminent of its Fathers, as Clemens Alexandrinus, Origen, Athanasius.

The library in the Museum was burnt during the siege of Alexandria by Julius Caesar. To make amends for this great loss, that collected by Eumenes, King of Pergamus, was presented by Mark Antony to Queen Cleopatra. Originally it was founded as a rival to that of the Ptolemies. It was added to the collection in the Serapion.

SCIENTIFIC SCHOOL OF THE MUSEUM. It remains now to describe briefly the philosophical basis of the Museum, and some of its contributions to the stock of human knowledge.

In memory of the illustrious founder of this most noble institution—an institution which antiquity delighted to call "The divine school of Alexandria"—we must mention in the first rank his "History of the Campaigns of Alexander." Great as a soldier and as a sovereign, Ptolemy Soter added to his glory by being an author. Time, which has not been able to destroy the memory of our obligations to him, has dealt unjustly by his work. It is not now extant.

As might be expected from the friendship that existed between Alexander, Ptolemy, and Aristotle, the Aristotelian philosophy was the intellectual corner-stone on which the Museum rested. King Philip had committed the education of Alexander to Aristotle, and during the Persian campaigns the conqueror contributed materially, not only in money, but otherwise, toward the "Natural History" then in preparation.

The essential principle of the Aristotelian philosophy was, to rise from the study of particulars to a knowledge of general principles or universals, advancing to them by induction. The induction is the more certain as the facts on which it is based are more numerous; its correctness is established if it should enable us to predict other facts until then unknown. This system implies endless toil in the collection of facts, both by experiment and observation; it implies also a close meditation on them. It is, therefore, essentially a method of labor and of reason, not a method of imagination. The failures that Aristotle himself so often exhibits are no proof of its unreliability, but rather of its trustworthiness. They are failures arising from want of a sufficiency of facts.

ETHICAL SCHOOL OF THE MUSEUM. Some of the general results at which Aristotle arrived are very grand. Thus, he concluded that every thing is ready to burst into life, and that the various organic forms presented to us by Nature are those which existing conditions permit. Should the conditions change, the forms will also change. Hence there is an unbroken chain from the simple element through plants and animals up to man, the different groups merging by insensible shades into each other.

The inductive philosophy thus established by Aristotle is a method of great power. To it all the modern advances in science are due. In its most improved form it rises by inductions from phenomena to their causes, and then, imitating the method of the Academy, it descends by deductions from those causes to the detail of phenomena.

While thus the Scientific School of Alexandria was founded on the maxims of one great Athenian philosopher, the Ethical School was founded on the maxims of another, for Zeno, though a Cypriote or Phoenician, had for many years been established at Athens. His disciples took the name of Stoics. His doctrines long survived him, and, in times when there was no other consolation for man, offered a support in the hour of trial, and an unwavering guide in the vicissitudes of life, not only to illustrious Greeks, but also to many of the great philosophers, statesmen, generals, and emperors of Rome.

THE PRINCIPLES OF STOICISM. The aim of Zeno was, to furnish a guide for the daily practice of life, to make men virtuous. He insisted that education is the true foundation of virtue, for, if we know what is good, we shall incline to do it. We must trust to sense, to furnish the data of knowledge, and reason will suitably combine them. In this the affinity of Zeno to Aristotle is plainly seen. Every appetite, lust, desire, springs from imperfect knowledge. Our nature is imposed upon us by Fate, but we must learn to control our passions, and live free, intelligent, virtuous, in all things in accordance with reason. Our existence should be intellectual, we should survey with equanimity all pleasures and all pains. We should never forget that we are freemen, not the slaves of society. "I possess," said the Stoic, "a treasure which not all the world can rob me of—no one can deprive me of death." We should remember that Nature in her operations aims at the universal, and never spares individuals, but uses them as means for the accomplishment of her ends. It is, therefore, for us to submit to Destiny, cultivating, as the things necessary to virtue, knowledge, temperance, fortitude, justice. We must remember that every thing around us is in mutation; decay follows reproduction, and reproduction decay, and that it is useless to repine at death in a world where every thing is dying. As a cataract shows from year to year an invariable shape, though the water composing it is perpetually changing, so the aspect of Nature is nothing more than a flow of matter presenting an impermanent form. The universe, considered as a whole, is unchangeable. Nothing is eternal but space, atoms, force. The forms of Nature that we see are essentially transitory, they must all pass away.

STOICISM IN THE MUSEUM. We must bear in mind that the majority of men are imperfectly educated, and hence we must not needlessly offend the religious ideas of our age. It is enough for us ourselves to know that, though there is a Supreme Power, there is no Supreme Being. There is an invisible principle, but not a personal God, to whom it would be not so much blasphemy as absurdity to impute the form, the sentiments, the passions of man. All revelation is, necessarily, a mere fiction. That which men call chance is only the effect of an unknown cause. Even of chances there is a law. There is no such thing as Providence, for Nature proceeds under irresistible laws, and in this respect the universe is only a vast automatic engine. The vital force which pervades the world is what the illiterate call God. The modifications through which all things are running take place in an irresistible way, and hence it may be said that the progress of the world is, under Destiny, like a seed, it can evolve only in a predetermined mode.

The soul of man is a spark of the vital flame, the general vital principle. Like heat, it passes from one to another, and is finally reabsorbed or reunited in the universal principle from which it came. Hence we must not expect annihilation, but reunion; and, as the tired man looks forward to the insensibility of sleep, so the philosopher, weary of the world, should look forward to the tranquillity of extinction. Of these things, however, we should think doubtingly, since the mind can produce no certain knowledge from its internal resources alone. It is unphilosophical to inquire into first causes; we must deal only with phenomena. Above all, we must never forget that man cannot ascertain absolute truth, and that the final result of human inquiry into the matter is, that we are incapable of perfect knowledge; that, even if the truth be in our possession, we cannot be sure of it.

What, then, remains for us? Is it not this—the acquisition of knowledge, the cultivation of virtue and of friendship, the observance of faith and truth, an unrepining submission to whatever befalls us, a life led in accordance with reason?

PLATONISM IN THE MUSEUM. But, though the Alexandrian Museum was especially intended for the cultivation of the Aristotelian philosophy, it must not be supposed that other systems were excluded. Platonism was not only carried to its full development, but in the end it supplanted Peripateticism, and through the New Academy left a permanent impress on Christianity. The philosophical method of Plato was the inverse of that of Aristotle. Its starting-point was universals, the very existence of which was a matter of faith, and from these it descended to particulars, or details. Aristotle, on the contrary, rose from particulars to universals, advancing to them by inductions.

Plato, therefore, trusted to the imagination, Aristotle to reason. The former descended from the decomposition of a primitive idea into particulars, the latter united particulars into a general conception. Hence the method of Plato was capable of quickly producing what seemed to be splendid, though in reality unsubstantial results; that of Aristotle was more tardy in its operation, but much more solid. It implied endless labor in the collection of facts, a tedious resort to experiment and observation, the application of demonstration. The philosophy of Plato is a gorgeous castle in the air; that of Aristotle a solid structure, laboriously, and with many failures, founded on the solid rock.

An appeal to the imagination is much more alluring than the employment of reason. In the intellectual decline of Alexandria, indolent methods were preferred to laborious observation and severe mental exercise. The schools of Neo-Platonism were crowded with speculative mystics, such as Ammonius Saccas and Plotinus. These took the place of the severe geometers of the old Museum.

PHYSICAL SCIENCE IN THE MUSEUM. The Alexandrian school offers the first example of that system which, in the hands of modern physicists, has led to such wonderful results. It rejected imagination, and made its theories the expression of facts obtained by experiment and observation, aided by mathematical discussion. It enforced the principle that the true method of studying Nature is by experimental interrogation. The researches of Archimedes in specific gravity, and the works of Ptolemy on optics, resemble our present investigations in experimental philosophy, and stand in striking contrast with the speculative vagaries of the older writers. Laplace says that the only observation which the history of astronomy offers us, made by the Greeks before the school of Alexandria, is that of the summer solstice of the year B.C. 432. by Meton and Euctemon. We have, for the first time, in that school, a combined system of observations made with instruments for the measurement of angles, and calculated by trigonometrical methods. Astronomy then took a form which subsequent ages could only perfect.

It does not accord with the compass or the intention of this work to give a detailed account of the contributions of the Alexandrian Museum to the stock of human knowledge. It is sufficient that the reader should obtain a general impression of their character. For particulars, I may refer him to the sixth chapter of my "History of the Intellectual Development of Europe."

EUCLID—ARCHIMEDES. It has just been remarked that the Stoical philosophy doubted whether the mind can ascertain absolute truth. While Zeno was indulging in such doubts, Euclid was preparing his great work, destined to challenge contradiction from the whole human race. After more than twenty-two centuries it still survives, a model of accuracy, perspicuity, and a standard of exact demonstration. This great geometer not only wrote on other mathematical topics, such as Conic Sections and Prisms, but there are imputed to him treatises on Harmonics and Optics, the latter subject being discussed on the hypothesis of rays issuing from the eye to the object.

With the Alexandrian mathematicians and physicists must be classed Archimedes, though he eventually resided in Sicily. Among his mathematical works were two books on the Sphere and Cylinder, in which he gave the demonstration that the solid content of a sphere is two-thirds that of its circumscribing cylinder. So highly did he esteem this, that he directed the diagram to be engraved on his tombstone. He also treated of the quadrature of the circle and of the parabola; he wrote on Conoids and Spheroids, and on the spiral that bears his name, the genesis of which was suggested to him by his friend Conon the Alexandrian. As a mathematician, Europe produced no equal to him for nearly two thousand years. In physical science he laid the foundation of hydrostatics; invented a method for the determination of specific gravities; discussed the equilibrium of floating bodies; discovered the true theory of the lever, and invented a screw, which still bears his name, for raising the water of the Nile. To him also are to be attributed the endless screw, and a peculiar form of burning-mirror, by which, at the siege of Syracuse, it is said that he set the Roman fleet on fire.

ERATOSTHENES—APOLLONIUS—HIPPARCHUS. Eratosthenes, who at one time had charge of the library, was the author of many important works. Among them may be mentioned his determination of the interval between the tropics, and an attempt to ascertain the size of the earth. He considered the articulation and expansion of continents, the position of mountain-chains, the action of clouds, the geological submersion of lands, the elevation of ancient sea-beds, the opening of the Dardanelles and the straits of Gibraltar, and the relations of the Euxine Sea. He composed a complete system of the earth, in three books—physical, mathematical, historical—accompanied by a map of all the parts then known. It is only of late years that the fragments remaining of his "Chronicles of the Theban Kings" have been justly appreciated. For many centuries they were thrown into discredit by the authority of our existing absurd theological chronology.

It is unnecessary to adduce the arguments relied upon by the Alexandrians to prove the globular form of the earth. They had correct ideas respecting the doctrine of the sphere, its poles, axis, equator, arctic and antarctic circles, equinoctial points, solstices, the distribution of climates, etc. I cannot do more than merely allude to the treatises on Conic Sections and on Maxima and Minima by Apollonius, who is said to have been the first to introduce the words ellipse and hyperbola. In like manner I must pass the astronomical observations of Alistyllus and Timocharis. It was to those of the latter on Spica Virginis that Hipparchus was indebted for his great discovery of the precession of the eqninoxes. Hipparchus also determined the first inequality of the moon, the equation of the centre. He adopted the theory of epicycles and eccentrics, a geometrical conception for the purpose of resolving the apparent motions of the heavenly bodies on the principle of circular movement. He also undertook to make a catalogue of the stars by the method of alineations—that is, by indicating those that are in the same apparent straight line. The number of stars so catalogued was 1,080. If he thus attempted to depict the aspect of the sky, he endeavored to do the same for the surface of the earth, by marking the position of towns and other places by lines of latitude and longitude. He was the first to construct tables of the sun and moon.

THE SYNTAXIS OF PTOLEMY. In the midst of such a brilliant constellation of geometers, astronomers, physicists, conspicuously shines forth Ptolemy, the author of the great work, "Syntaxis," "a Treatise on the Mathematical Construction of the Heavens." It maintained its ground for nearly fifteen hundred years, and indeed was only displaced by the immortal "Principia" of Newton. It commences with the doctrine that the earth is globular and fixed in space, it describes the construction of a table of chords, and instruments for observing the solstices, it deduces the obliquity of the ecliptic, it finds terrestrial latitudes by the gnomon, describes climates, shows how ordinary may be converted into sidereal time, gives reasons for preferring the tropical to the sidereal year, furnishes the solar theory on the principle of the sun's orbit being a simple eccentric, explains the equation of time, advances to the discussion of the motions of the moon, treats of the first inequality, of her eclipses, and the motion of her nodes. It then gives Ptolemy's own great discovery—that which has made his name immortal—the discovery of the moon's evection or second inequality, reducing it to the epicyclic theory. It attempts the determination of the distances of the sun and moon from the earth—with, however, only partial success. It considers the precession of the equinoxes, the discovery of Hipparchus, the full period of which is twenty-five thousand years. It gives a catalogue of 1,022 stars, treats of the nature of the milky-way, and discusses in the most masterly manner the motions of the planets. This point constitutes another of Ptolemy's claims to scientific fame. His determination of the planetary orbits was accomplished by comparing his own observations with those of former astronomers, among them the observations of Timocharis on the planet Venus.

INVENTION OF THE STEAM-ENGINE. In the Museum of Alexandria, Ctesibius invented the fire-engine. His pupil, Hero, improved it by giving it two cylinders. There, too, the first steam-engine worked. This also was the invention of Hero, and was a reaction engine, on the principle of the eolipile. The silence of the halls of Serapis was broken by the water-clocks of Ctesibius and Apollonius, which drop by drop measured time. When the Roman calendar had fallen into such confusion that it had become absolutely necessary to rectify it, Julius Caesar brought Sosigenes the astronomer from Alexandria. By his advice the lunar year was abolished, the civil year regulated entirely by the sun, and the Julian calendar introduced.

The Macedonian rulers of Egypt have been blamed for the manner in which they dealt with the religious sentiment of their time. They prostituted it to the purpose of state-craft, finding in it a means of governing their lower classes. To the intelligent they gave philosophy.

POLICY OF THE PTOLEMIES. But doubtless they defended this policy by the experience gathered in those great campaigns which had made the Greeks the foremost nation of the world. They had seen the mythological conceptions of their ancestral country dwindle into fables; the wonders with which the old poets adorned the Mediterranean had been discovered to be baseless illusions. From Olympus its divinities had disappeared; indeed, Olympus itself had proved to be a phantom of the imagination. Hades had lost its terrors; no place could be found for it.

From the woods and grottoes and rivers of Asia Minor the local gods and goddesses had departed; even their devotees began to doubt whether they had ever been there. If still the Syrian damsels lamented, in their amorous ditties, the fate of Adonis, it was only as a recollection, not as a reality. Again and again had Persia changed her national faith. For the revelation of Zoroaster she had substituted Dualism; then under new political influences she had adopted Magianism. She had worshiped fire, and kept her altars burning on mountain-tops.

She had adored the sun. When Alexander came, she was fast falling into pantheism.

On a country to which in its political extremity the indigenous gods have been found unable to give any protection, a change of faith is impending. The venerable divinities of Egypt, to whose glory obelisks had been raised and temples dedicated, had again and again submitted to the sword of a foreign conqueror. In the land of the Pyramids, the Colossi, the Sphinx, the images of the gods had ceased to represent living realities. They had ceased to be objects of faith. Others of more recent birth were needful, and Serapis confronted Osiris. In the shops and streets of Alexandria there were thousands of Jews who had forgotten the God that had made his habitation behind the veil of the temple.

Tradition, revelation, time, all had lost their influence. The traditions of European mythology, the revelations of Asia, the time-consecrated dogmas of Egypt, all had passed or were fast passing away. And the Ptolemies recognized how ephemeral are forms of faith.

But the Ptolemies also recognized that there is something more durable than forms of faith, which, like the organic forms of geological ages, once gone, are clean gone forever, and have no restoration, no return. They recognized that within this world of transient delusions and unrealities there is a world of eternal truth.

That world is not to be discovered through the vain traditions that have brought down to us the opinions of men who lived in the morning of civilization, nor in the dreams of mystics who thought that they were inspired. It is to be discovered by the investigations of geometry, and by the practical interrogation of Nature. These confer on humanity solid, and innumerable, and inestimable blessings.

The day will never come when any one of the propositions of Euclid will be denied; no one henceforth will call in question the globular shape of the earth, as recognized by Eratosthenes; the world will not permit the great physical inventions and discoveries made in Alexandria and Syracuse to be forgotten. The names of Hipparchus, of Apollonius, of Ptolemy, of Archimedes, will be mentioned with reverence by men of every religious profession, as long as there are men to speak.

THE MUSEUM AND MODERN SCIENCE. The Museum of Alexandria was thus the birthplace of modern science. It is true that, long before its establishment, astronomical observations had been made in China and Mesopotamia; the mathematics also had been cultivated with a certain degree of success in India. But in none of these countries had investigation assumed a connected and consistent form; in none was physical experimentation resorted to. The characteristic feature of Alexandrian, as of modern science, is, that it did not restrict itself to observation, but relied on a practical interrogation of Nature.

CHAPTER II.

THE ORIGIN OF CHRISTIANITY.—ITS TRANSFORMATION ON ATTAINING IMPERIAL POWER.—ITS RELATIONS TO SCIENCE.

Religious condition of the Roman Republic.—The adoption of imperialism leads to monotheism.—Christianity spreads over the Roman Empire.—The circumstances under which it attained imperial power make its union with Paganism a political necessity.—Tertullian's description of its doctrines and practices.—Debasing effect of the policy of Constantine on it.—Its alliance with the civil power.—Its incompatibility with science.—Destruction of the Alexandrian Library and prohibition of philosophy.—Exposition of the Augustinian philosophy and Patristic science generally.—The Scriptures made the standard of science.

IN a political sense, Christianity is the bequest of the Roman Empire to the world.

At the epoch of the transition of Rome from the republican to the imperial form of government, all the independent nationalities around the Mediterranean Sea had been brought under the control of that central power. The conquest that had befallen them in succession had been by no means a disaster. The perpetual wars they had maintained with each other came to an end; the miseries their conflicts had engendered were exchanged for universal peace.

Not only as a token of the conquest she had made but also as a gratification to her pride, the conquering republic brought the gods of the vanquished peoples to Rome. With disdainful toleration, she permitted the worship of them all. That paramount authority exercised by each divinity in his original seat disappeared at once in the crowd of gods and goddesses among whom he had been brought. Already, as we have seen, through geographical discoveries and philosophical criticism, faith in the religion of the old days had been profoundly shaken. It was, by this policy of Rome, brought to an end.

MONOTHEISM IN THE ROMAN EMPIRE. The kings of all the conquered provinces had vanished; in their stead one emperor had come. The gods also had disappeared. Considering the connection which in all ages has existed between political and religious ideas, it was then not at all strange that polytheism should manifest a tendency to pass into monotheism. Accordingly, divine honors were paid at first to the deceased and at length to the living emperor.

The facility with which gods were thus called into existence had a powerful moral effect. The manufacture of a new one cast ridicule on the origin of the old Incarnation in the East and apotheosis in the West were fast filling Olympus with divinities. In the East, gods descended from heaven, and were made incarnate in men; in the West, men ascended from earth, and took their seat among the gods. It was not the importation of Greek skepticism that made Rome skeptical. The excesses of religion itself sapped the foundations of faith.

Not with equal rapidity did all classes of the population adopt monotheistic views. The merchants and lawyers and soldiers, who by the nature of their pursuits are more familiar with the vicissitudes of life, and have larger intellectual views, were the first to be affected, the land laborers and farmers the last.

THE RISE OF CHRISTIANITY When the empire in a military and political sense had reached its culmination, in a religious and social aspect it had attained its height of immorality. It had become thoroughly epicurean; its maxim was, that life should be made a feast, that virtue is only the seasoning of pleasure, and temperance the means of prolonging it. Dining-rooms glittering with gold and incrusted with gems, slaves in superb apparel, the fascinations of female society where all the women were dissolute, magnificent baths, theatres, gladiators, such were the objects of Roman desire. The conquerors of the world had discovered that the only thing worth worshiping is Force. By it all things might be secured, all that toil and trade had laboriously obtained. The confiscation of goods and lands, the taxation of provinces, were the reward of successful warfare; and the emperor was the symbol of force. There was a social splendor, but it was the phosphorescent corruption of the ancient Mediterranean world.

In one of the Eastern provinces, Syria, some persons in very humble life had associated themselves together for benevolent and religious purposes. The doctrines they held were in harmony with that sentiment of universal brotherhood arising from the coalescence of the conquered kingdoms. They were doctrines inculcated by Jesus.

The Jewish people at that time entertained a belief, founded on old traditions, that a deliverer would arise among them, who would restore them to their ancient splendor. The disciples of Jesus regarded him as this long-expected Messiah. But the priesthood, believing that the doctrines he taught were prejudicial to their interests, denounced him to the Roman governor, who, to satisfy their clamors, reluctantly delivered him over to death.

His doctrines of benevolence and human brotherhood outlasted that event. The disciples, instead of scattering, organized. They associated themselves on a principle of communism, each throwing into the common stock whatever property he possessed, and all his gains. The widows and orphans of the community were thus supported, the poor and the sick sustained. From this germ was developed a new, and as the events proved, all-powerful society—the Church; new, for nothing of the kind had existed in antiquity; powerful, for the local churches, at first isolated, soon began to confederate for their common interest. Through this organization Christianity achieved all her political triumphs.

As we have said, the military domination of Rome had brought about universal peace, and had generated a sentiment of brotherhood among the vanquished nations. Things were, therefore, propitious for the rapid diffusion of the newly-established—the Christian—principle throughout the empire. It spread from Syria through all Asia Minor, and successively reached Cyprus, Greece, Italy, eventually extending westward as far as Gaul and Britain.

Its propagation was hastened by missionaries who made it known in all directions. None of the ancient classical philosophies had ever taken advantage of such a means.

Political conditions determined the boundaries of the new religion. Its limits were eventually those of the Roman Empire; Rome, doubtfully the place of death of Peter, not Jerusalem, indisputably the place of the death of our Savior, became the religious capital. It was better to have possession of the imperial seven hilled city, than of Gethsemane and Calvary with all their holy souvenirs.

IT GATHERS POLITICAL POWER. For many years Christianity manifested itself as a system enjoining three things—toward God veneration, in personal life purity, in social life benevolence. In its early days of feebleness it made proselytes only by persuasion, but, as it increased in numbers and influence, it began to exhibit political tendencies, a disposition to form a government within the government, an empire within the empire. These tendencies it has never since lost. They are, in truth, the logical result of its development. The Roman emperors, discovering that it was absolutely incompatible with the imperial system, tried to put it down by force. This was in accordance with the spirit of their military maxims, which had no other means but force for the establishment of conformity.

In the winter A.D. 302-'3, the Christian soldiers in some of the legions refused to join in the time-honored solemnities for propitiating the gods. The mutiny spread so quickly, the emergency became so pressing, that the Emperor Diocletian was compelled to hold a council for the purpose of determining what should be done. The difficulty of the position may perhaps be appreciated when it is understood that the wife and the daughter of Diocletian himself were Christians. He was a man of great capacity and large political views; he recognized in the opposition that must be made to the new party a political necessity, yet he expressly enjoined that there should be no bloodshed. But who can control an infuriated civil commotion? The church of Nicomedia was razed to the ground; in retaliation the imperial palace was set on fire, an edict was openly insulted and torn down. The Christian officers in the army were cashiered; in all directions, martyrdoms and massacres were taking place. So resistless was the march of events, that not even the emperor himself could stop the persecution.

THE FIRST CHRISTIAN EMPEROR. It had now become evident that the Christians constituted a powerful party in the state, animated with indignation at the atrocities they had suffered, and determined to endure them no longer. After the abdication of Diocletian (A.D. 305), Constantine, one of the competitors for the purple, perceiving the advantages that would accrue to him from such a policy, put himself forth as the head of the Christian party. This gave him, in every part of the empire, men and women ready to encounter fire and sword in his behalf; it gave him unwavering adherents in every legion of the armies. In a decisive battle, near the Milvian bridge, victory crowned his schemes. The death of Maximin, and subsequently that of Licinius, removed all obstacles. He ascended the throne of the Caesars—the first Christian emperor.

Place, profit, power—these were in view of whoever now joined the conquering sect. Crowds of worldly persons, who cared nothing about its religious ideas, became its warmest supporters. Pagans at heart, their influence was soon manifested in the paganization of Christianity that forthwith ensued. The emperor, no better than they, did nothing to check their proceedings. But he did not personally conform to the ceremonial requirements of the Church until the close of his evil life, A.D. 337.

TERTULLIAN'S EXPOSITION OF CHRISTIANITY. That we may clearly appreciate the modifications now impressed on Christianity—modifications which eventually brought it in conflict with science—we must have, as a means of comparison, a statement of what it was in its purer days. Such, fortunately, we find in the "Apology or Defense of the Christians against the Accusations of the Gentiles," written by Tertullian, at Rome, during the persecution of Severus. He addressed it, not to the emperor, but to the magistrates who sat in judgment on the accused. It is a solemn and most earnest expostulation, setting forth all that could be said in explanation of the subject, a representation of the belief and cause of the Christians made in the imperial city in the face of the whole world, not a querulous or passionate ecclesiastical appeal, but a grave historical document. It has ever been looked upon as one of the ablest of the early Christian works. Its date is about A.D. 200.

With no inconsiderable skill Tertullian opens his argument. He tells the magistrates that Christianity is a stranger upon earth, and that she expects to meet with enemies in a country which is not her own. She only asks that she may not be condemned unheard, and that Roman magistrates will permit her to defend herself; that the laws of the empire will gather lustre, if judgment be passed upon her after she has been tried but not if she is sentenced without a hearing of her cause; that it is unjust to hate a thing of which we are ignorant, even though it may be a thing worthy of hate; that the laws of Rome deal with actions, not with mere names; but that, notwithstanding this, persons have been punished because they were called Christians, and that without any accusation of crime.

He then advances to an exposition of the origin, the nature, and the effects of Christianity, stating that it is founded on the Hebrew Scriptures, which are the most venerable of all books. He says to the magistrates: "The books of Moses, in which God has inclosed, as in a treasure, all the religion of the Jews, and consequently all the Christian religion, reach far beyond the oldest you have, even beyond all your public monuments, the establishment of your state, the foundation of many great cities—all that is most advanced by you in all ages of history, and memory of times; the invention of letters, which are the interpreters of sciences and the guardians of all excellent things. I think I may say more—beyond your gods, your temples, your oracles and sacrifices. The author of those books lived a thousand years before the siege of Troy, and more than fifteen hundred before Homer." Time is the ally of truth, and wise men believe nothing but what is certain, and what has been verified by time. The principal authority of these Scriptures is derived from their venerable antiquity. The most learned of the Ptolemies, who was surnamed Philadelphus, an accomplished prince, by the advice of Demetrius Phalareus, obtained a copy of these holy books. It may be found at this day in his library. The divinity of these Scriptures is proved by this, that all that is done in our days may be found predicted in them; they contain all that has since passed in the view of men.

Is not the accomplishment of a prophecy a testimony to its truth? Seeing that events which are past have vindicated these prophecies, shall we be blamed for trusting them in events that are to come? Now, as we believe things that have been prophesied and have come to pass, so we believe things that have been told us, but not yet come to pass, because they have all been foretold by the same Scriptures, as well those that are verified every day as those that still remain to be fulfilled.

These Holy Scriptures teach us that there is one God, who made the world out of nothing, who, though daily seen, is invisible; his infiniteness is known only to himself; his immensity conceals, but at the same time discovers him. He has ordained for men, according to their lives, rewards and punishments; he will raise all the dead that have ever lived from the creation of the world, will command them to reassume their bodies, and thereupon adjudge them to felicity that has so end, or to eternal flames. The fires of hell are those hidden flames which the earth shuts up in her bosom. He has in past times sent into the world preachers or prophets. The prophets of those old times were Jews; they addressed their oracles, for such they were, to the Jews, who have stored them up in the Scriptures. On them, as has been said, Christianity is founded, though the Christian differs in his ceremonies from the Jew. We are accused of worshiping a man, and not the God of the Jews. Not so. The honor we bear to Christ does not derogate from the honor we bear to God.

On account of the merit of these ancient patriarchs, the Jews were the only beloved people of God; he delighted to be in communication with them by his own mouth. By him they were raised to admirable greatness. But with perversity they wickedly ceased to regard him; they changed his laws into a profane worship. He warned them that he would take to himself servants more faithful than they, and, for their crime, punished them by driving them forth from their country. They are now spread all over the world; they wander in all parts; they cannot enjoy the air they breathed at their birth; they have neither man nor God for their king. As he threatened them, so he has done. He has taken, in all nations and countries of the earth, people more faithful than they. Through his prophets he had declared that these should have greater favors, and that a Messiah should come, to publish a new law among them. This Messiah was Jesus, who is also God. For God may be derived from God, as the light of a candle may be derived from the light of another candle. God and his Son are the self-same God—a light is the same light as that from which it was taken.

The Scriptures make known two comings of the Son of God; the first in humility, the second at the day of judgment, in power. The Jews might have known all this from the prophets, but their sins have so blinded them that they did not recognize him at his first coming, and are still vainly expecting him. They believed that all the miracles wrought by him were the work of magic. The doctors of the law and the chief priests were envious of him; they denounced him to Pilate. He was crucified, died, was buried, and after three days rose again. For forty days he remained among his disciples. Then he was environed in a cloud, and rose up to heaven—a truth far more certain than any human testimonies touching the ascension of Romulus or of any other Roman prince mounting up to the same place.

Tertullian then describes the origin and nature of devils, who, under Satan, their prince, produce diseases, irregularities of the air, plagues, and the blighting of the blossoms of the earth, who seduce men to offer sacrifices, that they may have the blood of the victims, which is their food. They are as nimble as the birds, and hence know every thing that is passing upon earth; they live in the air, and hence can spy what is going on in heaven; for this reason they can impose on men reigned prophecies, and deliver oracles. Thus they announced in Rome that a victory would be obtained over King Perseus, when in truth they knew that the battle was already won. They falsely cure diseases; for, taking possession of the body of a man, they produce in him a distemper, and then ordaining some remedy to be used, they cease to afflict him, and men think that a cure has taken place.

Though Christians deny that the emperor is a god, they nevertheless pray for his prosperity, because the general dissolution that threatens the universe, the conflagration of the world, is retarded so long as the glorious majesty of the triumphant Roman Empire shall last. They desire not to be present at the subversion of all Nature. They acknowledge only one republic, but it is the whole world; they constitute one body, worship one God, and all look forward to eternal happiness. Not only do they pray for the emperor and the magistrates, but also for peace. They read the Scriptures to nourish their faith, lift up their hope, and strengthen the confidence they have in God. They assemble to exhort one another; they remove sinners from their societies; they have bishops who preside over them, approved by the suffrages of those whom they are to conduct. At the end of each month every one contributes if he will, but no one is constrained to give; the money gathered in this manner is the pledge of piety; it is not consumed in eating and drinking, but in feeding the poor, and burying them, in comforting children that are destitute of parents and goods, in helping old men who have spent the best of their days in the service of the faithful, in assisting those who have lost by shipwreck what they had, and those who are condemned to the mines, or have been banished to islands, or shut up in prisons, because they professed the religion of the true God. There is but one thing that Christians have not in common, and that one thing is their wives. They do not feast as if they should die to-morrow, nor build as if they should never die. The objects of their life are innocence, justice, patience, temperance, chastity.

To this noble exposition of Christian belief and life in his day, Tertullian does not hesitate to add an ominous warning to the magistrates he is addressing—ominous, for it was a forecast of a great event soon to come to pass: "Our origin is but recent, yet already we fill all that your power acknowledges—cities, fortresses, islands, provinces, the assemblies of the people, the wards of Rome, the palace, the senate, the public places, and especially the armies. We have left you nothing but your temples. Reflect what wars we are able to undertake! With what promptitude might we not arm ourselves were we not restrained by our religion, which teaches us that it is better to be killed than to kill!"

Before he closes his defense, Tertullian renews an assertion which, carried into practice, as it subsequently was, affected the intellectual development of all Europe. He declares that the Holy Scriptures are a treasure from which all the true wisdom in the world has been drawn; that every philosopher and every poet is indebted to them. He labors to show that they are the standard and measure of all truth, and that whatever is inconsistent with them must necessarily be false.

From Tertullian's able work we see what Christianity was while it was suffering persecution and struggling for existence. We have now to see what it became when in possession of imperial power. Great is the difference between Christianity under Severus and Christianity after Constantine. Many of the doctrines which at the latter period were preeminent, in the former were unknown.

PAGANIZATION OF CHRISTIANITY. Two causes led to the amalgamation of Christianity with paganism: 1. The political necessities of the new dynasty; 2. The policy adopted by the new religion to insure its spread.

1. Though the Christian party had proved itself sufficiently strong to give a master to the empire, it was never sufficiently strong to destroy its antagonist, paganism. The issue of the struggle between them was an amalgamation of the principles of both. In this, Christianity differed from Mohammedanism, which absolutely annihilated its antagonist, and spread its own doctrines without adulteration.

Constantine continually showed by his acts that he felt he must be the impartial sovereign of all his people, not merely the representative of a successful faction. Hence, if he built Christian churches, he also restored pagan temples; if he listened to the clergy, he also consulted the haruspices; if he summoned the Council of Nicea, he also honored the statue of Fortune; if he accepted the rite of baptism, he also struck a medal bearing his title of "God." His statue, on the top of the great porphyry pillar at Constantinople, consisted of an ancient image of Apollo, whose features were replaced by those of the emperor, and its head surrounded by the nails feigned to have been used at the crucifixion of Christ, arranged so as to form a crown of glory.

Feeling that there must be concessions to the defeated pagan party, in accordance with its ideas, he looked with favor on the idolatrous movements of his court. In fact, the leaders of these movements were persons of his own family.

CHRISTIANITY UNDER CONSTANTINE. 2. To the emperor—a mere worldling—a man without any religious convictions, doubtless it appeared best for himself, best for the empire, and best for the contending parties, Christian and pagan, to promote their union or amalgamation as much as possible. Even sincere Christians do not seem to have been averse to this; perhaps they believed that the new doctrines would diffuse most thoroughly by incorporating in themselves ideas borrowed from the old, that Truth would assert her self in the end, and the impurity be cast off. In accomplishing this amalgamation, Helena, the empress-mother, aided by the court ladies, led the way. For her gratification there were discovered, in a cavern at Jerusalem, wherein they had lain buried for more than three centuries, the Savior's cross, and those of the two thieves, the inscription, and the nails that had been used. They were identified by miracle. A true relic-worship set in. The superstition of the old Greek times reappeared; the times when the tools with which the Trojan horse was made might still be seen at Metapontum, the sceptre of Pelops at Chaeroneia, the spear of Achilles at Phaselis, the sword of Memnon at Nicomedia, when the Tegeates could show the hide of the Calydonian boar and very many cities boasted their possession of the true palladium of Troy; when there were statues of Minerva that could brandish spears, paintings that could blush, images that could sweat, and endless shrines and sanctuaries at which miracle-cures could be performed.

As years passed on, the faith described by Tertullian was transmuted into one more fashionable and more debased. It was incorporated with the old Greek mythology. Olympus was restored, but the divinities passed under other names. The more powerful provinces insisted on the adoption of their time-honored conceptions. Views of the Trinity, in accordance with Egyptian traditions, were established. Not only was the adoration of Isis under a new name restored, but even her image, standing on the crescent moon, reappeared. The well-known effigy of that goddess, with the infant Horus in her arms, has descended to our days in the beautiful, artistic creations of the Madonna and Child. Such restorations of old conceptions under novel forms were everywhere received with delight. When it was announced to the Ephesians that the Council of that place, headed by Cyril, had decreed that the Virgin should be called "the Mother of God," with tears of joy they embraced the knees of their bishop; it was the old instinct peeping out; their ancestors would have done the same for Diana.

This attempt to conciliate worldly converts, by adopting their ideas and practices, did not pass without remonstrance from those whose intelligence discerned the motive. "You have," says Faustus to Augustine, "substituted your agapae for the sacrifices of the pagans; for their idols your martyrs, whom you serve with the very same honors. You appease the shades of the dead with wine and feasts; you celebrate the solemn festivities of the Gentiles, their calends, and their solstices; and, as to their manners, those you have retained without any alteration. Nothing distinguishes you from the pagans, except that you hold your assemblies apart from them." Pagan observances were everywhere introduced. At weddings it was the custom to sing hymns to Venus.

INTRODUCTION OF ROMAN RITES. Let us pause here a moment, and see, in anticipation, to what a depth of intellectual degradation this policy of paganization eventually led. Heathen rites were adopted, a pompous and splendid ritual, gorgeous robes, mitres, tiaras, wax-tapers, processional services, lustrations, gold and silver vases, were introduced. The Roman lituus, the chief ensign of the augurs, became the crozier. Churches were built over the tombs of martyrs, and consecrated with rites borrowed from the ancient laws of the Roman pontiffs. Festivals and commemorations of martyrs multiplied with the numberless fictitious discoveries of their remains. Fasting became the grand means of repelling the devil and appeasing God; celibacy the greatest of the virtues. Pilgrimages were made to Palestine and the tombs of the martyrs. Quantities of dust and earth were brought from the Holy Land and sold at enormous prices, as antidotes against devils. The virtues of consecrated water were upheld. Images and relics were introduced into the churches, and worshiped after the fashion of the heathen gods. It was given out that prodigies and miracles were to be seen in certain places, as in the heathen times. The happy souls of departed Christians were invoked; it was believed that they were wandering about the world, or haunting their graves. There was a multiplication of temples, altars, and penitential garments. The festival of the purification of the Virgin was invented to remove the uneasiness of heathen converts on account of the loss of their Lupercalia, or feasts of Pan. The worship of images, of fragments of the cross, or bones, nails, and other relics, a true fetich worship, was cultivated. Two arguments were relied on for the authenticity of these objects—the authority of the Church, and the working of miracles. Even the worn-out clothing of the saints and the earth of their graves were venerated. From Palestine were brought what were affirmed to be the skeletons of St. Mark and St. James, and other ancient worthies. The apotheosis of the old Roman times was replaced by canonization; tutelary saints succeed to local mythological divinities. Then came the mystery of transubstantiation, or the conversion of bread and wine by the priest into the flesh and blood of Christ. As centuries passed, the paganization became more and more complete. Festivals sacred to the memory of the lance with which the Savior's side was pierced, the nails that fastened him to the cross, and the crown of thorns, were instituted. Though there were several abbeys that possessed this last peerless relic, no one dared to say that it was impossible they could all be authentic.

We may read with advantage the remarks made by Bishop Newton on this paganization of Christianity. He asks: "Is not the worship of saints and angels now in all respects the same that the worship of demons was in former times? The name only is different, the thing is identically the same,... the deified men of the Christians are substituted for the deified men of the heathens. The promoters of this worship were sensible that it was the same, and that the one succeeded to the other; and, as the worship is the same, so likewise it is performed with the same ceremonies. The burning of incense or perfumes on several altars at one and the same time; the sprinkling of holy water, or a mixture of salt and common water, at going into and coming out of places of public worship; the lighting up of a great number of lamps and wax-candles in broad daylight before altars and statues of these deities; the hanging up of votive offerings and rich presents as attestations of so many miraculous cures and deliverances from diseases and dangers; the canonization or deification of deceased worthies; the assigning of distinct provinces or prefectures to departed heroes and saints; the worshiping and adoring of the dead in their sepulchres, shrines, and relics; the consecrating and bowing down to images; the attributing of miraculous powers and virtues to idols; the setting up of little oratories, altars, and statues in the streets and highways, and on the tops of mountains; the carrying of images and relics in pompous procession, with numerous lights and with music and singing; flagellations at solemn seasons under the notion of penance; a great variety of religious orders and fraternities of priests; the shaving of priests, or the tonsure as it is called, on the crown of their heads; the imposing of celibacy and vows of chastity on the religious of both sexes—all these and many more rites and ceremonies are equally parts of pagan and popish superstition. Nay, the very same temples, the very same images, which were once consecrated to Jupiter and the other demons, are now consecrated to the Virgin Mary and the other saints. The very same rites and inscriptions are ascribed to both, the very same prodigies and miracles are related of these as of those. In short, almost the whole of paganism is converted and applied to popery; the one is manifestly formed upon the same plan and principles as the other; so that there is not only a conformity, but even a uniformity, in the worship of ancient and modern, of heathen and Christian Rome."

DEBASEMENT OF CHRISTIANITY. Thus far Bishop Newton; but to return to the times of Constantine: though these concessions to old and popular ideas were permitted and even encouraged, the dominant religious party never for a moment hesitated to enforce its decisions by the aid of the civil power—an aid which was freely given. Constantine thus carried into effect the acts of the Council of Nicea. In the affair of Arius, he even ordered that whoever should find a book of that heretic, and not burn it, should be put to death. In like manner Nestor was by Theodosius the Younger banished to an Egyptian oasis.

The pagan party included many of the old aristocratic families of the empire; it counted among its adherents all the disciples of the old philosophical schools. It looked down on its antagonist with contempt. It asserted that knowledge is to be obtained only by the laborious exercise of human observation and human reason.

The Christian party asserted that all knowledge is to be found in the Scriptures and in the traditions of the Church; that, in the written revelation, God had not only given a criterion of truth, but had furnished us all that he intended us to know. The Scriptures, therefore, contain the sum, the end of all knowledge. The clergy, with the emperor at their back, would endure no intellectual competition.

Thus came into prominence what were termed sacred and profane knowledge; thus came into presence of each other two opposing parties, one relying on human reason as its guide, the other on revelation. Paganism leaned for support on the learning of its philosophers, Christianity on the inspiration of its Fathers.

The Church thus set herself forth as the depository and arbiter of knowledge; she was ever ready to resort to the civil power to compel obedience to her decisions. She thus took a course which determined her whole future career: she became a stumbling-block in the intellectual advancement of Europe for more than a thousand years.

The reign of Constantine marks the epoch of the transformation of Christianity from a religion into a political system; and though, in one sense, that system was degraded into an idolatry, in another it had risen into a development of the old Greek mythology. The maxim holds good in the social as well as in the mechanical world, that, when two bodies strike, the form of both is changed. Paganism was modified by Christianity; Christianity by Paganism.

THE TRINITARIAN DISPUTE. In the Trinitarian controversy, which first broke out in Egypt—Egypt, the land of Trinities—the chief point in discussion was to define the position of "the Son." There lived in Alexandria a presbyter of the name of Arius, a disappointed candidate for the office of bishop. He took the ground that there was a time when, from the very nature of sonship, the Son did not exist, and a time at which he commenced to be, asserting that it is the necessary condition of the filial relation that a father must be older than his son. But this assertion evidently denied the coeternity of the three persons of the Trinity; it suggested a subordination or inequality among them, and indeed implied a time when the Trinity did not exist. Hereupon, the bishop, who had been the successful competitor against Arius, displayed his rhetorical powers in public debates on the question, and, the strife spreading, the Jews and pagans, who formed a very large portion of the population of Alexandria, amused themselves with theatrical representations of the contest on the stage—the point of their burlesques being the equality of age of the Father and his Son.

Such was the violence the controversy at length assumed, that the matter had to be referred to the emperor. At first he looked upon the dispute as altogether frivolous, and perhaps in truth inclined to the assertion of Arius, that in the very nature of the thing a father must be older than his son. So great, however, was the pressure laid upon him, that he was eventually compelled to summon the Council of Nicea, which, to dispose of the conflict, set forth a formulary or creed, and attached to it this anathema: "The Holy Catholic and Apostolic Church anathematizes those who say that there was a time when the Son of God was not, and that, before he was begotten, he was not, and that he was made out of nothing, or out of another substance or essence, and is created, or changeable, or alterable." Constantine at once enforced the decision of the council by the civil power.

A few years subsequently the Emperor Theodosius prohibited sacrifices, made the inspection of the entrails of animals a capital offense, and forbade any one entering a temple. He instituted Inquisitors of Faith, and ordained that all who did not accord with the belief of Damasus, the Bishop of Rome, and Peter, the Bishop of Alexandria, should be driven into exile, and deprived of civil rights. Those who presumed to celebrate Easter on the same day as the Jews, he condemned to death. The Greek language was now ceasing to be known in the West, and true learning was becoming extinct.

At this time the bishopric of Alexandria was held by one Theophilus. An ancient temple of Osiris having been given to the Christians of the city for the site of a church, it happened that, in digging the foundation for the new edifice, the obscene symbols of the former worship chanced to be found. These, with more zeal than modesty, Theophilus exhibited in the market-place to public derision. With less forbearance than the Christian party showed when it was insulted in the theatre during the Trinitarian dispute, the pagans resorted to violence, and a riot ensued. They held the Serapion as their headquarters. Such were the disorder and bloodshed that the emperor had to interfere. He dispatched a rescript to Alexandria, enjoining the bishop, Theophilus, to destroy the Serapion; and the great library, which had been collected by the Ptolemies, and had escaped the fire of Julius Caesar, was by that fanatic dispersed.

THE MURDER OF HYPATIA. The bishopric thus held by Theophilus was in due time occupied by his nephew St. Cyril, who had commended himself to the approval of the Alexandrian congregations as a successful and fashionable preacher. It was he who had so much to do with the introduction of the worship of the Virgin Mary. His hold upon the audiences of the giddy city was, however, much weakened by Hypatia, the daughter of Theon, the mathematician, who not only distinguished herself by her expositions of the doctrines of Plato and Aristotle, but also by her comments on the writings of Apollonius and other geometers. Each day before her academy stood a long train of chariots; her lecture-room was crowded with the wealth and fashion of Alexandria. They came to listen to her discourses on those questions which man in all ages has asked, but which never yet have been answered: "What am I? Where am I? What can I know?"

Hypatia and Cyril! Philosophy and bigotry. They cannot exist together. So Cyril felt, and on that feeling he acted. As Hypatia repaired to her academy, she was assaulted by Cyril's mob—a mob of many monks. Stripped naked in the street, she was dragged into a church, and there killed by the club of Peter the Reader. The corpse was cut to pieces, the flesh was scraped from the bones with shells, and the remnants cast into a fire. For this frightful crime Cyril was never called to account. It seemed to be admitted that the end sanctified the means.

So ended Greek philosophy in Alexandria, so came to an untimely close the learning that the Ptolemies had done so much to promote. The "Daughter Library," that of the Serapion, had been dispersed. The fate of Hypatia was a warning to all who would cultivate profane knowledge. Henceforth there was to be no freedom for human thought. Every one must think as the ecclesiastical authority ordered him, A.D. 414. In Athens itself philosophy awaited its doom. Justinian at length prohibited its teaching, and caused all its schools in that city to be closed.

PELAGIUS. While these events were transpiring in the Eastern provinces of the Roman Empire, the spirit that had produced them was displaying itself in the West. A British monk, who had assumed the name of Pelagius, passed through Western Europe and Northern Africa, teaching that death was not introduced into the world by the sin of Adam; that on the contrary he was necessarily and by nature mortal, and had he not sinned he would nevertheless have died; that the consequences of his sins were confined to himself, and did not affect his posterity. From these premises Pelagius drew certain important theological conclusions.

At Rome, Pelagius had been received with favor; at Carthage, at the instigation of St. Augustine, he was denounced. By a synod, held at Diospolis, he was acquitted of heresy, but, on referring the matter to the Bishop of Rome, Innocent I., he was, on the contrary, condemned. It happened that at this moment Innocent died, and his successor, Zosimus, annulled his judgment and declared the opinions of Pelagius to be orthodox. These contradictory decisions are still often referred to by the opponents of papal infallibility. Things were in this state of confusion, when the wily African bishops, through the influence of Count Valerius, procured from the emperor an edict denouncing Pelagins as a heretic; he and his accomplices were condemned to exile and the forfeiture of their goods. To affirm that death was in the world before the fall of Adam, was a state crime.

CONDEMNATION OF PELAGIUS. It is very instructive to consider the principles on which this strange decision was founded. Since the question was purely philosophical, one might suppose that it would have been discussed on natural principles; instead of that, theological considerations alone were adduced. The attentive reader will have remarked, in Tertullian's statement of the principles of Christianity, a complete absence of the doctrines of original sin, total depravity, predestination, grace, and atonement. The intention of Christianity, as set forth by him, has nothing in common with the plan of salvation upheld two centuries subsequently. It is to St. Augustine, a Carthaginian, that we are indebted for the precision of our views on these important points.

In deciding whether death had been in the world before the fall of Adam, or whether it was the penalty inflicted on the world for his sin, the course taken was to ascertain whether the views of Pelagius were accordant or discordant not with Nature but with the theological doctrines of St. Augustine. And the result has been such as might be expected. The doctrine declared to be orthodox by ecclesiastical authority is overthrown by the unquestionable discoveries of modern science. Long before a human being had appeared upon earth, millions of individuals—nay, more, thousands of species and even genera—had died; those which remain with us are an insignificant fraction of the vast hosts that have passed away.

A consequence of great importance issued from the decision of the Pelagian controversy. The book of Genesis had been made the basis of Christianity. If, in a theological point of view, to its account of the sin in the garden of Eden, and the transgression and punishment of Adam, so much weight had been attached, it also in a philosophical point of view became the grand authority of Patristic science. Astronomy, geology, geography, anthropology, chronology, and indeed all the various departments of human knowledge, were made to conform to it.

ST. AUGUSTINE. As the doctrines of St. Augustine have had the effect of thus placing theology in antagonism with science, it may be interesting to examine briefly some of the more purely philosophical views of that great man. For this purpose, we may appropriately select portions of his study of the first chapter of Genesis, as contained in the eleventh, twelfth, and thirteenth books of his "Confessions."

These consist of philosophical discussions, largely interspersed with rhapsodies. He prays that God will give him to understand the Scriptures, and will open their meaning to him; he declares that in them there is nothing superfluous, but that the words have a manifold meaning.

The face of creation testifies that there has been a Creator; but at once arises the question, "How and when did he make heaven and earth? They could not have been made IN heaven and earth, the world could not have been made IN the world, nor could they have been made when there was nothing to make them of." The solution of this fundamental inquiry St. Augustine finds in saying, "Thou spakest, and they were made."

But the difficulty does not end here. St. Augustine goes on to remark that the syllables thus uttered by God came forth in succession, and there must have been some created thing to express the words. This created thing must, therefore, have existed before heaven and earth, and yet there could have been no corporeal thing before heaven and earth. It must have been a creature, because the words passed away and came to an end but we know that "the word of the Lord endureth forever."

Moreover, it is plain that the words thus spoken could not have been spoken successively, but simultaneously, else there would have been time and change—succession in its nature implying time; whereas there was then nothing but eternity and immortality. God knows and says eternally what takes place in time.

CRITICISM OF ST. AUGUSTINE. St. Augustine then defines, not without much mysticism, what is meant by the opening words of Genesis: "In the beginning." He is guided to his conclusion by another scriptural passage: "How wonderful are thy works, O Lord! in wisdom hast thou made them all." This "wisdom" is "the beginning," and in that beginning the Lord created the heaven and the earth.

"But," he adds, "some one may ask, 'What was God doing before he made the heaven and the earth? for, if at any particular moment he began to employ himself, that means time, not eternity. In eternity nothing transpires—the whole is present.'" In answering this question, he cannot forbear one of those touches of rhetoric for which he was so celebrated: "I will not answer this question by saying that he was preparing hell for priers into his mysteries. I say that, before God made heaven and earth, he did not make any thing, for no creature could be made before any creature was made. Time itself is a creature, and hence it could not possibly exist before creation.

"What, then, is time? The past is not, the future is not, the present—who can tell what it is, unless it be that which has no duration between two nonentities? There is no such thing as 'a long time,' or 'a short time,' for there are no such things as the past and the future. They have no existence, except in the soul."

The style in which St. Augustine conveyed his ideas is that of a rhapsodical conversation with God. His works are an incoherent dream. That the reader may appreciate this remark, I might copy almost at random any of his paragraphs. The following is from the twelfth book:

"This then, is what I conceive, O my God, when I hear thy Scripture saying, In the beginning God made heaven and earth: and the earth was invisible and without form, and darkness was upon the deep, and not mentioning what day thou createdst them; this is what I conceive, that because of the heaven of heavens—that intellectual heaven, whose intelligences know all at once, not in part, not darkly, not through a glass, but as a whole, in manifestation, face to face; not this thing now, and that thing anon; but (as I said) know all at once, without any succession of times; and because of the earth, invisible and without form, without any succession of times, which succession presents 'this thing now, that thing anon;' because, where there is no form, there is no distinction of things; it is, then, on account of these two, a primitive formed, and a primitive formless; the one, heaven, but the heaven of heavens; the other, earth, but the earth movable and without form; because of these two do I conceive, did thy Scripture say without mention of days, In the beginning God created the heaven and the earth. For, forthwith it subjoined what earth it spake of; and also in that the firmament is recorded to be created the second day, and called heaven, it conveys to us of which heaven he before spake, without mention of days.

"Wondrous depth of thy words! whose surface behold! is before us, inviting to little ones; yet are they a wondrous depth, O my God, a wondrous depth! It is awful to look therein; an awfulness of honor, and a trembling of love. The enemies thereof I hate vehemently; O that thou wouldst slay them with thy two-edged sword, that they might no longer be enemies to it: for so do I love to have them slain unto themselves, that they may live unto thee."

As an example of the hermeneutical manner in which St. Augustine unfolded the concealed facts of the Scriptures, I may cite the following from the thirteenth book of the "Confessions;" his object is to show that the doctrine of the Trinity is contained in the Mosaic narrative of the creation:

"Lo, now the Trinity appears unto me in a glass darkly, which is thou my God, because thou, O Father, in him who is the beginning of our wisdom, which is thy wisdom, born of thyself, equal unto thee and coeternal, that is, in thy Son, createdst heaven and earth. Much now have we said of the heaven of heavens, and of the earth invisible and without form, and of the darksome deep, in reference to the wandering instability of its spiritual deformity, unless it had been converted unto him, from whom it had its then degree of life, and by his enlightening became a beauteous life, and the heaven of that heaven, which was afterward set between water and water. And under the name of God, I now held the Father, who made these things; and under the name of the beginning, the Son, in whom he made these things; and believing, as I did, my God as the Trinity, I searched further in his holy words, and lo! thy Spirit moved upon the waters. Behold the Trinity, my God!—Father, and Son, and Holy Ghost Creator of all creation."

That I might convey to my reader a just impression of the character of St. Augustine's philosophical writings, I have, in the two quotations here given, substituted for my own translation that of the Rev. Dr. Pusey, as contained in Vol. I. of the "Library of Fathers of the Holy Catholic Church," published at Oxford, 1840.

Considering the eminent authority which has been attributed to the writings of St. Augustine by the religious world for nearly fifteen centuries, it is proper to speak of them with respect. And indeed it is not necessary to do otherwise. The paragraphs here quoted criticise themselves. No one did more than this Father to bring science and religion into antagonism; it was mainly he who diverted the Bible from its true office—a guide to purity of life—and placed it in the perilous position of being the arbiter of human knowledge, an audacious tyranny over the mind of man. The example once set, there was no want of followers; the works of the great Greek philosophers were stigmatized as profane; the transcendently glorious achievements of the Museum of Alexandria were hidden from sight by a cloud of ignorance, mysticism, and unintelligible jargon, out of which there too often flashed the destroying lightnings of ecclesiastical vengeance.

A divine revelation of science admits of no improvement, no change, no advance. It discourages as needless, and indeed as presumptuous, all new discovery, considering it as an unlawful prying into things which it was the intention of God to conceal.

What, then, is that sacred, that revealed science, declared by the Fathers to be the sum of all knowledge?

It likened all phenomena, natural and spiritual, to human acts. It saw in the Almighty, the Eternal, only a gigantic man.

THE PATRISTIC PHILOSOPHY. As to the earth, it affirmed that it is a flat surface, over which the sky is spread like a dome, or, as St. Augustine tells us, is stretched like a skin. In this the sun and moon and stars move, so that they may give light by day and by night to man. The earth was made of matter created by God out of nothing, and, with all the tribes of animals and plants inhabiting it, was finished in six days. Above the sky or firmament is heaven; in the dark and fiery space beneath the earth is hell. The earth is the central and most important body of the universe, all other things being intended for and subservient to it.

As to man, he was made out of the dust of the earth. At first he was alone, but subsequently woman was formed from one of his ribs. He is the greatest and choicest of the works of God. He was placed in a paradise near the banks of the Euphrates, and was very wise and very pure; but, having tasted of the forbidden fruit, and thereby broken the commandment given to him, he was condemned to labor and to death.

The descendants of the first man, undeterred by his punishment, pursued such a career of wickedness that it became necessary to destroy them. A deluge, therefore, flooded the face of the earth, and rose over the tops of the mountains. Having accomplished its purpose, the water was dried up by a wind.

From this catastrophe Noah and his three sons, with their wives, were saved in an ark. Of these sons, Shem remained in Asia and repeopled it. Ham peopled Africa; Japhet, Europe. As the Fathers were not acquainted with the existence of America, they did not provide an ancestor for its people.

Let us listen to what some of these authorities say in support of their assertions. Thus Lactantius, referring to the heretical doctrine of the globular form of the earth, remarks: "Is it possible that men can be so absurd as to believe that the crops and the trees on the other side of the earth hang downward, and that men have their feet higher than their heads? If you ask them how they defend these monstrosities, how things do not fall away from the earth on that side, they reply that the nature of things is such that heavy bodies tend toward the centre, like the spokes of a wheel, while light bodies, as clouds, smoke, fire, tend from the centre to the heavens on all sides. Now, I am really at a loss what to say of those who, when they have once gone wrong, steadily persevere in their folly, and defend one absurd opinion by another." On the question of the antipodes, St. Augustine asserts that "it is impossible there should be inhabitants on the opposite side of the earth, since no such race is recorded by Scripture among the descendants of Adam." Perhaps, however, the most unanswerable argument against the sphericity of the earth was this, that "in the day of judgment, men on the other side of a globe could not see the Lord descending through the air."

It is unnecessary for me to say any thing respecting the introduction of death into the world, the continual interventions of spiritual agencies in the course of events, the offices of angels and devils, the expected conflagration of the earth, the tower of Babel, the confusion of tongues, the dispersion of mankind, the interpretation of natural phenomena, as eclipses, the rainbow, etc. Above all, I abstain from commenting on the Patristic conceptions of the Almighty; they are too anthropomorphic, and wanting in sublimity.

Perhaps, however, I may quote from Cosmas Indicopleustes the views that were entertained in the sixth century. He wrote a work entitled "Christian Topography," the chief intent of which was to confute the heretical opinion of the globular form of the earth, and the pagan assertion that there is a temperate zone on the southern side of the torrid. He affirms that, according to the true orthodox system of geography, the earth is a quadrangular plane, extending four hundred days' journey east and west, and exactly half as much north and south; that it is inclosed by mountains, on which the sky rests; that one on the north side, huger than the others, by intercepting the rays of the sun, produces night; and that the plane of the earth is not set exactly horizontally, but with a little inclination from the north: hence the Euphrates, Tigris, and other rivers, running southward, are rapid; but the Nile, having to run up-hill, has necessarily a very slow current.

The Venerable Bede, writing in the seventh century, tells us that "the creation was accomplished in six days, and that the earth is its centre and its primary object. The heaven is of a fiery and subtile nature, round, and equidistant in every part, as a canopy from the centre of the earth. It turns round every day with ineffable rapidity, only moderated by the resistance of the seven planets, three above the sun—Saturn, Jupiter, Mars—then the sun; three below—Venus, Mercury, the moon. The stars go round in their fixed courses, the northern perform the shortest circle. The highest heaven has its proper limit; it contains the angelic virtues who descend upon earth, assume ethereal bodies, perform human functions, and return. The heaven is tempered with glacial waters, lest it should be set on fire. The inferior heaven is called the firmament, because it separates the superincumbent waters from the waters below. The firmamental waters are lower than the spiritual heaven, higher than all corporeal beings, reserved, some say, for a second deluge; others, more truly, to temper the fire of the fixed stars."

Was it for this preposterous scheme—this product of ignorance and audacity—that the works of the Greek philosophers were to be given up? It was none too soon that the great critics who appeared at the Reformation, by comparing the works of these writers with one another, brought them to their proper level, and taught us to look upon them all with contempt.

Of this presumptuous system, the strangest part was its logic, the nature of its proofs. It relied upon miracle-evidence. A fact was supposed to be demonstrated by an astounding illustration of something else! An Arabian writer, referring to this, says: "If a conjurer should say to me, 'Three are more than ten, and in proof of it I will change this stick into a serpent,' I might be surprised at his legerdemain, but I certainly should not admit his assertion." Yet, for more than a thousand years, such was the accepted logic, and all over Europe propositions equally absurd were accepted on equally ridiculous proof.

Since the party that had become dominant in the empire could not furnish works capable of intellectual competition with those of the great pagan authors, and since it was impossible for it to accept a position of inferiority, there arose a political necessity for the discouragement, and even persecution, of profane learning. The persecution of the Platonists under Valentinian was due to that necessity. They were accused of magic, and many of them were put to death. The profession of philosophy had become dangerous—it was a state crime. In its stead there arose a passion for the marvelous, a spirit of superstition. Egypt exchanged the great men, who had made her Museum immortal, for bands of solitary monks and sequestered virgins, with which she was overrun.

CHAPTER III.

CONFLICT RESPECTING THE DOCTRINE OF THE UNITY OF GOD.—THE FIRST OR SOUTHERN REFORMATION.

The Egyptians insist on the introduction of the worship of the Virgin Mary—They are resisted by Nestor, the Patriarch of Constantinople, but eventually, through their influence with the emperor, cause Nestor's exile and the dispersion of his followers.

Prelude to the Southern Reformation—The Persian attack; its moral effects.

The Arabian Reformation.—Mohammed is brought in contact with the Nestorians—He adopts and extends their principles, rejecting the worship of the Virgin, the doctrine of the Trinity, and every thing in opposition to the unity of God.—He extinguishes idolatry in Arabia, by force, and prepares to make war on the Roman Empire.—His successors conquer Syria, Egypt, Asia Minor, North Africa, Spain, and invade France.

As the result of this conflict, the doctrine of the unity of God was established in the greater part of the Roman Empire—The cultivation of science was restored, and Christendom lost many of her most illustrious capitals, as Alexandria, Carthage, and, above all, Jerusalem.

THE policy of the Byzantine court had given to primitive Christianity a paganized form, which it had spread over all the idolatrous populations constituting the empire. There had been an amalgamation of the two parties. Christianity had modified paganism, paganism had modified Christianity. The limits of this adulterated religion were the confines of the Roman Empire. With this great extension there had come to the Christian party political influence and wealth. No insignificant portion of the vast public revenues found their way into the treasuries of the Church. As under such circumstances must ever be the case, there were many competitors for the spoils—men who, under the mask of zeal for the predominant faith, sought only the enjoyment of its emoluments.

ECCLESIASTICAL DISPUTES. Under the early emperors, conquest had reached its culmination; the empire was completed; there remained no adequate objects for military life; the days of war-peculation, and the plundering of provinces, were over. For the ambitious, however, another path was open; other objects presented. A successful career in the Church led to results not unworthy of comparison with those that in former days had been attained by a successful career in the army.

The ecclesiastical, and indeed, it may be said, much of the political history of that time, turns on the struggles of the bishops of the three great metropolitan cities—Constantinople, Alexandria, Rome—for supremacy: Constantinople based her claims on the fact that she was the existing imperial city; Alexandria pointed to her commercial and literary position; Rome, to her souvenirs. But the Patriarch of Constantinople labored under the disadvantage that he was too closely under the eye, and, as he found to his cost, too often under the hand, of the emperor. Distance gave security to the episcopates of Alexandria and Rome.

ECCLESIASTICAL DISPUTES. Religious disputations in the East have generally turned on diversities of opinion respecting the nature and attributes of God; in the West, on the relations and life of man. This peculiarity has been strikingly manifested in the transformations that Christianity has undergone in Asia and Europe respectively. Accordingly, at the time of which we are speaking, all the Eastern provinces of the Roman Empire exhibited an intellectual anarchy. There were fierce quarrels respecting the Trinity, the essence of God, the position of the Son, the nature of the Holy Spirit, the influences of the Virgin Mary. The triumphant clamor first of one then of another sect was confirmed, sometimes by miracle-proof, sometimes by bloodshed. No attempt was ever made to submit the rival opinions to logical examination. All parties, however, agreed in this, that the imposture of the old classical pagan forms of faith was demonstrated by the facility with which they had been overthrown. The triumphant ecclesiastics proclaimed that the images of the gods had failed to defend themselves when the time of trial came.

Polytheistic ideas have always been held in repute by the southern European races, the Semitic have maintained the unity of God. Perhaps this is due to the fact, as a recent author has suggested, that a diversified landscape of mountains and valleys, islands, and rivers, and gulfs, predisposes man to a belief in a multitude of divinities. A vast sandy desert, the illimitable ocean, impresses him with an idea of the oneness of God.

Political reasons had led the emperors to look with favor on the admixture of Christianity and paganism, and doubtless by this means the bitterness of the rivalry between those antagonists was somewhat abated. The heaven of the popular, the fashionable Christianity was the old Olympus, from which the venerable Greek divinities had been removed. There, on a great white throne, sat God the Father, on his right the Son, and then the blessed Virgin, clad in a golden robe, and "covered with various female adornments;" on the left sat God the Holy Ghost. Surrounding these thrones were hosts of angels with their harps. The vast expanse beyond was filled with tables, seated at which the happy spirits of the just enjoyed a perpetual banquet.

If, satisfied with this picture of happiness, illiterate persons never inquired how the details of such a heaven were carried out, or how much pleasure there could be in the ennui of such an eternally unchanging, unmoving scene, it was not so with the intelligent. As we are soon to see, there were among the higher ecclesiastics those who rejected with sentiments of horror these carnal, these materialistic conceptions, and raised their protesting voices in vindication of the attributes of the Omnipresent, the Almighty God.

EGYPTIAN DOCTRINES. In the paganization of religion, now in all directions taking place, it became the interest of every bishop to procure an adoption of the ideas which, time out of mind, had been current in the community under his charge. The Egyptians had already thus forced on the Church their peculiar Trinitarian views; and now they were resolved that, under the form of the adoration of the Virgin Mary, the worship of Isis should be restored.

THE NESTORIANS. It so happened that Nestor, the Bishop of Antioch, who entertained the philosophical views of Theodore of Mopsuestia, had been called by the Emperor Theodosius the Younger to the Episcopate of Constantinople (A.D. 427). Nestor rejected the base popular anthropomorphism, looking upon it as little better than blasphemous, and pictured to himself an awful eternal Divinity, who pervaded the universe, and had none of the aspects or attributes of man. Nestor was deeply imbued with the doctrines of Aristotle, and attempted to coordinate them with what he considered to be orthodox Christian tenets. Between him and Cyril, the Bishop or Patriarch of Alexandria, a quarrel accordingly arose. Cyril represented the paganizing, Nestor the philosophizing party of the Church. This was that Cyril who had murdered Hypatia. Cyril was determined that the worship of the Virgin as the Mother of God should be recognized, Nestor was determined that it should not. In a sermon delivered in the metropolitan church at Constantinople, he vindicated the attributes of the Eternal, the Almighty God. "And can this God have a mother?" he exclaimed. In other sermons and writings, he set forth with more precision his ideas that the Virgin should be considered not as the Mother of God, but as the mother of the human portion of Christ, that portion being as essentially distinct from the divine as is a temple from its contained deity.

PERSECUTION AND DEATH OF NESTOR. Instigated by the monks of Alexandria, the monks of Constantinople took up arms in behalf of "the Mother of God." The quarrel rose to such a pitch that the emperor was constrained to summon a council to meet at Ephesus. In the mean time Cyril had given a bribe of many pounds of gold to the chief eunuch of the imperial court, and had thereby obtained the influence of the emperor's sister. "The holy virgin of the court of heaven thus found an ally of her own sex in the holy virgin of the emperor's court." Cyril hastened to the council, attended by a mob of men and women of the baser sort. He at once assumed the presidency, and in the midst of a tumult had the emperor's rescript read before the Syrian bishops could arrive. A single day served to complete his triumph. All offers of accommodation on the part of Nestor were refused, his explanations were not read, he was condemned unheard. On the arrival of the Syrian ecclesiastics, a meeting of protest was held by them. A riot, with much bloodshed, ensued in the cathedral of St. John. Nestor was abandoned by the court, and eventually exiled to an Egyptian oasis. His persecutors tormented him as long as he lived, by every means in their power, and at his death gave out that "his blasphemous tongue had been devoured by worms, and that from the heats of an Egyptian desert he had escaped only into the hotter torments of hell!"

The overthrow and punishment of Nestor, however, by no means destroyed his opinions. He and his followers, insisting on the plain inference of the last verse of the first chapter of St. Matthew, together with the fifty-fifth and fifty-sixth verses of the thirteenth of the same gospel, could never be brought to an acknowledgment of the perpetual virginity of the new queen of heaven. Their philosophical tendencies were soon indicated by their actions. While their leader was tormented in an African oasis, many of them emigrated to the Euphrates, and established the Chaldean Church. Under their auspices the college of Edessa was founded. From the college of Nisibis issued those doctors who spread Nestor's tenets through Syria, Arabia, India, Tartary, China, Egypt. The Nestorians, of course, adopted the philosophy of Aristotle, and translated the works of that great writer into Syriac and Persian. They also made similar translations of later works, such as those of Pliny. In connection with the Jews they founded the medical college of Djondesabour. Their missionaries disseminated the Nestorian form of Christianity to such an extent over Asia, that its worshipers eventually outnumbered all the European Christians of the Greek and Roman Churches combined. It may be particularly remarked that in Arabia they had a bishop.

THE PERSIAN CAMPAIGN. The dissensions between Constantinople and Alexandria had thus filled all Western Asia with sectaries, ferocious in their contests with each other, and many of them burning with hatred against the imperial power for the persecutions it had inflicted on them. A religious revolution, the consequences of which are felt in our own times, was the result. It affected the whole world.

We shall gain a clear view of this great event, if we consider separately the two acts into which it may be decomposed: 1. The temporary overthrow of Asiatic Christianity by the Persians; 2. The decisive and final reformation under the Arabians.

1. It happened (A.D. 590) that, by one of those revolutions so frequent in Oriental courts, Chosroes, the lawful heir to the Persian throne, was compelled to seek refuge in the Byzantine Empire, and implore the aid of the Emperor Maurice. That aid was cheerfully given. A brief and successful campaign restored Chosroes to the throne of his ancestors.

But the glories of this generous campaign could not preserve Maurice himself. A mutiny broke out in the Roman army, headed by Phocas, a centurion. The statues of the emperor were overthrown. The Patriarch of Constantinople, having declared that he had assured himself of the orthodoxy of Phocas, consecrated him emperor. The unfortunate Maurice was dragged from a sanctuary, in which he had sought refuge; his five sons were beheaded before his eyes, and then he was put to death. His empress was inveigled from the church of St. Sophia, tortured, and with her three young daughters beheaded. The adherents of the massacred family were pursued with ferocious vindictiveness; of some the eyes were blinded, of others the tongues were torn out, or the feet and hands cut off, some were whipped to death, others were burnt.

When the news reached Rome, Pope Gregory received it with exultation, praying that the hands of Phocas might be strengthened against all his enemies. As an equivalent for this subserviency, he was greeted with the title of "Universal Bishop." The cause of his action, as well as of that of the Patriarch of Constantinople, was doubtless the fact that Maurice was suspected of Magrian tendencies, into which he had been lured by the Persians. The mob of Constantinople had hooted after him in the streets, branding him as a Marcionite, a sect which believed in the Magian doctrine of two conflicting principles.

With very different sentiments Chosroes heard of the murder of his friend. Phocas had sent him the heads of Maurice and his sons. The Persian king turned from the ghastly spectacle with horror, and at once made ready to avenge the wrongs of his benefactor by war.

THE EXPEDITION OF HERACLIUS. The Exarch of Africa, Heraclius, one of the chief officers of the state, also received the shocking tidings with indignation. He was determined that the imperial purple should not be usurped by an obscure centurion of disgusting aspect. "The person of this Phocas was diminutive and deformed; the closeness of his shaggy eyebrows, his red hair, his beardless chin, were in keeping with his cheek, disfigured and discolored by a formidable scar. Ignorant of letters, of laws, and even of arms, he indulged in an ample privilege of lust and drunkenness." At first Heraclius refused tribute and obedience to him; then, admonished by age and infirmities, he committed the dangerous enterprise of resistance to his son of the same name. A prosperous voyage from Carthage soon brought the younger Heraclius in front of Constantinople. The inconstant clergy, senate, and people of the city joined him, the usurper was seized in his palace and beheaded.

INVASION OF CHOSROES. But the revolution that had taken place in Constantinople did not arrest the movements of the Persian king. His Magian priests had warned him to act independently of the Greeks, whose superstition, they declared, was devoid of all truth and justice. Chosroes, therefore, crossed the Euphrates; his army was received with transport by the Syrian sectaries, insurrections in his favor everywhere breaking out. In succession, Antioch, Caesarea, Damascus fell; Jerusalem itself was taken by storm; the sepulchre of Christ, the churches of Constantine and of Helena were given to the flames; the Savior's cross was sent as a trophy to Persia; the churches were rifled of their riches; the sacred relics, collected by superstition, were dispersed. Egypt was invaded, conquered, and annexed to the Persian Empire; the Patriarch of Alexandria escaped by flight to Cyprus; the African coast to Tripoli was seized. On the north, Asia Minor was subdued, and for ten years the Persian forces encamped on the shores of the Bosporus, in front of Constantinople.

In his extremity Heraclius begged for peace. "I will never give peace to the Emperor of Rome," replied the proud Persian, "till he has abjured his crucified God, and embraced the worship of the sun." After a long delay terms were, however, secured, and the Roman Empire was ransomed at the price of "a thousand talents of gold, a thousand talents of silver, a thousand silk robes, a thousand horses, and a thousand virgins."

But Heraclius submitted only for a moment. He found means not only to restore his affairs but to retaliate on the Persian Empire. The operations by which he achieved this result were worthy of the most brilliant days of Rome.

INVASION OF CHOSROES Though her military renown was thus recovered, though her territory was regained, there was something that the Roman Empire had irrecoverably lost. Religious faith could never be restored. In face of the world Magianism had insulted Christianity, by profaning her most sacred places—Bethlehem, Gethsemane, Calvary—by burning the sepulchre of Christ, by rifling and destroying the churches, by scattering to the winds priceless relics, by carrying off, with shouts of laughter, the cross.

Miracles had once abounded in Syria, in Egypt, in Asia Minor; there was not a church which had not its long catalogue of them. Very often they were displayed on unimportant occasions and in insignificant cases. In this supreme moment, when such aid was most urgently demanded, not a miracle was worked.

Amazement filled the Christian populations of the East when they witnessed these Persian sacrileges perpetrated with impunity. The heavens should have rolled asunder, the earth should have opened her abysses, the sword of the Almighty should have flashed in the sky, the fate of Sennacherib should have been repeated. But it was not so. In the land of miracles, amazement was followed by consternation—consternation died out in disbelief.

2. But, dreadful as it was, the Persian conquest was but a prelude to the great event, the story of which we have now to relate—the Southern revolt against Christianity. Its issue was the loss of nine-tenths of her geographical possessions—Asia, Africa, and part of Europe.

MOHAMMED. In the summer of 581 of the Christian era, there came to Bozrah, a town on the confines of Syria, south of Damascus, a caravan of camels. It was from Mecca, and was laden with the costly products of South Arabia—Arabia the Happy. The conductor of the caravan, one Abou Taleb, and his nephew, a lad of twelve years, were hospitably received and entertained at the Nestorian convent of the town.

The monks of this convent soon found that their young visitor, Halibi or Mohammed, was the nephew of the guardian of the Caaba, the sacred temple of the Arabs. One of them, by name Bahira, spared no pains to secure his conversion from the idolatry in which he had been brought up. He found the boy not only precociously intelligent, but eagerly desirous of information, especially on matters relating to religion.

In Mohammed's own country the chief object of Meccan worship was a black meteoric stone, kept in the Caaba, with three hundred and sixty subordinate idols, representing the days of the year, as the year was then counted.

At this time, as we have seen, the Christian Church, through the ambition and wickedness of its clergy, had been brought into a condition of anarchy. Councils had been held on various pretenses, while the real motives were concealed. Too often they were scenes of violence, bribery, corruption. In the West, such were the temptations of riches, luxury, and power, presented by the episcopates, that the election of a bishop was often disgraced by frightful murders. In the East, in consequence of the policy of the court of Constantinople, the Church had been torn in pieces by contentions and schisms. Among a countless host of disputants may be mentioned Arians, Basilidians, Carpocratians, Collyridians, Eutychians, Gnostics, Jacobites, Marcionites, Marionites, Nestorians, Sabellians, Valentinians. Of these, the Marionites regarded the Trinity as consisting of God the Father, God the Son, and God the Virgin Mary; the Collyridians worshiped the Virgin as a divinity, offering her sacrifices of cakes; the Nestorians, as we have seen, denied that God had "a mother." They prided themselves on being the inheritors, the possessors of the science of old Greece.

But, though they were irreconcilable in matters of faith, there was one point in which all these sects agreed—ferocious hatred and persecution of each other. Arabia, an unconquered land of liberty, stretching from the Indian Ocean to the Desert of Syria, gave them all, as the tide of fortune successively turned, a refuge. It had been so from the old times. Thither, after the Roman conquest of Palestine, vast numbers of Jews escaped; thither, immediately after his conversion, St. Paul tells the Galatians that he retired. The deserts were now filled with Christian anchorites, and among the chief tribes of the Arabs many proselytes had been made. Here and there churches had been built. The Christian princes of Abyssinia, who were Nestorians, held the southern province of Arabia—Yemen—in possession.

By the monk Bahira, in the convent at Bozrah, Mohammed was taught the tenets of the Nestorians; from them the young Arab learned the story of their persecutions. It was these interviews which engendered in him a hatred of the idolatrous practices of the Eastern Church, and indeed of all idolatry; that taught him, in his wonderful career, never to speak of Jesus as the Son of God, but always as "Jesus, the son of Mary." His untutored but active mind could not fail to be profoundly impressed not only with the religious but also with the philosophical ideas of his instructors, who gloried in being the living representatives of Aristotelian science. His subsequent career shows how completely their religious thoughts had taken possession of him, and repeated acts manifest his affectionate regard for them. His own life was devoted to the expansion and extension of their theological doctrine, and, that once effectually established, his successors energetically adopted and diffused their scientific, their Aristotelian opinions.

As Mohammed grew to manhood, he made other expeditions to Syria. Perhaps, we may suppose, that on these occasions the convent and its hospitable in mates were not forgotten. He had a mysterious reverence for that country. A wealthy Meccan widow Chadizah, had intrusted him with the care of her Syrian trade. She was charmed with his capacity and fidelity, and (since he is said to have been characterized by the possession of singular manly beauty and a most courteous demeanor) charmed with his person. The female heart in all ages and countries is the same. She caused a slave to intimate to him what was passing in her mind, and, for the remaining twenty-four years of her life, Mohammed was her faithful husband. In a land of polygamy, he never insulted her by the presence of a rival. Many years subsequently, in the height of his power, Ayesha, who was one of the most beautiful women in Arabia, said to him: "Was she not old? Did not God give you in me a better wife in her place?" "No, by God!" exclaimed Mohammed, and with a burst of honest gratitude, "there never can be a better. She believed in me when men despised me, she relieved me when I was poor and persecuted by the world."

His marriage with Chadizah placed him in circumstances of ease, and gave him an opportunity of indulging his inclination to religious meditation. It so happened that her cousin Waraka, who was a Jew, had turned Christian. He was the first to translate the Bible into Arabic. By his conversation Mohammed's detestation of idolatry was confirmed.

After the example of the Christian anchorites in their hermitages in the desert, Mohammed retired to a grotto in Mount Hera, a few miles from Mecca, giving himself up to meditation and prayer. In this seclusion, contemplating the awful attributes of the Omnipotent and Eternal God, he addressed to his conscience the solemn inquiry, whether he could adopt the dogmas then held in Asiatic Christendom respecting the Trinity, the sonship of Jesus as begotten by the Almighty, the character of Mary as at once a virgin, a mother, and the queen of heaven, without incurring the guilt and the peril of blasphemy.

By his solitary meditations in the grotto Mohammed was drawn to the conclusion that, through the cloud of dogmas and disputations around him, one great truth might be discerned —the unity of God. Leaning against the stem of a palm-tree, he unfolded his views on this subject to his neighbors and friends, and announced to them that he should dedicate his life to the preaching of that truth. Again and again, in his sermons and in the Koran, he declared: "I am nothing but a public preacher.... I preach the oneness of God." Such was his own conception of his so-called apostleship. Henceforth, to the day of his death, he wore on his finger a seal-ring on which was engraved, "Mohammed, the messenger of God."

VICTORIES OF MOHAMMED. It is well known among physicians that prolonged fasting and mental anxiety inevitably give rise to hallucination. Perhaps there never has been any religious system introduced by self-denying, earnest men that did not offer examples of supernatural temptations and supernatural commands. Mysterious voices encouraged the Arabian preacher to persist in his determination; shadows of strange forms passed before him. He heard sounds in the air like those of a distant bell. In a nocturnal dream he was carried by Gabriel from Mecca to Jerusalem, and thence in succession through the six heavens. Into the seventh the angel feared to intrude and Mohammed alone passed into the dread cloud that forever enshrouds the Almighty. "A shiver thrilled his heart as he felt upon his shoulder the touch of the cold hand of God."

His public ministrations met with much resistance and little success at first. Expelled from Mecca by the upholders of the prevalent idolatry, he sought refuge in Medina, a town in which there were many Jews and Nestorians; the latter at once became proselytes to his faith. He had already been compelled to send his daughter and others of his disciples to Abyssinia, the king of which was a Nestorian Christian. At the end of six years he had made only fifteen hundred converts. But in three little skirmishes, magnified in subsequent times by the designation of the battles of Beder, of Ohud, and of the Nations, Mohammed discovered that his most convincing argument was his sword. Afterward, with Oriental eloquence, he said, "Paradise will be found in the shadow of the crossing of swords." By a series of well-conducted military operations, his enemies were completely overthrown. Arabian idolatry was absolutely exterminated; the doctrine he proclaimed, that "there is but one God," was universally adopted by his countrymen, and his own apostleship accepted.

DEATH OF MOHAMMED. Let us pass over his stormy life, and hear what he says when, on the pinnacle of earthly power and glory, he was approaching its close.

Steadfast in his declaration of the unity of God, he departed from Medina on his last pilgrimage to Mecca, at the head of one hundred and fourteen thousand devotees, with camels decorated with garlands of flowers and fluttering streamers. When he approached the holy city, he uttered the solemn invocation: "Here am I in thy service, O God! Thou hast no companion. To thee alone belongeth worship. Thine alone is the kingdom. There is none to share it with thee."

With his own hand he offered up the camels in sacrifice. He considered that primeval institution to be equally sacred as prayer, and that no reason can be alleged in support of the one which is not equally strong in support of the other.

From the pulpit of the Caaba he reiterated, "O my hearers, I am only a man like yourselves." They remembered that he had once said to one who approached him with timid steps: "Of what dost thou stand in awe? I am no king. I am nothing but the son of an Arab woman, who ate flesh dried in the sun."

He returned to Medina to die. In his farewell to his congregation, he said: "Every thing happens according to the will of God, and has its appointed time, which can neither be hastened nor avoided. I return to him who sent me, and my last command to you is, that ye love, honor, and uphold each other, that ye exhort each other to faith and constancy in belief, and to the performance of pious deeds. My life has been for your good, and so will be my death."

In his dying agony, his head was reclined on the lap of Ayesha. From time to time he had dipped his hand in a vase of water, and moistened his face. At last he ceased, and, gazing steadfastly upward, said, in broken accents: "O God—forgive my sins—be it so. I come."

Shall we speak of this man with disrespect? His precepts are, at this day, the religious guide of one-third of the human race.

DOCTRINES OF MOHAMMED. In Mohammed, who had already broken away from the ancient idolatrous worship of his native country, preparation had been made for the rejection of those tenets which his Nestorian teachers had communicated to him, inconsistent with reason and conscience. And, though, in the first pages of the Koran, he declares his belief in what was delivered to Moses and Jesus, and his reverence for them personally, his veneration for the Almighty is perpetually displayed. He is horror-stricken at the doctrine of the divinity of Jesus, the Worship of Mary as the mother of God, the adoration of images and paintings, in his eyes a base idolatry. He absolutely rejects the Trinity, of which he seems to have entertained the idea that it could not be interpreted otherwise than as presenting three distinct Gods.

His first and ruling idea was simply religious reform—to overthrow Arabian idolatry, and put an end to the wild sectarianism of Christianity. That he proposed to set up a new religion was a calumny invented against him in Constantinople, where he was looked upon with detestation, like that with which in after ages Luther was regarded in Rome.

But, though he rejected with indignation whatever might seem to disparage the doctrine of the unity of God, he was not able to emancipate himself from anthropomorphic conceptions. The God of the Koran is altogether human, both corporeally and mentally, if such expressions may with propriety be used. Very soon, however, the followers of Mohammed divested themselves of these base ideas and rose to nobler ones.

The view here presented of the primitive character of Mohammedanism has long been adopted by many competent authorities. Sir William Jones, following Locke, regards the main point in the divergence of Mohammedanism from Christianity to consist "in denying vehemently the character of our Savior as the Son, and his equality as God with the Father, of whose unity and attributes the Mohammedans entertain and express the most awful ideas." This opinion has been largely entertained in Italy. Dante regarded Mohammed only as the author of a schism, and saw in Islamism only an Arian sect. In England, Whately views it as a corruption of Christianity. It was an offshoot of Nestorianism, and not until it had overthrown Greek Christianity in many great battles, was spreading rapidly over Asia and Africa, and had become intoxicated with its wonderful successes, did it repudiate its primitive limited intentions, and assert itself to be founded on a separate and distinct revelation.

THE FIRST KHALIF. Mohammed's life had been almost entirely consumed in the conversion or conquest of his native country. Toward its close, however, he felt himself strong enough to threaten the invasion of Syria and Persia. He had made no provision for the perpetuation of his own dominion, and hence it was not without a struggle that a successor was appointed. At length Abubeker, the father of Ayesha, was selected. He was proclaimed the first khalif, or successor of the Prophet.

There is a very important difference between the spread of Mohammedanism and the spread of Christianity. The latter was never sufficiently strong to over throw and extirpate idolatry in the Roman Empire. As it advanced, there was an amalgamation, a union. The old forms of the one were vivified by the new spirit of the other, and that paganization to which reference has already been made was the result.

THE MOHAMMEDAN HEAVEN. But, in Arabia, Mohammed overthrew and absolutely annihilated the old idolatry. No trace of it is found in the doctrines preached by him and his successors. The black stone that had fallen from heaven—the meteorite of the Caaba—and its encircling idols, passed totally out of view. The essential dogma of the new faith—"There is but one God"—spread without any adulteration. Military successes had, in a worldly sense made the religion of the Koran profitable; and, no matter what dogmas may be, when that is the case, there will be plenty of converts.

As to the popular doctrines of Mohammedanism, I shall here have nothing to say. The reader who is interested in that matter will find an account of them in a review of the Koran in the eleventh chapter of my "History of the Intellectual Development of Europe." It is enough now to remark that their heaven was arranged in seven stories, and was only a palace of Oriental carnal delight. It was filled with black-eyed concubines and servants. The form of God was, perhaps, more awful than that of paganized Christianity. Anthropomorphism will, however, never be obliterated from the ideas of the unintellectual. Their God, at the best, will never be any thing more than the gigantic shadow of a man—a vast phantom of humanity—like one of those Alpine spectres seen in the midst of the clouds by him who turns his back on the sun.

Abubeker had scarcely seated himself in the khalifate, when he put forth the following proclamation:

In the name of the most merciful God! Abubeker to the rest of the true believers, health and happiness. The mercy and blessing of God be upon you. I praise the most high God. I pray for his prophet Mohammed.

INVASION OF SYRIA. "This is to inform you that I intend to send the true believers into Syria, to take it out of the hands of the infidels. And I would have you know that the fighting for religion is an act of obedience to God."

On the first encounter, Khaled, the Saracen general, hard pressed, lifted up his hands in the midst of his army and said: "O God! these vile wretches pray with idolatrous expressions and take to themselves another God besides thee, but we acknowledge thy unity and affirm that there is no other God but thee alone. Help us, we beseech thee, for the sake of thy prophet Mohammed, against these idolaters." On the part of the Saracens the conquest of Syria was conducted with ferocious piety. The belief of the Syrian Christians aroused in their antagonists sentiments of horror and indignation. "I will cleave the skull of any blaspheming idolater who says that the Most Holy God, the Almighty and Eternal, has begotten a son." The Khalif Omar, who took Jerusalem, commences a letter to Heraclius, the Roman emperor: "In the name of the most merciful God! Praise be to God, the Lord of this and of the other world, who has neither female consort nor son." The Saracens nicknamed the Christians "Associators," because they joined Mary and Jesus as partners with the Almighty and Most Holy God.

It was not the intention of the khalif to command his army; that duty was devolved on Abou Obeidah nominally, on Khaled in reality. In a parting review the khalif enjoined on his troops justice, mercy, and the observance of fidelity in their engagements he commanded them to abstain from all frivolous conversation and from wine, and rigorously to observe the hours of prayer; to be kind to the common people among whom they passed, but to show no mercy to their priests.

FALL OF BOZRAH. Eastward of the river Jordan is Bozrah, a strong town where Mohammed had first met his Nestorian Christian instructors. It was one of the Roman forts with which the country was dotted over. Before this place the Saracen army encamped. The garrison was strong, the ramparts were covered with holy crosses and consecrated banners. It might have made a long defense. But its governor, Romanus, betrayed his trust, and stealthily opened its gates to the besiegers. His conduct shows to what a deplorable condition the population of Syria had come. After the surrender, in a speech he made to the people he had betrayed, he said: "I renounce your society, both in this world and that to come. And I deny him that was crucified, and whosoever worships him. And I choose God for my Lord, Islam for my faith, Mecca for my temple, the Moslems for my brethren, Mohammed for my prophet, who was sent to lead us in the right way, and to exalt the true religion in spite of those who join partners with God." Since the Persian invasion, Asia Minor, Syria, and even Palestine, were full of traitors and apostates, ready to join the Saracens. Romanus was but one of many thousands who had fallen into disbelief through the victories of the Persians.

FALL OF DAMASCUS. From Bozrah it was only seventy miles northward to Damascus, the capital of Syria. Thither, without delay, the Saracen army marched. The city was at once summoned to take its option—conversion, tribute, or the sword. In his palace at Antioch, barely one hundred and fifty miles still farther north, the Emperor Heraclius received tidings of the alarming advance of his assailants. He at once dispatched an army of seventy thousand men. The Saracens were compelled to raise the siege. A battle took place in the plains of Aiznadin, the Roman army was overthrown and dispersed. Khaled reappeared before

Damascus with his standard of the black eagle, and after a renewed investment of seventy days Damascus surrendered.

From the Arabian historians of these events we may gather that thus far the Saracen armies were little better than a fanatic mob. Many of the men fought naked. It was not unusual for a warrior to stand forth in front and challenge an antagonist to mortal duel. Nay, more, even the women engaged in the combats. Picturesque narratives have been handed down to us relating the gallant manner in which they acquitted themselves.

FALL OF JERUSALEM. From Damascus the Saracen army advanced northward, guided by the snow-clad peaks of Libanus and the beautiful river Orontes. It captured on its way Baalbec, the capital of the Syrian valley, and Emesa, the chief city of the eastern plain. To resist its further progress, Heraclius collected an army of one hundred and forty thousand men. A battle took place at Yermuck; the right wing of the Saracens was broken, but the soldiers were driven back to the field by the fanatic expostulations of their women. The conflict ended in the complete overthrow of the Roman army. Forty thousand were taken prisoners, and a vast number killed. The whole country now lay open to the victors. The advance of their army had been east of the Jordan. It was clear that, before Asia Minor could be touched, the strong and important cities of Palestine, which was now in their rear, must be secured. There was a difference of opinion among the generals in the field as to whether Caesarea or Jerusalem should be assailed first. The matter was referred to the khalif, who, rightly preferring the moral advantages of the capture of Jerusalem to the military advantages of the capture of Caesarea, ordered the Holy City to be taken, and that at any cost. Close siege was therefore laid to it. The inhabitants, remembering the atrocities inflicted by the Persians, and the indignities that had been offered to the Savior's sepulchre, prepared now for a vigorous defense. But, after an investment of four months, the Patriarch Sophronius appeared on the wall, asking terms of capitulation. There had been misunderstandings among the generals at the capture of Damascus, followed by a massacre of the fleeing inhabitants. Sophronius, therefore, stipulated that the surrender of Jerusalem should take place in presence of the khalif himself Accordingly, Omar, the khalif, came from Medina for that purpose. He journeyed on a red camel, carrying a bag of corn and one of dates, a wooden dish, and a leathern water-bottle. The Arab conqueror entered the Holy City riding by the side of the Christian patriarch and the transference of the capital of Christianity to the representative of Mohammedanism was effected without tumult or outrage. Having ordered that a mosque should be built on the site of the temple of Solomon, the khalif returned to the tomb of the Prophet at Medina.

Heraclius saw plainly that the disasters which were fast settling on Christianity were due to the dissensions of its conflicting sects; and hence, while he endeavored to defend the empire with his armies, he sedulously tried to compose those differences. With this view he pressed for acceptance the Monothelite doctrine of the nature of Christ. But it was now too late. Aleppo and Antioch were taken. Nothing could prevent the Saracens from overrunning Asia Minor. Heraclius himself had to seek safety in flight. Syria, which had been added by Pompey the Great, the rival of Caesar, to the provinces of Rome, seven hundred years previously—Syria, the birthplace of Christianity, the scene of its most sacred and precious souvenirs, the land from which Heraclius himself had once expelled the Persian intruder—was irretrievably lost. Apostates and traitors had wrought this calamity. We are told that, as the ship which bore him to Constantinople parted from the shore, Heraclius gazed intently on the receding hills, and in the bitterness of anguish exclaimed, "Farewell, Syria, forever farewell!"

It is needless to dwell on the remaining details of the Saracen conquest: how Tripoli and Tyre were betrayed; how Caesarea was captured; how with the trees of Libanus and the sailors of Phoenicia a Saracen fleet was equipped, which drove the Roman navy into the Hellespont; how Cyprus, Rhodes, and the Cyclades, were ravaged, and the Colossus, which was counted as one of the wonders of the world, sold to a Jew, who loaded nine hundred camels with its brass; how the armies of the khalif advanced to the Black Sea, and even lay in front of Constantinople—all this was as nothing after the fall of Jerusalem.

OVERTHROW OF THE PERSIANS. The fall of Jerusalem! the loss of the metropolis of Christianity! In the ideas of that age the two antagonistic forms of faith had submitted themselves to the ordeal of the judgment of God. Victory had awarded the prize of battle, Jerusalem, to the Mohammedan; and, notwithstanding the temporary successes of the Crusaders, after much more than a thousand years in his hands it remains to this day. The Byzantine historians are not without excuse for the course they are condemned for taking: "They have wholly neglected the great topic of the ruin of the Eastern Church." And as for the Western Church, even the debased popes of the middle ages—the ages of the Crusades—could not see without indignation that they were compelled to rest the claims of Rome as the metropolis of Christendom on a false legendary story of a visit of St. Peter to that city; while the true metropolis, the grand, the sacred place of the birth, the life, the death of Christ himself, was in the hands of the infidels! It has not been the Byzantine historians alone who have tried to conceal this great catastrophe. The Christian writers of Europe on all manner of subjects, whether of history, religion, or science, have followed a similar course against their conquering antagonists. It has been their constant practice to hide what they could not depreciate, and depreciate what they could not hide.

INVASION OF EGYPT. I have not space, nor indeed does it comport with the intention of this work, to relate, in such detail as I have given to the fall of Jerusalem, other conquests of the Saracens—conquests which eventually established a Mohammedan empire far exceeding in geographical extent that of Alexander, and even that of Rome. But, devoting a few words to this subject, it may be said that Magianism received a worse blow than that which had been inflicted on Christianity; The fate of Persia was settled at the battle of Cadesia. At the sack of Ctesiphon, the treasury, the royal arms, and an unlimited spoil, fell into the hands of the Saracens. Not without reason do they call the battle of Nehavend the "victory of victories." In one direction they advanced to the Caspian, in the other southward along the Tigris to Persepolis. The Persian king fled for his life over the great Salt Desert, from the columns and statues of that city which had lain in ruins since the night of the riotous banquet of Alexander. One division of the Arabian army forced the Persian monarch over the Oxus. He was assassinated by the Turks. His son was driven into China, and became a captain in the Chinese emperor's guards. The country beyond the Oxus was reduced. It paid a tribute of two million pieces of gold. While the emperor at Peking was demanding the friendship of the khalif at Medina, the standard of the Prophet was displayed on the banks of the Indus.

Among the generals who had greatly distinguished themselves in the Syrian wars was Amrou, destined to be the conqueror of Egypt; for the khalifs, not content with their victories on the North and East, now turned their eyes to the West, and prepared for the annexation of Africa. As in the former cases, so in this, sectarian treason assisted them. The Saracen army was hailed as the deliverer of the Jacobite Church; the Monophysite Christians of Egypt, that is, they who, in the language of the Athanasian Creed, confounded the substance of the Son, proclaimed, through their leader, Mokaukas, that they desired no communion with the Greeks, either in this world or the next, that they abjured forever the Byzantine tyrant and his synod of Chalcedon. They hastened to pay tribute to the khalif, to repair the roads and bridges, and to supply provisions and intelligence to the invading army.

FALL OF ALEXANDRIA. Memphis, one of the old Pharaonic capitals, soon fell, and Alexandria was invested. The open sea behind gave opportunity to Heraclius to reenforce the garrison continually. On his part, Omar, who was now khalif sent to the succor of the besieging army the veteran troops of Syria. There were many assaults and many sallies. In one Amrou himself was taken prisoner by the besieged, but, through the dexterity of a slave, made his escape. After a siege of fourteen months, and a loss of twenty-three thousand men, the Saracens captured the city. In his dispatch to the Khalif, Amrou enumerated the splendors of the great city of the West "its four thousand palaces, four thousand baths, four hundred theatres, twelve thousand shops for the sale of vegetable food, and forty thousand tributary Jews."

So fell the second great city of Christendom—the fate of Jerusalem had fallen on Alexandria, the city of Athanasius, and Arius, and Cyril; the city that had imposed Trinitarian ideas and Mariolatry on the Church. In his palace at Constantinople Heraclius received the fatal tidings. He was overwhelmed with grief. It seemed as if his reign was to be disgraced by the downfall of Christianity. He lived scarcely a month after the loss of the town.

But if Alexandria had been essential to Constantinople in the supply of orthodox faith, she was also essential in the supply of daily food. Egypt was the granary of the Byzantines. For this reason two attempts were made by powerful fleets and armies for the recovery of the place, and twice had Amrou to renew his conquest. He saw with what facility these attacks could be made, the place being open to the sea; he saw that there was but one and that a fatal remedy. "By the living God, if this thing be repeated a third time I will make Alexandria as open to anybody as is the house of a prostitute!" He was better than his word, for he forthwith dismantled its fortifications, and made it an untenable place.

FALL OF CARTHAGE. It was not the intention of the khalifs to limit their conquest to Egypt. Othman contemplated the annexation of the entire North-African coast. His general, Abdallah, set out from Memphis with forty thousand men, passed through the desert of Barca, and besieged Tripoli. But, the plague breaking out in his army, he was compelled to retreat to Egypt.

All attempts were now suspended for more than twenty years. Then Akbah forced his way from the Nile to the Atlantic Ocean. In front of the Canary Islands he rode his horse into the sea, exclaiming: "Great God! if my course were not stopped by this sea, I would still go on to the unknown kingdoms of the West, preaching the unity of thy holy name, and putting to the sword the rebellious nations who worship any other gods than thee."

These Saracen expeditions had been through the interior of the country, for the Byzantine emperors, controlling for the time the Mediterranean, had retained possession of the cities on the coast. The Khalif Abdalmalek at length resolved on the reduction of Carthage, the most important of those cities, and indeed the capital of North Africa. His general, Hassan, carried it by escalade; but reenforcements from Constantinople, aided by some Sicilian and Gothic troops, compelled him to retreat. The relief was, however, only temporary. Hassan, in the course of a few months renewed his attack. It proved successful, and he delivered Carthage to the flames.

Jerusalem, Alexandria, Carthage, three out of the five great Christian capitals, were lost. The fall of Constantinople was only a question of time. After its fall, Rome alone remained.

In the development of Christianity, Carthage had played no insignificant part. It had given to Europe its Latin form of faith, and some of its greatest theologians. It was the home of St. Augustine.

Never in the history of the world had there been so rapid and extensive a propagation of any religion as Mohammedanism. It was now dominating from the Altai Mountains to the Atlantic Ocean, from the centre of Asia to the western verge of Africa.

CONQUEST OF SPAIN. The Khalif Alwalid next authorized the invasion of Europe, the conquest of Andalusia, or the Region of the Evening. Musa, his general, found, as had so often been the case elsewhere, two effective allies sectarianism and treason—the Archbishop of Toledo and Count Julian the Gothic general. Under their lead, in the very crisis of the battle of Xeres, a large portion of the army went over to the invaders; the Spanish king was compelled to flee from the field, and in the pursuit he was drowned in the waters of the Guadalquivir.

With great rapidity Tarik, the lieutenant of Musa, pushed forward from the battle-field to Toledo, and thence northward. On the arrival of Musa the reduction of the Spanish peninsula was completed, and the wreck of the Gothic army driven beyond the Pyrenees into France. Considering the conquest of Spain as only the first step in his victories, he announced his intention of forcing his way into Italy, and preaching the unity of God in the Vatican. Thence he would march to Constantinople, and, having put all end to the Roman Empire and Christianity, would pass into Asia and lay his victorious sword on the footstool of the khalif at Damascus.

But this was not to be. Musa, envious of his lieutenant, Tarik, had treated him with great indignity. The friends of Tarik at the court of the khalif found means of retaliation. An envoy from Damascus arrested Musa in his camp; he was carried before his sovereign, disgraced by a public whipping, and died of a broken heart.

INVASION OF FRANCE. Under other leaders, however, the Saracen conquest of France was attempted. In a preliminary campaign the country from the mouth of the Garonne to that of the Loire was secured. Then Abderahman, the Saracen commander, dividing his forces into two columns, with one on the east passed the Rhone, and laid siege to Arles. A Christian army, attempting the relief of the place, was defeated with heavy loss. His western column, equally successful, passed the Dordogne, defeated another Christian army, inflicting on it such dreadful loss that, according to its own fugitives, "God alone could number the slain." All Central France was now overrun; the banks of the Loire were reached; the churches and monasteries were despoiled of their treasures; and the tutelar saints, who had worked so many miracles when there was no necessity, were found to want the requisite power when it was so greatly needed.

The progress of the invaders was at length stopped by Charles Martel (A.D. 732). Between Tours and Poictiers, a great battle, which lasted seven days, was fought. Abderahman was killed, the Saracens retreated, and soon afterward were compelled to recross the Pyrenees.

The banks of the Loire, therefore, mark the boundary of the Mohammedan advance in Western Europe. Gibbon, in his narrative of these great events, makes this remark: "A victorious line of march had been prolonged above a thousand miles from the rock of Gibraltar to the banks of the Loire—a repetition of an equal space would have carried the Saracens to the confines of Poland and the Highlands of Scotland."

INSULT TO ROME. It is not necessary for me to add to this sketch of the military diffusion of Mohammedanism, the operations of the Saracens on the Mediterranean Sea, their conquest of Crete and Sicily, their insult to Rome. It will be found, however, that their presence in Sicily and the south of Italy exerted a marked influence on the intellectual development of Europe.

Their insult to Rome! What could be more humiliating than the circumstances under which it took place (A.D. 846)? An insignificant Saracen expedition entered the Tiber and appeared before the walls of the city. Too weak to force an entrance, it insulted and plundered the precincts, sacrilegiously violating the tombs of St. Peter and St. Paul. Had the city itself been sacked, the moral effect could not have been greater. From the church of St. Peter its altar of silver was torn away and sent to Africa—St. Peter's altar, the very emblem of Roman Christianity!

Constantinople had already been besieged by the Saracens more than once; its fall was predestined, and only postponed. Rome had received the direst insult, the greatest loss that could be inflicted upon it; the venerable churches of Asia Minor had passed out of existence; no Christian could set his foot in Jerusalem without permission; the Mosque of Omar stood on the site of the Temple of Solomon. Among the ruins of Alexandria the Mosque of Mercy marked the spot where a Saracen general, satiated with massacre, had, in contemptuous compassion, spared the fugitive relics of the enemies of Mohammed; nothing remained of Carthage but her blackened ruins. The most powerful religious empire that the world had ever seen had suddenly come into existence. It stretched from the Atlantic Ocean to the Chinese Wall, from the shores of the Caspian to those of the Indian Ocean, and yet, in one sense, it had not reached its culmination. The day was to come when it was to expel the successors of the Caesars from their capital, and hold the peninsula of Greece in subjection, to dispute with Christianity the empire of Europe in the very centre of that continent, and in Africa to extend its dogmas and faith across burning deserts and through pestilential forests from the Mediterranean to regions southward far beyond the equinoctial line.

DISSENSIONS OF THE ARABS. But, though Mohammedanism had not reached its culmination, the dominion of the khalifs had. Not the sword of Charles Martel, but the internal dissension of the vast Arabian Empire, was the salvation of Europe. Though the Ommiade Khalifs were popular in Syria, elsewhere they were looked upon as intruders or usurpers; the kindred of the apostle was considered to be the rightful representative of his faith. Three parties, distinguished by their colors, tore the khalifate asunder with their disputes, and disgraced it by their atrocities. The color of the Ommiades was white, that of the Fatimites green, that of the Abassides black; the last represented the party of Abbas, the uncle of Mohammed. The result of these discords was a tripartite division of the Mohammedan Empire in the tenth century into the khalifates of Bagdad, of Cairoan, and of Cordova. Unity in Mohammedan political action was at an end, and Christendom found its safeguard, not in supernatural help, but in the quarrels of the rival potentates. To internal animosities foreign pressures were eventually added and Arabism, which had done so much for the intellectual advancement of the world, came to an end when the Turks and the Berbers attained to power.

The Saracens had become totally regardless of European opposition—they were wholly taken up with their domestic quarrels. Ockley says with truth, in his history: "The Saracens had scarce a deputy lieutenant or general that would not have thought it the greatest affront, and such as ought to stigmatize him with indelible disgrace, if he should have suffered himself to have been insulted by the united forces of all Europe. And if any one asks why the Greeks did not exert themselves more, in order to the extirpation of these insolent invaders, it is a sufficient answer to any person that is acquainted with the characters of those men to say that Amrou kept his residence at Alexandria, and Moawyah at Damascus."

As to their contempt, this instance may suffice: Nicephorus, the Roman emperor, had sent to the Khalif Haroun-al-Raschid a threatening letter, and this was the reply: "In the name of the most merciful God, Haroun-al-Raschid, commander of the faithful, to Nicephorus, the Roman dog! I have read thy letter, O thou son of an unbelieving mother. Thou shalt not hear, thou shalt behold my reply!" It was written in letters of blood and fire on the plains of Phrygia.

POLITICAL EFFECT OF POLYGAMY. A nation may recover the confiscation of its provinces, the confiscation of its wealth; it may survive the imposition of enormous war-fines; but it never can recover from that most frightful of all war-acts, the confiscation of its women. When Abou Obeidah sent to Omar news of his capture of Antioch, Omar gently upbraided him that he had not let the troops have the women. "If they want to marry in Syria, let them; and let them have as many female slaves as they have occasion for." It was the institution of polygamy, based upon the confiscation of the women in the vanquished countries, that secured forever the Mohammedan rule. The children of these unions gloried in their descent from their conquering fathers. No better proof can be given of the efficacy of this policy than that which is furnished by North Africa. The irresistible effect of polygamy in consolidating the new order of things was very striking. In little more than a single generation, the Khalif was informed by his officers that the tribute must cease, for all the children born in that region were Mohammedans, and all spoke Arabic.

MOHAMMEDANISM. Mohammedanism, as left by its founder, was an anthropomorphic religion. Its God was only a gigantic man, its heaven a mansion of carnal pleasures. From these imperfect ideas its more intelligent classes very soon freed themselves, substituting for them others more philosophical, more correct. Eventually they attained to an accordance with those that have been pronounced in our own times by the Vatican Council as orthodox. Thus Al-Gazzali says: "A knowledge of God cannot be obtained by means of the knowledge a man has of himself, or of his own soul. The attributes of God cannot be determined from the attributes of man. His sovereignty and government can neither be compared nor measured."

CHAPTER IV.

THE RESTORATION OF SCIENCE IN THE SOUTH.

By the influence of the Nestorians and Jews, the Arabians are turned to the cultivation of Science.—They modify their views as to the destiny of man, and obtain true conceptions respecting the structure of the world.—They ascertain the size of the earth, and determine its shape.—Their khalifs collect great libraries, patronize every department of science and literature, establish astronomical observatories.—They develop the mathematical sciences, invent algebra, and improve geometry and trigonometry.—They collect and translate the old Greek mathematical and astronomical works, and adopt the inductive method of Aristotle.—They establish many colleges, and, with the aid of the Nestorians, organize a public-school system.—They introduce the Arabic numerals and arithmetic, and catalogue and give names to the stars.—They lay the foundation of modern astronomy, chemistry, and physics, and introduce great improvements in agriculture and manufactures.

"IN the course of my long life," said the Khalif Ali, "I have often observed that men are more like the times they live in than they are like their fathers." This profoundly philosophical remark of the son-in-law of Mohammed is strictly true; for, though the personal, the bodily lineaments of a man may indicate his parentage, the constitution of his mind, and therefore the direction of his thoughts, is determined by the environment in which he lives.

When Amrou, the lieutenant of the Khalif Omar, conquered Egypt, and annexed it to the Saracenic Empire, he found in Alexandria a Greek grammarian, John surnamed Philoponus, or the Labor-lover. Presuming on the friendship which had arisen between them, the Greek solicited as a gift the remnant of the great library—a remnant which war and time and bigotry had spared. Amrou, therefore, sent to the khalif to ascertain his pleasure. "If," replied the khalif, "the books agree with the Koran, the Word of God, they are useless, and need not be preserved; if they disagree with it, they are pernicious. Let them be destroyed." Accordingly, they were distributed among the baths of Alexandria, and it is said that six months were barely sufficient to consume them.

Although the fact has been denied, there can be little doubt that Omar gave this order. The khalif was an illiterate man; his environment was an environment of fanaticism and ignorance. Omar's act was an illustration of Ali's remark.

THE ALEXANDRIAN LIBRARY BURNT. But it must not be supposed that the books which John the Labor-lover coveted were those which constituted the great library of the Ptolemies, and that of Eumenes, King of Pergamus. Nearly a thousand years had elapsed since Philadelphus began his collection. Julius Caesar had burnt more than half; the Patriarchs of Alexandria had not only permitted but superintended the dispersion of almost all the rest. Orosius expressly states that he saw the empty cases or shelves of the library twenty years after Theophilus, the uncle of St. Cyril, had procured from the Emperor Theodosius a rescript for its destruction. Even had this once noble collection never endured such acts of violence, the mere wear and tear, and perhaps, I may add, the pilfering of a thousand years, would have diminished it sadly. Though John, as the surname he received indicates, might rejoice in a superfluity of occupation, we may be certain that the care of a library of half a million books would transcend even his well-tried powers; and the cost of preserving and supporting it, that had demanded the ample resources of the Ptolemies and the Caesars, was beyond the means of a grammarian. Nor is the time required for its combustion or destruction any indication of the extent of the collection. Of all articles of fuel, parchment is, perhaps, the most wretched. Paper and papyrus do excellently well as kindling-materials, but we may be sure that the bath-men of Alexandria did not resort to parchment so long as they could find any thing else, and of parchment a very large portion of these books was composed.

There can, then, be no more doubt that Omar did order the destruction of this library, under an impression of its uselessness or its irreligious tendency, than that the Crusaders burnt the library of Tripoli, fancifully said to have consisted of three million volumes. The first apartment entered being found to contain nothing but the Koran, all the other books were supposed to be the works of the Arabian impostor, and were consequently committed to the flames. In both cases the story contains some truth and much exaggeration. Bigotry, however, has often distinguished itself by such exploits. The Spaniards burnt in Mexico vast piles of American picture-writings, an irretrievable loss; and Cardinal Ximenes delivered to the flames, in the squares of Granada, eighty thousand Arabic manuscripts, many of them translations of classical authors.

We have seen how engineering talent, stimulated by Alexander's Persian campaign, led to a wonderful development of pure science under the Ptolemies; a similar effect may be noted as the result of the Saracenic military operations.

The friendship contracted by Amrou, the conqueror of Egypt, with John the Grammarian, indicates how much the Arabian mind was predisposed to liberal ideas. Its step from the idolatry of the Caaba to the monotheism of Mohammed prepared it to expatiate in the wide and pleasing fields of literature and philosophy. There were two influences to which it was continually exposed. They conspired in determining its path. These were—1. That of the Nestorians in Syria; 2. That of the Jews in Egypt.

INFLUENCE OF THE NESTORIANS AND JEWS. In the last chapter I have briefly related the persecution of Nestor and his disciples. They bore testimony to the oneness of God, through many sufferings and martyrdoms. They utterly repudiated an Olympus filled with gods and goddesses. "Away from us a queen of heaven!"

Such being their special views, the Nestorians found no difficulty in affiliating with their Saracen conquerors, by whom they were treated not only with the highest respect, but intrusted with some of the most important offices of the state. Mohammed, in the strongest manner, prohibited his followers from committing any injuries against them. Jesuiabbas, their pontiff, concluded treaties both with the Prophet and with Omar, and subsequently the Khalif Haroun-al-Raschid placed all his public schools under the superintendence of John Masue, a Nestorian.

To the influence of the Nestorians that of the Jews was added. When Christianity displayed a tendency to unite itself with paganism, the conversion of the Jews was arrested; it totally ceased when Trinitarian ideas were introduced. The cities of Syria and Egypt were full of Jews. In Alexandria alone, at the time of its capture by Amrou, there were forty thousand who paid tribute. Centuries of misfortune and persecution had served only to confirm them in their monotheism, and to strengthen that implacable hatred of idolatry which they had cherished ever since the Babylonian captivity. Associated with the Nestorians, they translated into Syriac many Greek and Latin philosophical works, which were retranslated into Arabic. While the Nestorian was occupied with the education of the children of the great Mohammedan families, the Jew found his way into them in the character of a physician.

FATALISM OF THE ARABIANS. Under these influences the ferocious fanaticism of the Saracens abated, their manners were polished, their thoughts elevated. They overran the realms of Philosophy and Science as quickly as they had overrun the provinces of the Roman Empire. They abandoned the fallacies of vulgar Mohammedanism, accepting in their stead scientific truth.

In a world devoted to idolatry, the sword of the Saracen had vindicated the majesty of God. The doctrine of fatalism, inculcated by the Koran, had powerfully contributed to that result. "No man can anticipate or postpone his predetermined end. Death will overtake us even in lofty towers. From the beginning God hath settled the place in which each man shall die." In his figurative language the Arab said: "No man can by flight escape his fate. The Destinies ride their horses by night.... Whether asleep in bed or in the storm of battle, the angel of death will find thee." "I am convinced," said Ali, to whose wisdom we have already referred—"I am convinced that the affairs of men go by divine decree, and not by our administration." The Mussulmen are those who submissively resign themselves to the will of God. They reconciled fate and free-will by saying, "The outline is given us, we color the picture of life as we will." They said that, if we would overcome the laws of Nature, we must not resist, we must balance them against each other.

This dark doctrine prepared its devotees for the accomplishment of great things—things such as the Saracens did accomplish. It converted despair into resignation, and taught men to disdain hope. There was a proverb among them that "Despair is a freeman, Hope is a slave."

But many of the incidents of war showed plainly that medicines may assuage pain, that skill may close wounds, that those who are incontestably dying may be snatched from the grave. The Jewish physician became a living, an accepted protest against the fatalism of the Koran. By degrees the sternness of predestination was mitigated, and it was admitted that in individual life there is an effect due to free-will; that by his voluntary acts man may within certain limits determine his own course. But, so far as nations are concerned, since they can yield no personal accountability to God, they are placed under the control of immutable law.

In this respect the contrast between the Christian and the Mohammedan nations was very striking: The Christian was convinced of incessant providential interventions; he believed that there was no such thing as law in the government of the world. By prayers and entreaties he might prevail with God to change the current of affairs, or, if that failed, he might succeed with Christ, or perhaps with the Virgin Mary, or through the intercession of the saints, or by the influence of their relics or bones. If his own supplications were unavailing, he might obtain his desire through the intervention of his priest, or through that of the holy men of the Church, and especially if oblations or gifts of money were added. Christendom believed that she could change the course of affairs by influencing the conduct of superior beings. Islam rested in a pious resignation to the unchangeable will of God. The prayer of the Christian was mainly an earnest intercession for benefits hoped for, that of the Saracen a devout expression of gratitude for the past. Both substituted prayer for the ecstatic meditation of India. To the Christian the progress of the world was an exhibition of disconnected impulses, of sudden surprises. To the Mohammedan that progress presented a very different aspect. Every corporeal motion was due to some preceding motion; every thought to some preceding thought; every historical event was the offspring of some preceding event; every human action was the result of some foregone and accomplished action. In the long annals of our race, nothing has ever been abruptly introduced. There has been an orderly, an inevitable sequence from event to event. There is an iron chain of destiny, of which the links are facts; each stands in its preordained place—not one has ever been disturbed, not one has ever been removed. Every man came into the world without his own knowledge, he is to depart from it perhaps against his own wishes. Then let him calmly fold his hands, and expect the issues of fate.

Coincidently with this change of opinion as to the government of individual life, there came a change as respects the mechanical construction of the world. According to the Koran, the earth is a square plane, edged with vast mountains, which serve the double purpose of balancing it in its seat, and of sustaining the dome of the sky. Our devout admiration of the power and wisdom of God should be excited by the spectacle of this vast crystalline brittle expanse, which has been safely set in its position without so much as a crack or any other injury. Above the sky, and resting on it, is heaven, built in seven stories, the uppermost being the habitation of God, who, under the form of a gigantic man, sits on a throne, having on either side winged bulls, like those in the palaces of old Assyrian kings.

THEY MEASURE THE EARTH. These ideas, which indeed are not peculiar to Mohammedanism, but are entertained by all men in a certain stage of their intellectual development as religious revelations, were very quickly exchanged by the more advanced Mohammedans for others scientifically correct. Yet, as has been the case in Christian countries, the advance was not made without resistance on the part of the defenders of revealed truth. Thus when Al-Mamun, having become acquainted with the globular form of the earth, gave orders to his mathematicians and astronomers to measure a degree of a great circle upon it, Takyuddin, one of the most celebrated doctors of divinity of that time, denounced the wicked khalif, declaring that God would assuredly punish him for presumptuously interrupting the devotions of the faithful by encouraging and diffusing a false and atheistical philosophy among them. Al-Mamun, however, persisted. On the shores of the Red Sea, in the plains of Shinar, by the aid of an astrolabe, the elevation of the pole above the horizon was determined at two stations on the same meridian, exactly one degree apart. The distance between the two stations was then measured, and found to be two hundred thousand Hashemite cubits; this gave for the entire circumference of the earth about twenty-four thousand of our miles, a determination not far from the truth. But, since the spherical form could not be positively asserted from one such measurement, the khalif caused another to be made near Cufa in Mesopotamia. His astronomers divided themselves into two parties, and, starting from a given point, each party measured an arc of one degree, the one northward, the other southward. Their result is given in cubits. If the cubit employed was that known as the royal cubit, the length of a degree was ascertained within one-third of a mile of its true value. From these measures the khalif concluded that the globular form was established.

THEIR PASSION FOR SCIENCE. It is remarkable how quickly the ferocious fanaticism of the Saracens was transformed into a passion for intellectual pursuits. At first the Koran was an obstacle to literature and science. Mohammed had extolled it as the grandest of all compositions, and had adduced its unapproachable excellence as a proof of his divine mission. But, in little more than twenty years after his death, the experience that had been acquired in Syria, Persia, Asia Minor, Egypt, had produced a striking effect, and Ali the khalif reigning at that time, avowedly encouraged all kinds of literary pursuits. Moawyah, the founder of the Ommiade dynasty, who followed in 661, revolutionized the government. It had been elective, he made it hereditary. He removed its seat from Medina to a more central position at Damascus, and entered on a career of luxury and magnificence. He broke the bonds of a stern fanaticism, and put himself forth as a cultivator and patron of letters. Thirty years had wrought a wonderful change. A Persian satrap who had occasion to pay homage to Omar, the second khalif, found him asleep among the beggars on the steps of the Mosque of Medina; but foreign envoys who had occasion to seek Moawyah, the sixth khalif, were presented to him in a magnificent palace, decorated with exquisite arabesques, and adorned with flower-gardens and fountains.

THEIR LITERATURE. In less than a century after the death of Mohammed, translations of the chief Greek philosophical authors had been made into Arabic; poems such as the "Iliad" and the "Odyssey," being considered to have an irreligious tendency from their mythological allusions, were rendered into Syriac, to gratify the curiosity of the learned. Almansor, during his khalifate (A.D. 753-775), transferred the seat of government to Bagdad, which he converted into a splendid metropolis; he gave much of his time to the study and promotion of astronomy, and established schools of medicine and law. His grandson, Haroun-al-Raschid (A.D. 786), followed his example, and ordered that to every mosque in his dominions a school should be attached. But the Augustan age of Asiatic learning was during the khalifate of Al-Mamun (A.D. 813-832). He made Bagdad the centre of science, collected great libraries, and surrounded himself with learned men.

The elevated taste thus cultivated continued after the division of the Saracen Empire by internal dissensions into three parts. The Abasside dynasty in Asia, the Fatimite in Egypt, and the Ommiade in Spain, became rivals not merely in politics, but also in letters and science.

THEY ORIGINATE CHEMISTRY. In letters the Saracens embraced every topic that can amuse or edify the mind. In later times, it was their boast that they had produced more poets than all other nations combined. In science their great merit consists in this, that they cultivated it after the manner of the Alexandrian Greeks, not after the manner of the European Greeks. They perceived that it can never be advanced by mere speculation; its only sure progress is by the practical interrogation of Nature. The essential characteristics of their method are experiment and observation. Geometry and the mathematical sciences they looked upon as instruments of reasoning. In their numerous writings on mechanics, hydrostatics, optics, it is interesting to remark that the solution of a problem is always obtained by performing an experiment, or by an instrumental observation. It was this that made them the originators of chemistry, that led them to the invention of all kinds of apparatus for distillation, sublimation, fusion, filtration, etc.; that in astronomy caused them to appeal to divided instruments, as quadrants and astrolabes; in chemistry, to employ the balance, the theory of which they were perfectly familiar with; to construct tables of specific gravities and astronomical tables, as those of Bagdad, Spain, Samarcand; that produced their great improvements in geometry, trigonometry, the invention of algebra, and the adoption of the Indian numeration in arithmetic. Such were the results of their preference of the inductive method of Aristotle, their declining the reveries of Plato.

THEIR GREAT LIBRARIES. For the establishment and extension of the public libraries, books were sedulously collected. Thus the khalif Al-Mamun is reported to have brought into Bagdad hundreds of camel-loads of manuscripts. In a treaty he made with the Greek emperor,

Michael III., he stipulated that one of the Constantinople libraries should be given up to him. Among the treasures he thus acquired was the treatise of Ptolemy on the mathematical construction of the heavens. He had it forthwith translated into Arabic, under the title of "Al-magest." The collections thus acquired sometimes became very large; thus the Fatimite Library at Cairo contained one hundred thousand volumes, elegantly transcribed and bound. Among these, there were six thousand five hundred manuscripts on astronomy and medicine alone. The rules of this library permitted the lending out of books to students resident at Cairo. It also contained two globes, one of massive silver and one of brass; the latter was said to have been constructed by Ptolemy, the former cost three thousand golden crowns. The great library of the Spanish khalifs eventually numbered six hundred thousand volumes; its catalogue alone occupied forty-four. Besides this, there were seventy public libraries in Andalusia. The collections in the possession of individuals were sometimes very extensive. A private doctor refused the invitation of a Sultan of Bokhara because the carriage of his books would have required four hundred camels.

There was in every great library a department for the copying or manufacture of translations. Such manufactures were also often an affair of private enterprise. Honian, a Nestorian physician, had an establishment of the kind at Bagdad (A.D. 850). He issued versions of Aristotle, Plato, Hippocrates, Galen, etc. As to original works, it was the custom of the authorities of colleges to require their professors to prepare treatises on prescribed topics. Every khalif had his own historian. Books of romances and tales, such as "The Thousand and One Arabian Nights' Entertainments," bear testimony to the creative fancy of the Saracens. Besides these, there were works on all kinds of subjects—history, jurisprudence, politics, philosophy, biographies not only of illustrious men, but also of celebrated horses and camels. These were issued without any censorship or restraint, though, in later times, works on theology required a license for publication. Books of reference abounded, geographical, statistical, medical, historical dictionaries, and even abridgments or condensations of them, as the "Encyclopedic Dictionary of all the Sciences," by Mohammed Abu Abdallah. Much pride was taken in the purity and whiteness of the paper, in the skillful intermixture of variously-colored inks, and in the illumination of titles by gilding and other adornments.

The Saracen Empire was dotted all over with colleges. They were established in Mongolia, Tartary, Persia, Mesopotamia, Syria, Egypt, North Africa, Morocco, Fez, Spain. At one extremity of this vast region, which far exceeded the Roman Empire in geographical extent, were the college and astronomical observatory of Samarcand, at the other the Giralda in Spain. Gibbon, referring to this patronage of learning, says: "The same royal prerogative was claimed by the independent emirs of the provinces, and their emulation diffused the taste and the rewards of science from Samarcand and Bokhara to Fez and Cordova. The vizier of a sultan consecrated a sum of two hundred thousand pieces of gold to the foundation of a college at Bagdad, which he endowed with an annual revenue of fifteen thousand dinars. The fruits of instruction were communicated, perhaps, at different times, to six thousand disciples of every degree, from the son of the noble to that of the mechanic; a sufficient allowance was provided for the indigent scholars, and the merit or industry of the professors was repaid with adequate stipends. In every city the productions of Arabic literature were copied and collected, by the curiosity of the studious and the vanity of the rich." The superintendence of these schools was committed with noble liberality sometimes to Nestorians, sometimes to Jews. It mattered not in what country a man was born, nor what were his religious opinions; his attainment in learning was the only thing to be considered. The great Khalif Al-Mamun had declared that "they are the elect of God, his best and most useful servants, whose lives are devoted to the improvement of their rational faculties; that the teachers of wisdom are the true luminaries and legislators of this world, which, without their aid, would again sink into ignorance and barbarism."

After the example of the medical college of Cairo, other medical colleges required their students to pass a rigid examination. The candidate then received authority to enter on the practice of his profession. The first medical college established in Europe was that founded by the Saracens at Salerno, in Italy. The first astronomical observatory was that erected by them at Seville, in Spain.

THE ARABIAN SCIENTIFIC MOVEMENT. It would far transcend the limits of this book to give an adequate statement of the results of this imposing scientific movement. The ancient sciences were greatly extended—new ones were brought into existence. The Indian method of arithmetic was introduced, a beautiful invention, which expresses all numbers by ten characters, giving them an absolute value, and a value by position, and furnishing simple rules for the easy performance of all kinds of calculations. Algebra, or universal arithmetic—the method of calculating indeterminate quantities, or investigating the relations that subsist among quantities of all kinds, whether arithmetical or geometrical—was developed from the germ that Diophantus had left. Mohammed Ben Musa furnished the solution of quadratic equations, Omar Ben Ibra him that of cubic equations. The Saracens also gave to trigonometry its modern form, substituting sines for chords, which had been previously used; they elevated it into a separate science. Musa, above mentioned, was the author of a "Treatise on Spherical Trigonometry." Al-Baghadadi left one on land-surveying, so excellent, that by some it has been declared to be a copy of Euclid's lost work on that subject.

ARABIAN ASTRONOMY. In astronomy, they not only made catalogues, but maps of the stars visible in their skies, giving to those of the larger magnitudes the Arabic names they still bear on our celestial globes. They ascertained, as we have seen, the size of the earth by the measurement of a degree on her surface, determined the obliquity of the ecliptic, published corrected tables of the sun and moon fixed the length of the year, verified the precession of the equinoxes. The treatise of Albategnius on "The Science of the Stars" is spoken of by Laplace with respect; he also draws attention to an important fragment of Ibn-Junis, the astronomer of Hakem, the Khalif of Egypt, A.D. 1000, as containing a long series of observations from the time of Almansor, of eclipses, equinoxes, solstices, conjunctions of planets, occultations of stars—observations which have cast much light on the great variations of the system of the world. The Arabian astronomers also devoted themselves to the construction and perfection of astronomical instruments, to the measurement of time by clocks of various kinds, by clepsydras and sun-dials. They were the first to introduce, for this purpose, the use of the pendulum.

In the experimental sciences, they originated chemistry; they discovered some of its most important reagents—sulphuric acid, nitric acid, alcohol. They applied that science in the practice of medicine, being the first to publish pharmacopoeias or dispensatories, and to include in them mineral preparations. In mechanics, they had determined the laws of falling bodies, had ideas, by no means indistinct, of the nature of gravity; they were familiar with the theory of the mechanical powers. In hydrostatics they constructed the first tables of the specific gravities of bodies, and wrote treatises on the flotation and sinking of bodies in water. In optics, they corrected the Greek misconception, that a ray proceeds from the eye, and touches the object seen, introducing the hypothesis that the ray passes from the object to the eye. They understood the phenomena of the reflection and refraction of light. Alhazen made the great discovery of the curvilinear path of a ray of light through the atmosphere, and proved that we see the sun and moon before they have risen, and after they have set.

AGRICULTURE AND MANUFACTURE. The effects of this scientific activity are plainly perceived in the great improvements that took place in many of the industrial arts. Agriculture shows it in better methods of irrigation, the skillful employment of manures, the raising of improved breeds of cattle, the enactment of wise codes of rural laws, the introduction of the culture of rice, and that of sugar and coffee. The manufactures show it in the great extension of the industries of silk, cotton, wool; in the fabrication of cordova and morocco leather, and paper; in mining, casting, and various metallurgic operations; in the making of Toledo blades.

Passionate lovers of poetry and music, they dedicated much of their leisure time to those elegant pursuits. They taught Europe the game of chess; they gave it its taste for works of fiction—romances and novels. In the graver domains of literature they took delight: they had many admirable compositions on such subjects as the instability of human greatness; the consequences of irreligion; the reverses of fortune; the origin, duration, and end of the world. Sometimes, not without surprise, we meet with ideas which we flatter ourselves have originated in our own times. Thus our modern doctrines of evolution and development were taught in their schools. In fact, they carried them much farther than we are disposed to do, extending them even to inorganic or mineral things. The fundamental principle of alchemy was the natural process of development of metalline bodies. "When common people," says Al-Khazini, writing in the twelfth century, "hear from natural philosophers that gold is a body which has attained to perfection of maturity, to the goal of completeness, they firmly believe that it is something which has gradually come to that perfection by passing through the forms of all other metallic bodies, so that its gold nature was originally lead, afterward it became tin, then brass, then silver, and finally reached the development of gold; not knowing that the natural philosophers mean, in saying this, only something like what they mean when they speak of man, and attribute to him a completeness and equilibrium in nature and constitution—not that man was once a bull, and was changed into an ass, and afterward into a horse, and after that into an ape, and finally became a man."

CHAPTER V.

CONFLICT RESPECTING THE NATURE OF THE SOUL.—DOCTRINE OF EMANATION AND ABSORPTION.

European ideas respecting the soul.—It resembles the form of the body.

Philosophical views of the Orientals.—The Vedic theology and Buddhism assert the doctrine of emanation and absorption.—It is advocated by Aristotle, who is followed by the Alexandrian school, and subsequently by the Jews and

Arabians.—It is found in the writings of Erigena.

Connection of this doctrine with the theory of conservation and correlation of force.—Parallel between the origin and destiny of the body and the soul.—The necessity of founding human on comparative psychology.

Averroism, which is based on these facts, is brought into Christendom through Spain and Sicily.

History of the repression of Averroism.—Revolt of Islam against it.—Antagonism of the Jewish synagogues.—Its destruction undertaken by the papacy.—Institution of the Inquisition in Spain.—Frightful persecutions and their results.—Expulsion of the Jews and Moors.—Overthrow of Averroism in Europe.—Decisive action of the late Vatican Council.

THE pagan Greeks and Romans believed that the spirit of man resembles his bodily form, varying its appearance with his variations, and growing with his growth. Heroes, to whom it had been permitted to descend into Hades, had therefore without difficulty recognized their former friends. Not only had the corporeal aspect been retained, but even the customary raiment.

THE SOUL. The primitive Christians, whose conceptions of a future life and of heaven and hell, the abodes of the blessed and the sinful, were far more vivid than those of their pagan predecessors, accepted and intensified these ancient ideas. They did not doubt that in the world to come they should meet their friends, and hold converse with them, as they had done here upon earth—an expectation that gives consolation to the human heart, reconciling it to the most sorrowful bereavements, and restoring to it its dead.

In the uncertainty as to what becomes of the soul in the interval between its separation from the body and the judgment-day, many different opinions were held. Some thought that it hovered over the grave, some that it wandered disconsolate through the air. In the popular belief, St. Peter sat as a door-keeper at the gate of heaven. To him it had been given to bind or to loose. He admitted or excluded the Spirits of men at his pleasure. Many persons, however, were disposed to deny him this power, since his decisions would be anticipatory of the judgment-day, which would thus be rendered needless. After the time of Gregory the Great, the doctrine of purgatory met with general acceptance. A resting-place was provided for departed spirits.

That the spirits of the dead occasionally revisit the living, or haunt their former abodes, has been in all ages, in all European countries, a fixed belief, not confined to rustics, but participated in by the intelligent. A pleasing terror gathers round the winter's-evening fireside at the stories of apparitions, goblins, ghosts. In the old times the Romans had their lares, or spirits of those who had led virtuous lives; their larvae or lemures, the spirits of the wicked; their manes, the spirits of those of whom the merits were doubtful. If human testimony on such subjects can be of any value, there is a body of evidence reaching from the remotest ages to the present time, as extensive and unimpeachable as is to be found in support of any thing whatever, that these shades of the dead congregate near tombstones, or take up their secret abode in the gloomy chambers of dilapidated castles, or walk by moonlight in moody solitude.

ASIATIC PSYCHOLOGICAL VIEWS. While these opinions have universally found popular acceptance in Europe, others of a very different nature have prevailed extensively in Asia, and indeed very generally in the higher regions of thought. Ecclesiastical authority succeeded in repressing them in the sixteenth century, but they never altogether disappeared. In our own times so silently and extensively have they been diffused in Europe, that it was found expedient in the papal Syllabus to draw them in a very conspicuous manner into the open light; and the Vatican Council, agreeing in that view of their obnoxious tendency and secret spread, has in an equally prominent and signal manner among its first canons anathematized all persons who hold them. "Let him be anathema who says that spiritual things are emanations of the divine substance, or that the divine essence by manifestation or development becomes all things." In view of this authoritative action, it is necessary now to consider the character and history of these opinions.

Ideas respecting the nature of God necessarily influence ideas respecting the nature of the soul. The eastern Asiatics had adopted the conception of an impersonal God, and, as regards the soul, its necessary consequence, the doctrine of emanation and absorption.

EMANATION AND ABSORPTION. Thus the Vedic theology is based on the acknowledgment of a universal spirit pervading all things. "There is in truth but one Deity, the supreme Spirit; he is of the same nature as the soul of man." Both the Vedas and the Institutes of Menu affirm that the soul is an emanation of the all-pervading Intellect, and that it is necessarily destined to be reabsorbed. They consider it to be without form, and that visible Nature, with all its beauties and harmonies, is only the shadow of God.

Vedaism developed itself into Buddhism, which has become the faith of a majority of the human race. This system acknowledges that there is a supreme Power, but denies that there is a supreme Being. It contemplates the existence of Force, giving rise as its manifestation to matter. It adopts the theory of emanation and absorption. In a burning taper it sees an effigy of man—an embodiment of matter, and an evolution of force. If we interrogate it respecting the destiny of the soul, it demands of us what has become of the flame when it is blown out, and in what condition it was before the taper was lighted. Was it a nonentity? Has it been annihilated? It admits that the idea of personality which has deluded us through life may not be instantaneously extinguished at death, but may be lost by slow degrees. On this is founded the doctrine of transmigration. But at length reunion with the universal Intellect takes place, Nirwana is reached, oblivion is attained, a state that has no relation to matter, space, or time, the state into which the departed flame of the extinguished taper has gone, the state in which we were before we were born. This is the end that we ought to hope for; it is reabsorption in the universal Force—supreme bliss, eternal rest.

Through Aristotle these doctrines were first introduced into Eastern Europe; indeed, eventually, as we shall see, he was regarded as the author of them. They exerted a dominating influence in the later period of the Alexandrian school. Philo, the Jew, who lived in the time of Caligula, based his philosophy on the theory of emanation. Plotinus not only accepted that theory as applicable to the soul of man, but as affording an illustration of the nature of the Trinity. For, as a beam of light emanates from the sun, and as warmth emanates from the beam when it touches material bodies, so from the Father the Son emanates, and thence the Holy Ghost. From these views Plotinus derived a practical religious system, teaching the devout how to pass into a condition of ecstasy, a foretaste of absorption into the universal mundane soul.

In that condition the soul loses its individual consciousness. In like manner Porphyry sought absorption in or union with God. He was a Tyrian by birth, established a school at Rome, and wrote against Christianity; his treatise on that subject was answered by Eusebius and St. Jerome, but the Emperor Theodosius silenced it more effectually by causing all the copies to be burnt. Porphyry bewails his own unworthiness, saying that he had been united to God in ecstasy but once in eighty-six years, whereas his master Plotinus had been so united six times in sixty years. A complete system of theology, based on the theory of emanation, was constructed by Proclus, who speculated on the manner in which absorption takes place: whether the soul is instantly reabsorbed and reunited in the moment of death, or whether it retains the sentiment of personality for a time, and subsides into complete reunion by successive steps.

ARABIC PSYCHOLOGY. From the Alexandrian Greeks these ideas passed to the Saracen philosophers, who very soon after the capture of the great Egyptian city abandoned to the lower orders their anthropomorphic notions of the nature of God and the simulachral form of the spirit of man. As Arabism developed itself into a distinct scientific system, the theories of emanation and absorption were among its characteristic features. In this abandonment of vulgar Mohammedanism, the example of the Jews greatly assisted. They, too, had given up the anthropomorphism of their ancestors; they had exchanged the God who of old lived behind the veil of the temple for an infinite Intelligence pervading the universe, and, avowing their inability to conceive that any thing which had on a sudden been called into existence should be capable of immortality, they affirmed that the soul of man is connected with a past of which there was no beginning, and with a future to which there is no end.

In the intellectual history of Arabism the Jew and the Saracen are continually seen together. It was the same in their political history, whether we consider it in Syria, in Egypt, or in Spain. From them conjointly Western Europe derived its philosophical ideas, which in the course of time culminated in Averroism; Averroism is philosophical Islamism. Europeans generally regarded Averroes as the author of these heresies, and the orthodox branded him accordingly, but he was nothing more than their collector and commentator. His works invaded Christendom by two routes: from Spain through Southern France they reached Upper Italy, engendering numerous heresies on their way; from Sicily they passed to Naples and South Italy, under the auspices of Frederick II.

But, long before Europe suffered this great intellectual invasion, there were what might, perhaps, be termed sporadic instances of Orientalism. As an example I may quote the views of John Erigena (A.D. 800) He had adopted and taught the philosophy of Aristotle had made a pilgrimage to the birthplace of that philosopher, and indulged a hope of uniting philosophy and religion in the manner proposed by the Christian ecclesiastics who were then studying in the Mohammedan universities of Spain. He was a native of Britain.

In a letter to Charles the Bald, Anastasius expresses his astonishment "how such a barbarian man, coming from the very ends of the earth, and remote from human conversation, could comprehend things so clearly, and transfer them into another language so well." The general intention of his writings was, as we have said, to unite philosophy with religion, but his treatment of these subjects brought him under ecclesiastical censure, and some of his works were adjudged to the flames. His most important book is entitled "De Divisione Nature."

Erigena's philosophy rests upon the observed and admitted fact that every living thing comes from something that had previously lived. The visible world, being a world of life, has therefore emanated necessarily from some primordial existence, and that existence is God, who is thus the originator and conservator of all. Whatever we see maintains itself as a visible thing through force derived from him, and, were that force withdrawn, it must necessarily disappear. Erigena thus conceives of the Deity as an unceasing participator in Nature, being its preserver, maintainer, upholder, and in that respect answering to the soul of the world of the Greeks. The particular life of individuals is therefore a part of general existence, that is, of the mundane soul.

If ever there were a withdrawal of the maintaining power, all things must return to the source from which they issued—that is, they must return to God, and be absorbed in him. All visible Nature must thus pass back into "the Intellect" at last. "The death of the flesh is the auspices of the restitution of things, and of a return to their ancient conservation. So sounds revert back to the air in which they were born, and by which they were maintained, and they are heard no more; no man knows what has become of them. In that final absorption which, after a lapse of time, must necessarily come, God will be all in all, and nothing exist but him alone." "I contemplate him as the beginning and cause of all things; all things that are and those that have been, but now are not, were created from him, and by him, and in him. I also view him as the end and intransgressible term of all things.... There is a fourfold conception of universal Nature —two views of divine Nature, as origin and end; two also of framed Nature, causes and effects. There is nothing eternal but God."

The return of the soul to the universal Intellect is designated by Erigena as Theosis, or Deification. In that final absorption all remembrance of its past experiences is lost. The soul reverts to the condition in which it was before it animated the body. Necessarily, therefore, Erigena fell under the displeasure of the Church.

It was in India that men first recognized the fact that force is indestructible and eternal. This implies ideas more or less distinct of that which we now term its "correlation and conservation." Considerations connected with the stability of the universe give strength to this view, since it is clear that, were there either an increase or a diminution, the order of the world must cease. The definite and invariable amount of energy in the universe must therefore be accepted as a scientific fact. The changes we witness are in its distribution.

But, since the soul must be regarded as an active principle, to call a new one into existence out of nothing is necessarily to add to the force previously in the world. And, if this has been done in the case of every individual who has been born, and is to be repeated for every individual hereafter, the totality of force must be continually increasing.

Moreover, to many devout persons there is something very revolting in the suggestion that the Almighty is a servitor to the caprices and lusts of man, and that, at a certain term after its origin, it is necessary for him to create for the embryo a soul.

Considering man as composed of two portions, a soul and a body, the obvious relations of the latter may cast much light on the mysterious, the obscure relations of the former. Now, the substance of which the body consists is obtained from the general mass of matter around us, and after death to that general mass it is restored. Has Nature, then, displayed before our eyes in the origin, mutations, and destiny of the material part, the body, a revelation that may guide us to a knowledge of the origin and destiny of the companion, the spiritual part, the soul?

Let us listen for a moment to one of the most powerful of Mohammedan writers:

"God has created the spirit of man out of a drop of his own light; its destiny is to return to him. Do not deceive yourself with the vain imagination that it will die when the body dies. The form you had on your entrance into this world, and your present form, are not the same; hence there is no necessity of your perishing, on account of the perishing of your body. Your spirit came into this world a stranger, it is only sojourning, in a temporary home. From the trials and tempests of this troublesome life, our refuge is in God. In reunion with him we shall find eternal rest—a rest without sorrow, a joy without pain, a strength without infirmity, a knowledge without doubt, a tranquil and yet an ecstatic vision of the source of life and light and glory, the source from which we came." So says the Saracen philosopher, Al-Gazzali (A.D. 1010).

In a stone the material particles are in a state of stable equilibrium; it may, therefore, endure forever. An animal is in reality only a form through which a stream of matter is incessantly flowing. It receives its supplies, and dismisses its wastes. In this it resembles a cataract, a river, a flame. The particles that compose it at one instant have departed from it the next. It depends for its continuance on exterior supplies. It has a definite duration in time, and an inevitable moment comes in which it must die.

In the great problem of psychology we cannot expect to reach a scientific result, if we persist in restricting ourselves to the contemplation of one fact. We must avail ourselves of all accessible facts. Human psychology can never be completely resolved except through comparative psychology. With Descartes, we must inquire whether the souls of animals be relations of the human soul, less perfect members in the same series of development. We must take account of what we discover in the intelligent principle of the ant, as well as what we discern in the intelligent principle of man. Where would human physiology be, if it were not illuminated by the bright irradiations of comparative physiology?

Brodie, after an exhaustive consideration of the facts, affirms that the mind of animals is essentially the same as that of man. Every one familiar with the dog will admit that that creature knows right from wrong, and is conscious when he has committed a fault. Many domestic animals have reasoning powers, and employ proper means for the attainment of ends. How numerous are the anecdotes related of the intentional actions of the elephant and the ape! Nor is this apparent intelligence due to imitation, to their association with man, for wild animals that have no such relation exhibit similar properties. In different species, the capacity and character greatly vary. Thus the dog is not only more intelligent, but has social and moral qualities that the cat does not possess; the former loves his master, the latter her home.

Du Bois-Reymond makes this striking remark: "With awe and wonder must the student of Nature regard that microscopic molecule of nervous substance which is the seat of the laborious, constructive, orderly, loyal, dauntless soul of the ant. It has developed itself to its present state through a countless series of generations." What an impressive inference we may draw from the statement of Huber, who has written so well on this subject: "If you will watch a single ant at work, you can tell what he will next do!" He is considering the matter, and reasoning as you are doing. Listen to one of the many anecdotes which Huber, at once truthful and artless, relates: "On the visit of an overseer ant to the works, when the laborers had begun the roof too soon, he examined it and had it taken down, the wall raised to the proper height, and a new ceiling constructed with the fragments of the old one." Surely these insects are not automata, they show intention. They recognize their old companions, who have been shut up from them for many months, and exhibit sentiments of joy at their return. Their antennal language is capable of manifold expression; it suits the interior of the nest, where all is dark.

While solitary insects do not live to raise their young, social insects have a longer term, they exhibit moral affections and educate their offspring. Patterns of patience and industry, some of these insignificant creatures will work sixteen or eighteen hours a day. Few men are capable of sustained mental application more than four or five hours.

Similarity of effects indicates similarity of causes; similarity of actions demands similarity of organs. I would ask the reader of these paragraphs, who is familiar with the habits of animals, and especially with the social relations of that wonderful insect to which reference has been made, to turn to the nineteenth chapter of my work on the "Intellectual Development of Europe," in which he will find a description of the social system of the Incas of Peru. Perhaps, then, in view of the similarity of the social institutions and personal conduct of the insect, and the social institutions and personal conduct of the civilized Indian—the one an insignificant speck, the other a man—he will not be disposed to disagree with me in the opinion that "from bees, and wasps, and ants, and birds, from all that low animal life on which he looks with supercilious contempt, man is destined one day to learn what in truth he really is."

The views of Descartes, who regarded all insects as automata, can scarcely be accepted without modification. Insects are automata only so far as the action of their ventral cord, and that portion of their cephalic ganglia which deals with contemporaneous impressions, is concerned.

It is one of the functions of vesicular-nervous material to retain traces or relics of impressions brought to it by the organs of sense; hence, nervous ganglia, being composed of that material, may be considered as registering apparatus. They also introduce the element of time into the action of the nervous mechanism. An impression, which without them might have forthwith ended in reflex action, is delayed, and with this duration come all those important effects arising through the interaction of many impressions, old and new, upon each other.

There is no such thing as a spontaneous, or self-originated, thought. Every intellectual act is the consequence of some preceding act. It comes into existence in virtue of something that has gone before. Two minds constituted precisely alike, and placed under the influence of precisely the same environment, must give rise to precisely the same thought. To such sameness of action we allude in the popular expression "common-sense"—a term full of meaning. In the origination of a thought there are two distinct conditions: the state of the organism as dependent on antecedent impressions, and on the existing physical circumstances.

In the cephalic ganglia of insects are stored up the relics of impressions that have been made upon the common peripheral nerves, and in them are kept those which are brought in by the organs of special sense—the visual, olfactive, auditory. The interaction of these raises insects above mere mechanical automata, in which the reaction instantly follows the impression.

In all cases the action of every nerve-centre, no matter what its stage of development may be, high or low, depends upon an essential chemical condition—oxidation. Even in man, if the supply of arterial blood be stopped but for a moment, the nerve-mechanism loses its power; if diminished, it correspondingly declines; if, on the contrary, it be increased—as when nitrogen monoxide is breathed—there is more energetic action. Hence there arises a need of repair, a necessity for rest and sleep.

Two fundamental ideas are essentially attached to all our perceptions of external things: they are SPACE and TIME, and for these provision is made in the nervous mechanism while it is yet in an almost rudimentary state. The eye is the organ of space, the ear of time; the perceptions of which by the elaborate mechanism of these structures become infinitely more precise than would be possible if the sense of touch alone were resorted to.

There are some simple experiments which illustrate the vestiges of ganglionic impressions. If on a cold, polished metal, as a new razor, any object, such as a wafer, be laid, and the metal be then breathed upon, and, when the moisture has had time to disappear, the wafer be thrown off, though now the most critical inspection of the polished surface can discover no trace of any form, if we breathe once more upon it, a spectral image of the wafer comes plainly into view; and this may be done again and again. Nay, more, if the polished metal be carefully put aside where nothing can deteriorate its surface, and be so kept for many months, on breathing again upon it the shadowy form emerges.

Such an illustration shows how trivial an impression may be thus registered and preserved. But, if, on such an inorganic surface, an impression may thus be indelibly marked, how much more likely in the purposely-constructed ganglion! A shadow never falls upon a wall without leaving thereupon a permanent trace, a trace which might be made visible by resorting to proper processes. Photographic operations are cases in point. The portraits of our friends, or landscape views, may be hidden on the sensitive surface from the eye, but they are ready to make their appearance as soon as proper developers are resorted to. A spectre is concealed on a silver or glassy surface until, by our necromancy, we make it come forth into the visible world. Upon the walls of our most private apartments, where we think the eye of intrusion is altogether shut out and our retirement can never be profaned, there exist the vestiges of all our acts, silhouettes of whatever we have done.

If, after the eyelids have been closed for some time, as when we first awake in the morning, we suddenly and steadfastly gaze at a brightly-illuminated object and then quickly close the lids again, a phantom image is perceived in the indefinite darkness beyond us. We may satisfy ourselves that this is not a fiction, but a reality, for many details that we had not time to identify in the momentary glance may be contemplated at our leisure in the phantom. We may thus make out the pattern of such an object as a lace curtain hanging in the window, or the branches of a tree beyond. By degrees the image becomes less and less distinct; in a minute or two it has disappeared. It seems to have a tendency to float away in the vacancy before us. If we attempt to follow it by moving the eyeball, it suddenly vanishes.

Such a duration of impressions on the retina proves that the effect of external influences on nerve-vesicles is not necessarily transitory. In this there is a correspondence to the duration, the emergence, the extinction, of impressions on photographic preparations. Thus, I have seen landscapes and architectural views taken in Mexico developed, as artists say, months subsequently in New York—the images coming out, after the long voyage, in all their proper forms and in all their proper contrast of light and shade. The photograph had forgotten nothing. It had equally preserved the contour of the everlasting mountains and the passing smoke of a bandit-fire.

Are there, then, contained in the brain more permanently, as in the retina more transiently, the vestiges of impressions that have been gathered by the sensory organs? Is this the explanation of memory—the Mind contemplating such pictures of past things and events as have been committed to her custody. In her silent galleries are there hung micrographs of the living and the dead, of scenes that we have visited, of incidents in which we have borne a part? Are these abiding impressions mere signal-marks, like the letters of a book, which impart ideas to the mind? or are they actual picture-images, inconceivably smaller than those made for us by artists, in which, by the aid of a microscope, we can see, in a space not bigger than a pinhole, a whole family group at a glance?

The phantom images of the retina are not perceptible in the light of the day. Those that exist in the sensorium in like manner do not attract our attention so long as the sensory organs are in vigorous operation, and occupied in bringing new impressions in. But, when those organs become weary or dull, or when we experience hours of great anxiety, or are in twilight reveries, or are asleep, the latent apparitions have their vividness increased by the contrast, and obtrude themselves on the mind. For the same reason they occupy us in the delirium of fevers, and doubtless also in the solemn moments of death. During a third part of our life, in sleep, we are withdrawn from external influences; hearing and sight and the other senses are inactive, but the never-sleeping Mind, that pensive, that veiled enchantress, in her mysterious retirement, looks over the ambrotypes she has collected—ambrotypes, for they are truly unfading impressions—and, combining them together, as they chance to occur, constructs from them the panorama of a dream.

Nature has thus implanted in the organization of every man means which impressively suggest to him the immortality of the soul and a future life. Even the benighted savage thus sees in his visions the fading forms of landscapes, which are, perhaps, connected with some of his most pleasant recollections; and what other conclusion can be possibly extract from those unreal pictures than that they are the foreshadowings of another land beyond that in which his lot is cast? At intervals he is visited in his dreams by the resemblances of those whom he has loved or hated while they were alive; and these manifestations are to him incontrovertible proofs of the existence and immortality of the soul. In our most refined social conditions we are never able to shake off the impressions of these occurrences, and are perpetually drawing from them the same conclusions that our uncivilized ancestors did. Our more elevated condition of life in no respect relieves us from the inevitable operation of our own organization, any more than it relieves us from infirmities and disease. In these respects, all over the globe men are on an equality. Savage or civilized, we carry within us a mechanism which presents us with mementoes of the most solemn facts with which we can be concerned. It wants only moments of repose or sickness, when the influence of external things is diminished, to come into full play, and these are precisely the moments when we are best prepared for the truths it is going to suggest. That mechanism is no respecter of persons. It neither permits the haughtiest to be free from the monitions, nor leaves the humblest without the consolation of a knowledge of another life. Open to no opportunities of being tampered with by the designing or interested, requiring no extraneous human agency for its effect, out always present with every man wherever he may go, it marvelously extracts from vestiges of the impressions of the past overwhelming proofs of the realities of the future, and, gathering its power from what would seem to be a most unlikely source, it insensibly leads us, no matter who or where we may be, to a profound belief in the immortal and imperishable, from phantoms which have scarcely made their appearance before they are ready to vanish away.

The insect differs from a mere automaton in this, that it is influenced by old, by registered impressions. In the higher forms of animated life that registration becomes more and more complete, memory becomes more perfect. There is not any necessary resemblance between an external form and its ganglionic impression, any more than there is between the words of a message delivered in a telegraphic office and the signals which the telegraph may give to the distant station; any more than there is between the letters of a printed page and the acts or scenes they describe, but the letters call up with clearness to the mind of the reader the events and scenes.

An animal without any apparatus for the retention of impressions must be a pure automaton

—it cannot have memory. From insignificant and uncertain beginnings, such an apparatus is gradually evolved, and, as its development advances, the intellectual capacity increases. In man, this retention or registration reaches perfection; he guides, himself by past as well as by present impressions; he is influenced by experience; his conduct is determined by reason.

A most important advance is made when the capability is acquired by any animal of imparting a knowledge of the impressions stored up in its own nerve-centres to another of the same kind. This marks the extension of individual into social life, and indeed is essential thereto. In the higher insects it is accomplished by antennal contacts, in man by speech. Humanity, in its earlier, its savage stages, was limited to this: the knowledge of one person could be transmitted to another by conversation. The acts and thoughts of one generation could be imparted to another, and influence its acts and thoughts.

But tradition has its limit. The faculty of speech makes society possible—nothing more.

Not without interest do we remark the progress of development of this function. The invention of the art of writing gave extension and durability to the registration or record of impressions. These, which had hitherto been stored up in the brain of one man, might now be imparted to the whole human race, and be made to endure forever. Civilization became possible—for civilization cannot exist without writing, or the means of record in some shape.

From this psychological point of view we perceive the real significance of the invention of printing—a development of writing which, by increasing the rapidity of the diffusion of ideas, and insuring their permanence, tends to promote civilization and to unify the human race.

In the foregoing paragraphs, relating to nervous impressions, their registry, and the consequences, that spring from them, I have given an abstract of views presented in my work on "Human Physiology," published in 1856, and may, therefore, refer the reader to the chapter on "Inverse Vision, or Cerebral Sight;" to Chapter XIV., Book I.; and to Chapter VIII., Book II.; of that work, for other particulars.

The only path to scientific human psychology is through comparative psychology. It is a long and wearisome path, but it leads to truth.

Is there, then, a vast spiritual existence pervading the universe, even as there is a vast existence of matter pervading it—a spirit which, as a great German author tells us, "sleeps in the stone, dreams in the animal, awakes in man?" Does the soul arise from the one as the body arises from the other? Do they in like manner return, each to the source from which it has come? If so, we can interpret human existence, and our ideas may still be in unison with scientific truth, and in accord with our conception of the stability, the unchangeability of the universe.

To this spiritual existence the Saracens, following Eastern nations, gave the designation "the Active Intellect." They believed that the soul of man emanated from it, as a rain-drop comes from the sea, and, after a season, returns. So arose among them the imposing doctrines of emanation and absorption. The active intellect is God.

In one of its forms, as we have seen, this idea was developed by Chakia Mouni, in India, in a most masterly manner, and embodied in the vast practical system of Buddhism; in another, it was with less power presented among the Saracens by Averroes.

But, perhaps we ought rather to say that Europeans hold Averroes as the author of this doctrine, because they saw him isolated from his antecedents. But Mohammedans gave him little credit for originality. He stood to them in the light of a commentator on Aristotle, and as presenting the opinions of the Alexandrian and other philosophical schools up to his time. The following excerpts from the "Historical Essay on Averroism," by M. Renan, will show how closely the Sarscenic ideas approached those presented above:

This system supposes that, at the death of an individual, his intelligent principle or soul no longer possesses a separate existence, but returns to or is absorbed in the universal mind, the active intelligence, the mundane soul, which is God; from whom, indeed, it had originally emanated or issued forth.

The universal, or active, or objective intellect, is uncreated, impassible, incorruptible, has neither beginning nor end; nor does it increase as the number of individual souls increases. It is altogether separate from matter. It is, as it were, a cosmic principle. This oneness of the active intellect, or reason, is the essential principle of the Averroistic theory, and is in harmony with the cardinal doctrine of Mohammedanism—the unity of God.

The individual, or passive, or subjective intellect, is an emanation from the universal, and constitutes what is termed the soul of man. In one sense it is perishable and ends with the body, but in a higher sense it endures; for, after death, it returns to or is absorbed in the universal soul, and thus of all human souls there remains at last but one—the aggregate of them all, life is not the property of the individual, it belongs to Nature. The end of, man is to enter into union more and more complete with the active intellect—reason. In that the happiness of the soul consists. Our destiny is quietude. It was the opinion of Averroes that the transition from the individual to the universal is instantaneous at death, but the Buddhists maintain that human personality continues in a declining manner for a certain term before nonentity, or Nirwana, is attained.

Philosophy has never proposed but two hypotheses to explain the system of the world: first, a personal God existing apart, and a human soul called into existence or created, and thenceforth immortal; second, an impersonal intelligence, or indeterminate God, and a soul emerging from and returning to him. As to the origin of beings, there are two opposite opinions: first, that they are created from nothing; second, that they come by development from pre-existing forms. The theory of creation belongs to the first of the above hypotheses, that of evolution to the last.

Philosophy among the Arabs thus took the same direction that it had taken in China, in India, and indeed throughout the East. Its whole spirit depended on the admission of the indestructibility of matter and force. It saw an analogy between the gathering of the material of which the body of man consists from the vast store of matter in Nature, and its final restoration to that store, and the emanation of the spirit of man from the universal Intellect, the Divinity, and its final reabsorption.

Having thus indicated in sufficient detail the philosophical characteristics of the doctrine of emanation and absorption, I have in the next place to relate its history. It was introduced into Europe by the Spanish Arabs. Spain was the focal point from which, issuing forth, it affected the ranks of intelligence and fashion all over Europe, and in Spain it had a melancholy end.

The Spanish khalifs had surrounded themselves with all the luxuries of Oriental life. They had magnificent palaces, enchanting gardens, seraglios filled with beautiful women. Europe at the present day does not offer more taste, more refinement, more elegance, than might have been seen, at the epoch of which we are speaking, in the capitals of the Spanish Arabs. Their streets were lighted and solidly paved. The houses were frescoed and carpeted; they were warmed in winter by furnaces, and cooled in summer with perfumed air brought by underground pipes from flower-beds. They had baths, and libraries, and dining-halls, fountains of quicksilver and water. City and country were full of conviviality, and of dancing to the lute and mandolin. Instead of the drunken and gluttonous wassail orgies of their Northern neighbors, the feasts of the Saracens were marked by sobriety. Wine was prohibited. The enchanting moonlight evenings of Andalusia were spent by the Moors in sequestered, fairy-like gardens or in orange-groves, listening to the romances of the story-teller, or engaged in philosophical discourse; consoling themselves for the disappointments of this life by such reflections as that, if virtue were rewarded in this world, we should be without expectations in the life to come; and reconciling themselves to their daily toil by the expectation that rest will be found after death—a rest never to be succeeded by labor.

In the tenth century the Khalif Hakein II. had made beautiful Andalusia the paradise of the world. Christians, Mussulmen, Jews, mixed together without restraint. There, among many celebrated names that have descended to our times, was Gerbert, destined subsequently to become pope. There, too, was Peter the Venerable, and many Christian ecclesiastics. Peter says that he found learned men even from Britain pursuing astronomy. All learned men, no matter from what country they came, or what their religious views, were welcomed. The khalif had in his palace a manufactory of books, and copyists, binders, illuminators. He kept book-buyers in all the great cities of Asia and Africa. His library contained four hundred thousand volumes, superbly bound and illuminated.

Throughout the Mohammedan dominions in Asia, in Africa, and in Spain, the lower order of Mussulmen entertained a fanatical hatred against learning. Among the more devout—those who claimed to be orthodox—there were painful doubts as to the salvation of the great Khalif Al-Mamun—the wicked khalif, as they called him—for he had not only disturbed the people by introducing the writings of Aristotle and other Greek heathens, but had even struck at the existence of heaven and hell by saying that the earth is a globe, and pretending that he could measure its size. These persons, from their numbers, constituted a political power.

Almansor, who usurped the khalifate to the prejudice of Hakem's son, thought that his usurpation would be sustained if he put himself at the head of the orthodox party. He therefore had the library of Hakem searched, and all works of a scientific or philosophical nature carried into the public places and burnt, or thrown into the cisterns of the palace. By a similar court revolution Averroes, in his old age—he died A.D. 1193—was expelled from Spain; the religious party had triumphed over the philosophical. He was denounced as a traitor to religion. An opposition to philosophy had been organized all over the Mussulman world. There was hardly a philosopher who was not punished. Some were put to death, and the consequence was, that Islam was full of hypocrites.

Into Italy, Germany, England, Averroism had silently made its way. It found favor in the eyes of the Franciscans, and a focus in the University of Paris. By very many of the leading minds it had been accepted. But at length the Dominicans, the rivals of the Franciscans, sounded an alarm. They said it destroys all personality, conducts to fatalism, and renders inexplicable the difference and progress of individual intelligences. The declaration that there is but one intellect is an error subversive of the merits of the saints, it is an assertion that there is no difference among men. What! is there no difference between the holy soul of Peter and the damned soul of Judas? are they identical? Averroes in this his blasphemous doctrine denies creation, providence, revelation, the Trinity, the efficacy of prayers, of alms, and of litanies; he disbelieves in the resurrection and immortality; he places the summum bonum in mere pleasure.

So, too, among the Jews who were then the leading intellects of the world, Averroism had been largely propagated. Their great writer Maimonides had thoroughly accepted it; his school was spreading it in all directions. A furious persecution arose on the part of the orthodox Jews.

Of Maimonides it had been formerly their delight to declare that he was "the Eagle of the Doctors, the Great Sage, the Glory of the West, the Light of the East, second only to Moses." Now, they proclaimed that he had abandoned the faith of Abraham; had denied the possibility of creation, believed in the eternity of the world; had given himself up to the manufacture of atheists; had deprived God of his attributes; made a vacuum of him; had declared him inaccessible to prayer, and a stranger to the government of the world. The works of Maimonides were committed to the flames by the synagogues of Montpellier, Barcelona, and Toledo.

Scarcely had the conquering arms of Ferdinand and Isabella overthrown the Arabian dominion in Spain, when measures were taken by the papacy to extinguish these opinions, which, it was believed, were undermining European Christianity.

Until Innocent IV. (1243), there was no special tribunal against heretics, distinct from those of the bishops. The Inquisition, then introduced, in accordance with the centralization of the times, was a general and papal tribunal, which displaced the old local ones. The bishops, therefore, viewed the innovation with great dislike, considering it as an intrusion on their rights. It was established in Italy, Spain, Germany, and the southern provinces of France.

The temporal sovereigns were only too desirous to make use of this powerful engine for their own political purposes. Against this the popes strongly protested. They were not willing that its use should pass out of the ecclesiastical hand.

The Inquisition, having already been tried in the south of France, had there proved to be very effective for the suppression of heresy. It had been introduced into Aragon. Now was assigned to it the duty of dealing with the Jews.

In the old times under Visigothic rule these people had greatly prospered, but the leniency that had been shown to them was succeeded by atrocious persecution, when the Visigoths abandoned their Arianism and became orthodox. The most inhuman ordinances were issued against them—a law was enacted condemning them all to be slaves. It was not to be wondered at that, when the Saracen invasion took place, the Jews did whatever they could to promote its success. They, like the Arabs, were an Oriental people, both traced their lineage to Abraham, their common ancestor; both were believers in the unity of God. It was their defense of that doctrine that had brought upon them the hatred of their Visigothic masters.

Under the Saracen rule they were treated with the highest consideration. They became distinguished for their wealth and their learning. For the most part they were Aristotelians. They founded many schools and colleges. Their mercantile interests led them to travel all over the world. They particularly studied the science of medicine. Throughout the middle ages they were the physicians and bankers of Europe. Of all men they saw the course of human affairs from the most elevated point of view. Among the special sciences they became proficient in mathematics and astronomy; they composed the tables of Alfonso, and were the cause of the voyage of De Gama. They distinguished themselves greatly in light literature. From the tenth to the fourteenth century their literature was the first in Europe. They were to be found in the courts of princes as physicians, or as treasurers managing the public finances.

The orthodox clergy in Navarre had excited popular prejudices against them. To escape the persecutions that arose, many of them feigned to turn Christians, and of these many apostatized to their former faith. The papal nuncio at the court of Castile raised a cry for the establishment of the Inquisition. The poorer Jews were accused of sacrificing Christian children at the Passover, in mockery of the crucifixion; the richer were denounced as Averroists. Under the influence of Torquemada, a Dominican monk, the confessor of Queen Isabella, that princess solicited a bull from the pope for the establishment of the Holy Office. A bull was accordingly issued in November, 1478, for the detection and suppression of heresy. In the first year of the operation of the Inquisition, 1481, two thousand victims were burnt in Andalusia; besides these, many thousands were dug up from their graves and burnt; seventeen thousand were fined or imprisoned for life. Whoever of the persecuted race could flee, escaped for his life. Torquemada, now appointed inquisitor-general for Castile and Leon, illustrated his office by his ferocity. Anonymous accusations were received, the accused was not confronted by witnesses, torture was relied upon for conviction; it was inflicted in vaults where no one could hear the cries of the tormented. As, in pretended mercy, it was forbidden to inflict torture a second time, with horrible duplicity it was affirmed that the torment had not been completed at first, but had only been suspended out of charity until the following day! The families of the convicted were plunged into irretrievable ruin. Llorente, the historian of the Inquisition, computes that Torquemada and his collaborators, in the course of eighteen years, burnt at the stake ten thousand two hundred and twenty persons, six thousand eight hundred and sixty in effigy, and otherwise punished ninety-seven thousand three hundred and twenty-one. This frantic priest destroyed Hebrew Bibles wherever he could find them, And burnt six thousand volumes of Oriental literature at Salamanca, under an imputation that they inculcated Judaism. With unutterable disgust and indignation, we learn that the papal government realized much money by selling to the rich dispensations to secure them from the Inquisition.

But all these frightful atrocities proved failures. The conversions were few. Torquemada, therefore, insisted on the immediate banishment of every unbaptized Jew. On March 30, 1492, the edict of expulsion was signed. All unbaptized Jews, of whatever age, sex, or condition, were ordered to leave the realm by the end of the following July. If they revisited it, they should suffer death. They might sell their effects and take the proceeds in merchandise or bills of exchange, but not in gold or silver. Exiled thus suddenly from the land of their birth, the land of their ancestors for hundreds of years, they could not in the glutted market that arose sell what they possessed. Nobody would purchase what could be got for nothing after July. The Spanish clergy occupied themselves by preaching in the public squares sermons filled with denunciations against their victims, who, when the time for expatriation came, swarmed in the roads and filled the air with their cries of despair. Even the Spanish onlookers wept at the scene of agony. Torquemada, however, enforced the ordinance that no one should afford them any help.

Of the banished persons some made their way into Africa, some into Italy; the latter carried with them to Naples ship-fever, which destroyed not fewer than twenty thousand in that city, and devastated that peninsula; some reached Turkey, a few England. Thousands, especially mothers with nursing children, infants, and old people, died by the way; many of them in the agonies of thirst.

This action against the Jews was soon followed by one against the Moors. A pragmatica was issued at Seville, February, 1502, setting forth the obligations of the Castilians to drive the enemies of God from the land, and ordering that all unbaptized Moors in the kingdoms of Castile and Leon above the age of infancy should leave the country by the end of April. They might sell their property, but not take away any gold or silver; they were forbidden to emigrate to the Mohammedan dominions; the penalty of disobedience was death. Their condition was thus worse than that of the Jews, who had been permitted to go where they chose. Such was the fiendish intolerance of the Spaniards, that they asserted the government would be justified in taking the lives of all the Moors for their shameless infidelity.

What an ungrateful return for the toleration that the Moors in their day of power had given to the Christians! No faith was kept with the victims. Granada had surrendered under the solemn guarantee of the full enjoyment of civil and religious liberty. At the instigation of Cardinal Ximenes that pledge was broken, and, after a residence of eight centuries, the Mohammedans were driven out of the land.

The coexistence of three religions in Andalusia—the Christian, the Mohammedan, the Mosaic—had given opportunity for the development of Averroism or philosophical Arabism. This was a repetition of what had occurred at Rome, when the gods of all the conquered countries were confronted in that capital, and universal disbelief in them all ensued. Averroes himself was accused of having been first a Mussulman, then a Christian, then a Jew, and finally a misbeliever. It was affirmed that he was the author of the mysterious book "De Tribus Impostoribus."

In the middle ages there were two celebrated heretical books, "The Everlasting Gospel," and the "De Tribus Impostoribus." The latter was variously imputed to Pope Gerbert, to Frederick II., and to Averroes. In their unrelenting hatred the Dominicans fastened all the blasphemies current in those times on Averroes; they never tired of recalling the celebrated and outrageous one respecting the eucharist. His writings had first been generally made known to Christian Europe by the translation of Michael Scot in the beginning of the thirteenth century, but long before his time the literature of the West, like that of Asia, was full of these ideas. We have seen how broadly they were set forth by Erigena. The Arabians, from their first cultivation of philosophy, had been infected by them; they were current in all the colleges of the three khalifates. Considered not as a mode of thought, that will spontaneously occur to all men at a certain stage of intellectual development, but as having originated with Aristotle, they continually found favor with men of the highest culture. We see them in Robert Grostete, in Roger Bacon, and eventually in Spinoza. Averroes was not their inventor, he merely gave them clearness and expression. Among the Jews of the thirteenth century, he had completely supplanted his imputed master. Aristotle had passed away from their eyes; his great commentator, Averroes, stood in his place. So numerous were the converts to the doctrine of emanation in Christendom, that Pope Alexander IV. (1255) found it necessary to interfere. By his order, Albertus Magnus composed a work against the "Unity of the Intellect." Treating of the origin and nature of the soul, he attempted to prove that the theory of "a separate intellect, enlightening man by irradiation anterior to the individual and surviving the individual, is a detestable error." But the most illustrious antagonist of the great commentator was St. Thomas Aquinas, the destroyer of all such heresies as the unity of the intellect, the denial of Providence, the impossibility of creation; the victories of "the Angelic Doctor" were celebrated not only in the disputations of the Dominicans, but also in the works of art of the painters of Florence and Pisa. The indignation of that saint knew no bounds when Christians became the disciples of an infidel, who was worse than a Mohammedan. The wrath of the Dominicans, the order to which St. Thomas belonged, was sharpened by the fact that their rivals, the Franciscans, inclined to Averroistic views; and Dante, who leaned to the Dominicans, denounced Averroes as the author of a most dangerous system. The theological odium of all three dominant religions was put upon him; he was pointed out as the originator of the atrocious maxim that "all religions are false, although all are probably useful." An attempt was made at the Council of Vienne to have his writings absolutely suppressed, and to forbid all Christians reading them. The Dominicans, armed with the weapons of the Inquisition, terrified Christian Europe with their unrelenting persecutions. They imputed all the infidelity of the times to the Arabian philosopher. But he was not without support. In Paris and in the cities of Northern Italy the Franciscans sustained his views, and all Christendom was agitated with these disputes.

Under the inspiration of the Dominicans, Averroes became to the Italian painters the emblem of unbelief. Many of the Italian towns had pictures or frescoes of the Day of Judgment and of Hell. In these Averroes not unfrequently appears. Thus, in one at Pisa, he figures with Arius, Mohammed, and Antichrist. In another he is represented as overthrown by St. Thomas. He had become an essential element in the triumphs of the great Dominican doctor. He continued thus to be familiar to the Italian painters until the sixteenth century. His doctrines were maintained in the University of Padua until the seventeenth.

Such is, in brief, the history of Averroism as it invaded Europe from Spain. Under the auspices of Frederick II., it, in a less imposing manner, issued from Sicily. That sovereign bad adopted it fully. In his "Sicilian Questions" he had demanded light on the eternity of the world, and on the nature of the soul, and supposed he had found it in the replies of Ibn Sabin, an upholder of these doctrines. But in his conflict with the papacy be was overthrown, and with him these heresies were destroyed.

In Upper Italy, Averroism long maintained its ground. It was so fashionable in high Venetian society that every gentleman felt constrained to profess it. At length the Church took decisive action against it. The Lateran Council, A.D. 1512, condemned the abettors of these detestable doctrines to be held as heretics and infidels. As we have seen, the late Vatican Council has anathematized them. Notwithstanding that stigma, it is to be borne in mind that these opinions are held to be true by a majority of the human race.

CHAPTER VI.

CONFLICT RESPECTING THE NATURE OF THE WORLD.

Scriptural view of the world: the earth a flat surface; location of heaven and hell.

Scientific view: the earth a globe; its size determined; its position in and relations to the solar system.—The three great voyages.—Columbus, De Gama, Magellan.—Circumnavigation of the earth.—Determination of its curvature by the measurement of a degree and by the pendulum.

The discoveries of Copernicus.—Invention of the telescope.—Galileo brought before the Inquisition.—His punishment.—Victory over the Church.

Attempts to ascertain the dimensions of the solar system.—

Determination of the sun's parallax by the transits of Venus.—Insignificance, of the earth and man.

Ideas respecting the dimensions of the universe.—Parallax of the stars.—The plurality of worlds asserted by Bruno.—He is seized and murdered by the Inquisition.

I HAVE now to present the discussions that arose respecting the third great philosophical problem—the nature of the world.

An uncritical observation of the aspect of Nature persuades us that the earth is an extended level surface which sustains the dome of the sky, a firmament dividing the waters above from the waters beneath; that the heavenly bodies—the sun, the moon, the stars—pursue their way, moving from east to west, their insignificant size and motion round the motionless earth proclaiming their inferiority. Of the various organic forms surrounding man none rival him in dignity, and hence he seems justified in concluding that every thing has been created for his use—the sun for the purpose of giving him light by day, the moon and stars by night.

Comparative theology shows us that this is the conception of Nature universally adopted in the early phase of intellectual life. It is the belief of all nations in all parts of the world in the beginning of their civilization: geocentric, for it makes the earth the centre of the universe; anthropocentric, for it makes man the central object of the earth. And not only is this the conclusion spontaneously come to from inconsiderate glimpses of the world, it is also the philosophical basis of various religious revelations, vouchsafed to man from time to time. These revelations, moreover, declare to him that above the crystalline dome of the sky is a region of eternal light and happiness—heaven—the abode of God and the angelic hosts, perhaps also his own abode after death; and beneath the earth a region of eternal darkness and misery, the habitation of those that are evil. In the visible world is thus seen a picture of the invisible.

On the basis of this view of the structure of the world great religious systems have been founded, and hence powerful material interests have been engaged in its support. These have resisted, sometimes by resorting to bloodshed, attempts that have been made to correct its incontestable errors—a resistance grounded on the suspicion that the localization of heaven and hell and the supreme value of man in the universe might be affected.

That such attempts would be made was inevitable. As soon as men began to reason on the subject at all, they could not fail to discredit the assertion that the earth is an indefinite plane. No one can doubt that the sun we see to-day is the self-same sun that we saw yesterday. His reappearance each morning irresistibly suggests that he has passed on the underside of the earth. But this is incompatible with the reign of night in those regions. It presents more or less distinctly the idea of the globular form of the earth.

The earth cannot extend indefinitely downward; for the sun cannot go through it, nor through any crevice or passage in it, Since he rises and sets in different positions at different seasons of the year. The stars also move under it in countless courses. There must, therefore, be a clear way beneath.

To reconcile revelation with these innovating facts, schemes, such as that of Cosmas Indicopleustes in his Christian Topography, were doubtless often adopted. To this in particular we have had occasion on a former page to refer. It asserted that in the northern parts of the flat earth there is an immense mountain, behind which the sun passes, and thus produces night.

At a very remote historical period the mechanism of eclipses had been discovered. Those of the moon demonstrated that the shadow of the earth is always circular. The form of the earth must therefore be globular. A body which in all positions casts a circular shadow must itself be spherical. Other considerations, with which every one is now familiar, could not fail to establish that such is her figure.

But the determination of the shape of the earth by no means deposed her from her position of superiority. Apparently vastly larger than all other things, it was fitting that she should be considered not merely as the centre of the world, but, in truth, as—the world. All other objects in their aggregate seemed utterly unimportant in comparison with her.

Though the consequences flowing from an admission of the globular figure of the earth affected very profoundly existing theological ideas, they were of much less moment than those depending on a determination of her size. It needed but an elementary knowledge of geometry to perceive that correct ideas on this point could be readily obtained by measuring a degree on her surface. Probably there were early attempts to accomplish this object, the results of which have been lost. But Eratosthenes executed one between Syene and Alexandria, in Egypt, Syene being supposed to be exactly under the tropic of Cancer. The two places are, however, not on the same meridian, and the distance between them was estimated, not measured. Two centuries later, Posidonius made another attempt between Alexandria and Rhodes; the bright star Canopus just grazed the horizon at the latter place, at Alexandria it rose 7 1/2 degrees. In this instance, also, since the direction lay across the sea, the distance was estimated, not measured. Finally, as we have already related, the Khalif Al-Mamun made two sets of measures, one on the shore of the Red Sea, the other near Cufa, in Mesopotamia. The general result of these various observations gave for the earth's diameter between seven and eight thousand miles.

This approximate determination of the size of the earth tended to depose her from her dominating position, and gave rise to very serious theological results. In this the ancient investigations of Aristarchus of Samos, one of the Alexandrian school, 280 B.C., powerfully aided. In his treatise on the magnitudes and distances of the sun and moon, he explains the ingenious though imperfect method to which he had resorted for the solution of that problem. Many ages previously a speculation had been brought from India to Europe by Pythagoras. It presented the sun as the centre of the system. Around him the planets revolved in circular orbits, their order of position being Mercury, Venus, Earth, Mars, Jupiter, Saturn, each of them being supposed to rotate on its axis as it revolved round the sun. According to Cicero, Nicetas suggested that, if it were admitted that the earth revolves on her axis, the difficulty presented by the inconceivable velocity of the heavens would be avoided.

There is reason to believe that the works of Aristarchus, in the Alexandrian Library, were burnt at the time of the fire of Caesar. The only treatise of his that has come down to us is that above mentioned, on the size and distance of the sun and moon.

Aristarchus adopted the Pythagorean system as representing the actual facts. This was the result of a recognition of the sun's amazing distance, and therefore of his enormous size. The heliocentric system, thus regarding the sun as the central orb, degraded the earth to a very subordinate rank, making her only one of a company of six revolving bodies.

But this is not the only contribution conferred on astronomy by Aristarchus, for, considering that the movement of the earth does not sensibly affect the apparent position of the stars, he inferred that they are incomparably more distant from us than the sun. He, therefore, of all the ancients, as Laplace remarks, had the most correct ideas of the grandeur of the universe. He saw that the earth is of absolutely insignificant size, when compared with the stellar distances.

He saw, too, that there is nothing above us but space and stars.

But the views of Aristarchus, as respects the emplacement of the planetary bodies, were not accepted by antiquity; the system proposed by Ptolemy, and incorporated in his "Syntaxis," was universally preferred. The physical philosophy of those times was very imperfect—one of Ptolemy's objections to the Pythagorean system being that, if the earth were in motion, it would leave the air and other light bodies behind it. He therefore placed the earth in the central position, and in succession revolved round her the Moon, Mercury, Venus, the Sun, Mars, Jupiter, Saturn; beyond the orbit of Saturn came the firmament of the fixed stars. As to the solid crystalline spheres, one moving from east to west, the other from north to south, these were a fancy of Eudoxus, to which Ptolemy does not allude.

The Ptolemaic system is, therefore, essentially a geocentric system. It left the earth in her position of superiority, and hence gave no cause of umbrage to religious opinions, Christian or Mohammedan. The immense reputation of its author, the signal ability of his great work on the mechanism of the heavens, sustained it for almost fourteen hundred years—that is, from the second to the sixteenth century.

In Christendom, the greater part of this long period was consumed in disputes respecting the nature of God, and in struggles for ecclesiastical power. The authority of the Fathers, and the prevailing belief that the Scriptures contain the sum, of all knowledge, discouraged any investigation of Nature. If by chance a passing interest was taken in some astronomical question, it was at once settled by a reference to such authorities as the writings of Augustine or Lactantius, not by an appeal to the phenomena of the heavens. So great was the preference given to sacred over profane learning that Christianity had been in existence fifteen hundred years, and had not produced a single astronomer.

The Mohammedan nations did much better. Their cultivation of science dates from the capture of Alexandria, A.D. 638. This was only six years after the death of the Prophet. In less than two centuries they had not only become acquainted with, but correctly appreciated, the Greek scientific writers. As we have already mentioned, by his treaty with Michael III., the khalif Al-Mamun had obtained a copy of the "Syntaxis" of Ptolemy. He had it forthwith translated into Arabic. It became at once the great authority of Saracen astronomy. From this basis the Saracens had advanced to the solution of some of the most important scientific problems. They had ascertained the dimensions of the earth; they had registered or catalogued all the stars visible in their heavens, giving to those of the larger magnitudes the names they still bear on our maps and globes; they determined the true length of the year, discovered astronomical refraction, invented the pendulum-clock, improved the photometry of the stars, ascertained the curvilinear path of a ray of light through the air, explained the phenomena of the horizontal sun and moon, and why we see those bodies before they have risen and after they have set; measured the height of the atmosphere, determining it to be fifty-eight miles; given the true theory of the twilight, and of the twinkling of the stars. They had built the first observatory in Europe. So accurate were they in their observations, that the ablest modern mathematicians have made use of their results. Thus Laplace, in his "Systeme du Monde," adduces the observations of Al-Batagni as affording incontestable proof of the diminution of the eccentricity of the earth's orbit. He uses those of Ibn-Junis in his discussion of the obliquity of the ecliptic, and also in the case of the problems of the greater inequalities of Jupiter and Saturn.

These represent but a part, and indeed but a small part, of the services rendered by the

Arabian astronomers, in the solution of the problem of the nature of the world. Meanwhile, such was the benighted condition of Christendom, such its deplorable ignorance, that it cared nothing about the matter. Its attention was engrossed by image-worship, transubstantiation, the merits of the saints, miracles, shrine-cures.

This indifference continued until the close of the fifteenth century. Even then there was no scientific inducement. The inciting motives were altogether of a different kind. They originated in commercial rivalries, and the question of the shape of the earth was finally settled by three sailors, Columbus, De Gama, and, above all, by Ferdinand Magellan.

The trade of Eastern Asia has always been a source of immense wealth to the Western nations who in succession have obtained it. In the middle ages it had centred in Upper Italy. It was conducted along two lines—a northern, by way of the Black and Caspian Seas, and camel-caravans beyond—the headquarters of this were at Genoa; and a southern, through the Syrian and Egyptian ports, and by the Arabian Sea, the headquarters of this being at Venice. The merchants engaged in the latter traffic had also made great gains in the transport service of the Crusade-wars.

The Venetians had managed to maintain amicable relations with the Mohammedan powers of Syria and Egypt; they were permitted to have consulates at Alexandria and Damascus, and, notwithstanding the military commotions of which those countries had been the scene, the trade was still maintained in a comparatively flourishing condition. But the northern or Genoese line had been completely broken up by the irruptions of the Tartars and the Turks, and the military and political disturbances of the countries through which it passed. The Eastern trade of Genoa was not merely in a precarious condition—it was on the brink of destruction.

The circular visible horizon and its dip at sea, the gradual appearance and disappearance of ships in the offing, cannot fail to incline intelligent sailors to a belief in the globular figure of the earth. The writings of the Mohammedan astronomers and philosophers had given currency to that doctrine throughout Western Europe, but, as might be expected, it was received with disfavor by theologians. When Genoa was thus on the very brink of ruin, it occurred to some of her mariners that, if this view were correct, her affairs might be re-established. A ship sailing through the straits of Gibraltar westward, across the Atlantic, would not fail to reach the East Indies. There were apparently other great advantages. Heavy cargoes might be transported without tedious and expensive land-carriage, and without breaking bulk.

Among the Genoese sailors who entertained these views was Christopher Columbus.

He tells us that his attention was drawn to this subject by the writings of Averroes, but among his friends he numbered Toscanelli, a Florentine, who had turned his attention to astronomy, and had become a strong advocate of the globular form. In Genoa itself Columbus met with but little encouragement. He then spent many years in trying to interest different princes in his proposed attempt. Its irreligious tendency was pointed out by the Spanish ecclesiastics, and condemned by the Council of Salamanca; its orthodoxy was confuted from the Pentateuch, the Psalms, the Prophecies, the Gospels, the Epistles, and the writings of the Fathers—St. Chrysostom, St. Augustine, St. Jerome, St. Gregory, St. Basil, St Ambrose.

At length, however, encouraged by the Spanish Queen Isabella, and substantially aided by a wealthy seafaring family, the Pinzons of Palos, some of whom joined him personally, he sailed on August 3, 1492, with three small ships, from Palos, carrying with him a letter from King Ferdinand to the Grand-Khan of Tartary, and also a chart, or map, constructed on the basis of that of Toscanelli. A little before midnight, October 11, 1492, he saw from the forecastle of his ship a moving light at a distance. Two hours subsequently a signal-gun from another of the ships announced that they had descried land. At sunrise Columbus landed in the New World.

On his return to Europe it was universally supposed that he had reached the eastern parts of Asia, and that therefore his voyage had been theoretically successful. Columbus himself died in that belief. But numerous voyages which were soon undertaken made known the general contour of the American coast-line, and the discovery of the Great South Sea by Balboa revealed at length the true facts of the case, and the mistake into which both Toscanelli and Columbus had fallen, that in a voyage to the West the distance from Europe to Asia could not exceed the distance passed over in a voyage from Italy to the Gulf of Guinea—a voyage that Columbus had repeatedly made.

In his first voyage, at nightfall on September 13, 1492, being then two and a half degrees east of Corvo, one of the Azores, Columbus observed that the compass needles of the ships no longer pointed a little to the east of north, but were varying to the west. The deviation became more and more marked as the expedition advanced. He was not the first to detect the fact of variation, but he was incontestably the first to discover the line of no variation. On the return-voyage the reverse was observed; the variation westward diminished until the meridian in question was reached, when the needles again pointed due north. Thence, as the coast of Europe was approached, the variation was to the east. Columbus, therefore, came to the conclusion that the line of no variation was a fixed geographical line, or boundary, between the Eastern and Western Hemispheres. In the bull of May, 1493, Pope Alexander VI. accordingly adopted this line as the perpetual boundary between the possessions of Spain and Portugal, in his settlement of the disputes of those nations. Subsequently, however, it was discovered that the line was moving eastward. It coincided with the meridian of London in 1662.

By the papal bull the Portuguese possessions were limited to the east of the line of no variation. Information derived from certain Egyptian Jews had reached that government, that it was possible to sail round the continent of Africa, there being at its extreme south a cape which could be easily doubled. An expedition of three ships under Vasco de Gama set sail, July 9, 1497; it doubled the cape on November 20th, and reached Calicut, on the coast of India, May 19, 1498. Under the bull, this voyage to the East gave to the Portuguese the right to the India trade.

Until the cape was doubled, the course of De Gama's ships was in a general manner southward. Very soon, it was noticed that the elevation of the pole-star above the horizon was diminishing, and, soon after the equator was reached, that star had ceased to be visible. Meantime other stars, some of them forming magnificent constellations, had come into view—the stars of the Southern Hemisphere. All this was in conformity to theoretical expectations founded on the admission of the globular form of the earth.

The political consequences that at once ensued placed the Papal Government in a position of great embarrassment. Its traditions and policy forbade it to admit any other than the flat figure of the earth, as revealed in the Scriptures. Concealment of the facts was impossible, sophistry was unavailing. Commercial prosperity now left Venice as well as Genoa. The front of Europe was changed. Maritime power had departed from the Mediterranean countries, and passed to those upon the Atlantic coast.

But the Spanish Government did not submit to the advantage thus gained by its commercial rival without an effort. It listened to the representations of one Ferdinand Magellan, that India and the Spice Islands could be reached by sailing to the west, if only a strait or passage through what had now been recognized as "the American Continent" could be discovered; and, if this should be accomplished, Spain, under the papal bull, would have as good a right to the India trade as Portugal. Under the command of Magellan, an expedition of five ships, carrying two hundred and thirty-seven men, was dispatched from Seville, August 10, 1519.

Magellan at once struck boldly for the South American coast, hoping to find some cleft or passage through the continent by which he might reach the great South Sea. For seventy days he was becalmed on the line; his sailors were appalled by the apprehension that they had drifted into a region where the winds never blew, and that it was impossible for them to escape. Calms, tempests, mutiny, desertion, could not shake his resolution. After more than a year he discovered the strait which now bears his name, and, as Pigafetti, an Italian, who was with him, relates, he shed fears of joy when he found that it had pleased God at length to bring him where he might grapple with the unknown dangers of the South Sea, "the Great and Pacific Ocean."

Driven by famine to eat scraps of skin and leather with which his rigging was here and there bound, to drink water that had gone putrid, his crew dying of hunger and scurvy, this man, firm in his belief of the globular figure of the earth, steered steadily to the northwest, and for nearly four months never saw inhabited land. He estimated that he had sailed over the Pacific not less than twelve thousand miles. He crossed the equator, saw once more the pole-star, and at length made land—the Ladrones. Here he met with adventurers from Sumatra. Among these islands he was killed, either by the savages or by his own men. His lieutenant, Sebastian d'Elcano, now took command of the ship, directing her course for the Cape of Good Hope, and encountering frightful hardships. He doubled the cape at last, and then for the fourth time crossed the equator. On September 7, 1522, after a voyage of more than three years, he brought his ship, the San Vittoria, to anchor in the port of St. Lucar, near Seville. She had accomplished the greatest achievement in the history of the human race. She had circumnavigated the earth.

The San Vittoria, sailing westward, had come back to her starting-point. Henceforth the theological doctrine of the flatness of the earth was irretrievably overthrown.

Five years after the completion of the voyage of Magellan, was made the first attempt in Christendom to ascertain the size of the earth. This was by Fernel, a French physician, who, having observed the height of the pole at Paris, went thence northward until he came to a place where the height of the pole was exactly one degree more than at that city. He measured the distance between the two stations by the number of revolutions of one of the wheels of his carriage, to which a proper indicator bad been attached, and came to the conclusion that the earth's circumference is about twenty-four thousand four hundred and eighty Italian miles.

Measures executed more and more carefully were made in many countries: by Snell in Holland; by Norwood between London and York in England; by Picard, under the auspices of the French Academy of Sciences, in France. Picard's plan was to connect two points by a series of triangles, and, thus ascertaining the length of the arc of a meridian intercepted between them, to compare it with the difference of latitudes found from celestial observations. The stations were Malvoisine in the vicinity of Paris, and Sourdon near Amiens. The difference of latitudes was determined by observing the zenith-distances, of delta Cassiopeia. There are two points of interest connected with Picard's operation: it was the first in which instruments furnished with telescopes were employed; and its result, as we shall shortly see, was to Newton the first confirmation of the theory of universal gravitation.

At this time it had become clear from mechanical considerations, more especially such as had been deduced by Newton, that, since the earth is a rotating body, her form cannot be that of a perfect sphere, but must be that of a spheroid, oblate or flattened at the poles. It would follow, from this, that the length of a degree must be greater near the poles than at the equator.

The French Academy resolved to extend Picard's operation, by prolonging the measures in each direction, and making the result the basis of a more accurate map of France. Delays, however, took place, and it was not until 1718 that the measures, from Dunkirk on the north to the southern extremity of France, were completed. A discussion arose as to the interpretation of these measures, some affirming that they indicated a prolate, others an oblate spheroid; the former figure may be popularly represented by a lemon, the latter by an orange. To settle this, the French Government, aided by the Academy, sent out two expeditions to measure degrees of the meridian—one under the equator, the other as far north as possible; the former went to Peru, the latter to Swedish Lapland. Very great difficulties were encountered by both parties. The Lapland commission, however, completed its observations long before the Peruvian, which consumed not less than nine years. The results of the measures thus obtained confirmed the theoretical expectation of the oblate form. Since that time many extensive and exact repetitions of the observation have been made, among which may be mentioned those of the English in England and in India, and particularly that of the French on the occasion of the introduction of the metric system of weights and measures. It was begun by Delambre and Mechain, from Dunkirk to Barcelona, and thence extended, by Biot and Arago, to the island of Formentera near Minorea. Its length was nearly twelve and a half degrees.

Besides this method of direct measurement, the figure of the earth may be determined from the observed number of oscillations made by a pendulum of invariable length in different latitudes. These, though they confirm the foregoing results, give a somewhat greater ellipticity to the earth than that found by the measurement of degrees. Pendulums vibrate more slowly the nearer they are to the equator. It follows, therefore, that they are there farther from the centre of the earth.

From the most reliable measures that have been made, the dimensions of the earth may be thus stated:

Greater or equatorial diameter..............7,925 miles.
Less or polar diameter......................7,899 "
Difference or polar compression............. 26 "

Such was the result of the discussion respecting the figure and size of the earth. While it was yet undetermined, another controversy arose, fraught with even more serious consequences. This was the conflict respecting the earth's position with regard to the sun and the planetary bodies.

Copernicus, a Prussian, about the year 1507, had completed a book "On the Revolutions of the Heavenly Bodies." He had journeyed to Italy in his youth, had devoted his attention to astronomy, and had taught mathematics at Rome. From a profound study of the Ptolemaic and Pythagorean systems, he had come to a conclusion in favor of the latter, the object of his book being to sustain it. Aware that his doctrines were totally opposed to revealed truth, and foreseeing that they would bring upon him the punishments of the Church, he expressed himself in a cautious and apologetic manner, saying that he had only taken the liberty of trying whether, on the supposition of the earth's motion, it was possible to find better explanations than the ancient ones of the revolutions of the celestial orbs; that in doing this he had only taken the privilege that had been allowed to others, of feigning what hypothesis they chose. The preface was addressed to Pope Paul III.

Full of misgivings as to what might be the result, he refrained from publishing his book for thirty-six years, thinking that "perhaps it might be better to follow the examples of the Pythagoreans and others, who delivered their doctrine only by tradition and to friends." At the entreaty of Cardinal Schomberg he at length published it in 1543. A copy of it was brought to him on his death-bed. Its fate was such as he had anticipated. The Inquisition condemned it as heretical. In their decree, prohibiting it, the Congregation of the Index denounced his system as "that false Pythagorean doctrine utterly contrary to the Holy Scriptures."

Astronomers justly affirm that the book of Copernicus, "De Revolutionibus," changed the face of their science. It incontestably established the heliocentric theory. It showed that the distance of the fixed stars is infinitely great, and that the earth is a mere point in the heavens. Anticipating Newton, Copernicus imputed gravity to the sun, the moon, and heavenly bodies, but he was led astray by assuming that the celestial motions must be circular. Observations on the orbit of Mars, and his different diameters at different times, had led Copernicus to his theory.

In thus denouncing the Copernican system as being in contradiction to revelation, the ecclesiastical authorities were doubtless deeply moved by inferential considerations. To dethrone the earth from her central dominating position, to give her many equals and not a few superiors, seemed to diminish her claims upon the Divine regard. If each of the countless myriads of stars was a sun, surrounded by revolving globes, peopled with responsible beings like ourselves, if we had fallen so easily and had been redeemed at so stupendous a price as the death of the Son of God, how was it with them? Of them were there none who had fallen or might fall like us? Where, then, for them could a Savior be found?

During the year 1608 one Lippershey, a Hollander, discovered that, by looking through two glass lenses, combined in a certain manner together, distant objects were magnified and rendered very plain. He had invented the telescope. In the following year Galileo, a Florentine, greatly distinguished by his mathematical and scientific writings, hearing of the circumstance, but without knowing the particulars of the construction, invented a form of the instrument for himself. Improving it gradually, he succeeded in making one that could magnify thirty times. Examining the moon, he found that she had valleys like those of the earth, and mountains casting shadows. It had been said in the old times that in the Pleiades there were formerly seven stars, but a legend related that one of them had mysteriously disappeared. On turning his telescope toward them, Galileo found that he could easily count not fewer than forty. In whatever direction he looked, he discovered stars that were totally invisible to the naked eye.

On the night of January 7, 1610, he perceived three small stars in a straight line, adjacent to the planet Jupiter, and, a few evenings later, a fourth. He found that these were revolving in orbits round the body of the planet, and, with transport, recognized that they presented a miniature representation of the Copernican system.

The announcement of these wonders at once attracted universal attention. The spiritual authorities were not slow to detect their tendency, as endangering the doctrine that the universe was made for man. In the creation of myriads of stars, hitherto invisible, there must surely have been some other motive than that of illuminating the nights for him.

It had been objected to the Copernican theory that, if the planets Mercury and Venus move round the sun in orbits interior to that of the earth, they ought to show phases like those of the moon; and that in the case of Venus, which is so brilliant and conspicuous, these phases should be very obvious. Copernicus himself had admitted the force of the objection, and had vainly tried to find an explanation. Galileo, on turning his telescope to the planet, discovered that the expected phases actually exist; now she was a crescent, then half-moon, then gibbous, then full. Previously to Copernicus, it was supposed that the planets shine by their own light, but the phases of Venus and Mars proved that their light is reflected. The Aristotelian notion, that celestial differ from terrestrial bodies in being incorruptible, received a rude shock from the discoveries of Galileo, that there are mountains and valleys in the moon like those of the earth, that the sun is not perfect, but has spots on his face, and that he turns on his axis instead of being in a state of majestic rest. The apparition of new stars had already thrown serious doubts on this theory of incorruptibility.

These and many other beautiful telescopic discoveries tended to the establishment of the truth of the Copernican theory and gave unbounded alarm to the Church. By the low and ignorant ecclesiastics they were denounced as deceptions or frauds. Some affirmed that the telescope might be relied on well enough for terrestrial objects, but with the heavenly bodies it was altogether a different affair. Others declared that its invention was a mere application of Aristotle's remark that stars could be seen in the daytime from the bottom of a deep well. Galileo was accused of imposture, heresy, blasphemy, atheism. With a view of defending himself, he addressed a letter to the Abbe Castelli, suggesting that the Scriptures were never intended to be a scientific authority, but only a moral guide. This made matters worse. He was summoned before the Holy Inquisition, under an accusation of having taught that the earth moves round the sun, a doctrine "utterly contrary to the Scriptures." He was ordered to renounce that heresy, on pain of being imprisoned. He was directed to desist from teaching and advocating the Copernican theory, and pledge himself that he would neither publish nor defend it for the future. Knowing well that Truth has no need of martyrs, he assented to the required recantation, and gave the promise demanded.

For sixteen years the Church had rest. But in 1632 Galileo ventured on the publication of his work entitled "The System of the World," its object being the vindication of the Copernican doctrine. He was again summoned before the Inquisition at Rome, accused of having asserted that the earth moves round the sun. He was declared to have brought upon himself the penalties of heresy. On his knees, with his hand on the Bible, he was compelled to abjure and curse the doctrine of the movement of the earth. What a spectacle! This venerable man, the most illustrious of his age, forced by the threat of death to deny facts which his judges as well as himself knew to be true! He was then committed to prison, treated with remorseless severity during the remaining ten years of his life, and was denied burial in consecrated ground. Must not that be false which requires for its support so much imposture, so much barbarity? The opinions thus defended by the Inquisition are now objects of derision to the whole civilized world.

One of the greatest of modern mathematicians, referring to this subject, says that the point here contested was one which is for mankind of the highest interest, because of the rank it assigns to the globe that we inhabit. If the earth be immovable in the midst of the universe, man has a right to regard himself as the principal object of the care of Nature. But if the earth be only one of the planets revolving round the sun, an insignificant body in the solar system, she will disappear entirely in the immensity of the heavens, in which this system, vast as it may appear to us, is nothing but an insensible point.

The triumphant establishment of the Copernican doctrine dates from the invention of the telescope. Soon there was not to be found in all Europe an astronomer who had not accepted the heliocentric theory with its essential postulate, the double motion of the earth—movement of rotation on her axis, and a movement of revolution round the sun. If additional proof of the latter were needed, it was furnished by Bradley's great discovery of the aberration of the fixed stars, an aberration depending partly on the progressive motion of light, and partly on the revolution of the earth. Bradley's discovery ranked in importance with that of the precession of the equinoxes. Roemer's discovery of the progressive motion of light, though denounced by Fontenelle as a seductive error, and not admitted by Cassini, at length forced its way to universal acceptance.

Next it was necessary to obtain correct ideas of the dimensions of the solar system, or, putting the problem under a more limited form, to determine the distance of the earth from the sun.

In the time of Copernicus it was supposed that the sun's distance could not exceed five million miles, and indeed there were many who thought that estimate very extravagant. From a review of the observations of Tycho Brahe, Kepler, however, concluded that the error was actually in the opposite direction, and that the estimate must be raised to at least thirteen million. In 1670 Cassini showed that these numbers were altogether inconsistent with the facts, and gave as his conclusion eighty-five million.

The transit of Venus over the face of the sun, June 3, 1769, had been foreseen, and its great value in the solution of this fundamental problem in astronomy appreciated. With commendable alacrity various governments contributed their assistance in making observations, so that in Europe there were fifty stations, in Asia six, in America seventeen. It was for this purpose that the English Government dispatched Captain Cook on his celebrated first voyage. He went to Otaheite. His voyage was crowned with success. The sun rose without a cloud, and the sky continued equally clear throughout the day. The transit at Cook's station lasted from about half-past nine in the morning until about half-past three in the afternoon, and all the observations were made in a satisfactory manner.

But, on the discussion of the observations made at the different stations, it was found that there was not the accordance that could have been desired—the result varying from eighty-eight to one hundred and nine million. The celebrated mathematician, Encke, therefore reviewed them in 1822-'24, and came to the conclusion that the sun's horizontal parallax, that is, the angle under which the semi-diameter of the earth is seen from the sun, is 8 576/1000 seconds; this gave as the distance 95,274,000 miles. Subsequently the observations were reconsidered by Hansen, who gave as their result 91,659,000 miles. Still later, Leverrier made it 91,759,000. Airy and Stone, by another method, made it 91,400,000; Stone alone, by a revision of the old observations, 91,730,000; and finally, Foucault and Fizeau, from physical experiments, determining the velocity of light, and therefore in their nature altogether differing from transit observations, 91,400,000. Until the results of the transit of next year (1874) are ascertained, it must therefore be admitted that the distance of the earth from the sun is somewhat less than ninety-two million miles.

This distance once determined, the dimensions of the solar system may be ascertained with ease and precision. It is enough to mention that the distance of Neptune from the sun, the most remote of the planets at present known, is about thirty times that of the earth.

By the aid of these numbers we may begin to gain a just appreciation of the doctrine of the human destiny of the universe—the doctrine that all things were made for man. Seen from the sun, the earth dwindles away to a mere speck, a mere dust-mote glistening in his beams. If the reader wishes a more precise valuation, let him hold a page of this book a couple of feet from his eye; then let him consider one of its dots or full stops; that dot is several hundred times larger in surface than is the earth as seen from the sun!

Of what consequence, then, can such an almost imperceptible particle be? One might think that it could be removed or even annihilated, and yet never be missed. Of what consequence is one of those human monads, of whom more than a thousand millions swarm on the surface of this all but invisible speck, and of a million of whom scarcely one will leave a trace that he has ever existed? Of what consequence is man, his pleasures or his pains?

Among the arguments brought forward against the Copernican system at the time of its promulgation, was one by the great Danish astronomer, Tycho Brahe, originally urged by Aristarchus against the Pythagorean system, to the effect that, if, as was alleged, the earth moves round the sun, there ought to be a change of the direction in which the fixed stars appear. At one time we are nearer to a particular region of the heavens by a distance equal to the whole diameter of the earth's orbit than we were six months previously, and hence there ought to be a change in the relative position of the stars; they should seem to separate as we approach them, and to close together as we recede from them; or, to use the astronomical expression, these stars should have a yearly parallax.

The parallax of a star is the angle contained between two lines drawn from it—one to the sun, the other to the earth.

At that time, the earth's distance from the sun was greatly under-estimated. Had it been known, as it is now, that that distance exceeds ninety million miles, or that the diameter of the orbit is more than one hundred and eighty million, that argument would doubtless have had very great weight.

In reply to Tycho, it was said that, since the parallax of a body diminishes as its distance increases, a star may be so far off that its parallax may be imperceptible. This answer proved to be correct. The detection of the parallax of the stars depended on the improvement of instruments for the measurement of angles.

The parallax of alpha Centauri, a fine double star of the Southern Hemisphere, at present considered to be the nearest of the fixed stars, was first determined by Henderson and Maclear at the Cape of Good Hope in 1832-'33. It is about nine-tenths of a second. Hence this star is almost two hundred and thirty thousand times as far from us as the sun. Seen from it, if the sun were even large enough to fill the whole orbit of the earth, or one hundred and eighty million miles in diameter, he would be a mere point. With its companion, it revolves round their common centre of gravity in eighty-one years, and hence it would seem that their conjoint mass is less than that of the sun.

The star 61 Cygni is of the sixth magnitude. Its parallax was first found by Bessel in 1838, and is about one-third of a second. The distance from us is, therefore, much more than five hundred thousand times that of the sun. With its companion, it revolves round their common centre of gravity in five hundred and twenty years. Their conjoint weight is about one-third that of the sun.

There is reason to believe that the great star Sirius, the brightest in the heavens, is about six times as far off as alpha Centauri. His probable diameter is twelve million miles, and the light he emits two hundred times more brilliant than that of the sun. Yet, even through the telescope, he has no measurable diameter; he looks merely like a very bright spark.

The stars, then, differ not merely in visible magnitude, but also in actual size. As the spectroscope shows, they differ greatly in chemical and physical constitution. That instrument is also revealing to us the duration of the life of a star, through changes in the refrangibility of the emitted light. Though, as we have seen, the nearest to us is at an enormous and all but immeasurable distance, this is but the first step—there are others the rays of which have taken thousands, perhaps millions, of years to reach us! The limits of our own system are far beyond the range of our greatest telescopes; what, then, shall we say of other systems beyond? Worlds are scattered like dust in the abysses in space.

Have these gigantic bodies—myriads of which are placed at so vast a distance that our unassisted eyes cannot perceive them—have these no other purpose than that assigned by theologians, to give light to us? Does not their enormous size demonstrate that, as they are centres of force, so they must be centres of motion—suns for other systems of worlds?

While yet these facts were very imperfectly known—indeed, were rather speculations than facts—Giordano Bruno, an Italian, born seven years after the death of Copernicus, published a work on the "Infinity of the Universe and of Worlds;" he was also the author of "Evening Conversations on Ash-Wednesday," an apology for the Copernican system, and of "The One Sole Cause of Things." To these may be added an allegory published in 1584, "The Expulsion of the Triumphant Beast." He had also collected, for the use of future astronomers, all the observations he could find respecting the new star that suddenly appeared in Cassiopeia, A.D. 1572, and increased in brilliancy, until it surpassed all the other stars. It could be plainly seen in the daytime. On a sudden, November 11th, it was as bright as Venus at her brightest. In the following March it was of the first magnitude. It exhibited various hues of color in a few months, and disappeared in March, 1574.

The star that suddenly appeared in Serpentarius, in Kepler's time (1604), was at first brighter than Venus. It lasted more than a year, and, passing through various tints of purple, yellow, red, became extinguished.

Originally, Bruno was intended for the Church. He had become a Dominican, but was led into doubt by his meditations on the subjects of transubstantiation and the immaculate conception. Not caring to conceal his opinions, he soon fell under the censure of the spiritual authorities, and found it necessary to seek refuge successively in Switzerland, France, England, Germany. The cold-scented sleuth-hounds of the Inquisition followed his track remorselessly, and eventually hunted him back to Italy. He was arrested in Venice, and confined in the Piombi for six years, without books, or paper, or friends.

In England he had given lectures on the plurality of worlds, and in that country had written, in Italian, his most important works. It added not a little to the exasperation against him, that he was perpetually declaiming against the insincerity; the impostures, of his persecutors—that wherever he went he found skepticism varnished over and concealed by hypocrisy; and that it was not against the belief of men, but against their pretended belief, that he was fighting; that he was struggling with an orthodoxy that had neither morality nor faith.

In his "Evening Conversations" he had insisted that the Scriptures were never intended to teach science, but morals only; and that they cannot be received as of any authority on astronomical and physical subjects. Especially must we reject the view they reveal to us of the constitution of the world, that the earth is a flat surface, supported on pillars; that the sky is a firmament—the floor of heaven. On the contrary, we must believe that the universe is infinite, and that it is filled with self-luminous and opaque worlds, many of them inhabited; that there is nothing above and around us but space and stars. His meditations on these subjects had brought him to the conclusion that the views of Averroes are not far from the truth—that there is an Intellect which animates the universe, and of this Intellect the visible world is only an emanation or manifestation, originated and sustained by force derived from it, and, were that force withdrawn, all things would disappear. This ever-present, all-pervading Intellect is God, who lives in all things, even such as seem not to live; that every thing is ready to become organized, to burst into life. God is, therefore, "the One Sole Cause of Things," "the All in All."

Bruno may hence be considered among philosophical writers as intermediate between Averroes and Spinoza. The latter held that God and the Universe are the same, that all events happen by an immutable law of Nature, by an unconquerable necessity; that God is the Universe, producing a series of necessary movements or acts, in consequence of intrinsic, unchangeable, and irresistible energy.

On the demand of the spiritual authorities, Bruno was removed from Venice to Rome, and confined in the prison of the Inquisition, accused not only of being a heretic, but also a heresiarch, who had written things unseemly concerning religion; the special charge against him being that he had taught the plurality of worlds, a doctrine repugnant to the whole tenor of Scripture and inimical to revealed religion, especially as regards the plan of salvation. After an imprisonment of two years he was brought before his judges, declared guilty of the acts alleged, excommunicated, and, on his nobly refusing to recant, was delivered over to the secular authorities to be punished "as mercifully as possible, and without the shedding of his blood," the horrible formula for burning a prisoner at the stake. Knowing well that though his tormentors might destroy his body, his thoughts would still live among men, he said to his judges, "Perhaps it is with greater fear that you pass the sentence upon me than I receive it." The sentence was carried into effect, and he was burnt at Rome, February 16th, A.D. 1600.

No one can recall without sentiments of pity the sufferings of those countless martyrs, who first by one party, and then by another, have been brought for their religious opinions to the stake. But each of these had in his supreme moment a powerful and unfailing support. The passage from this life to the next, though through a hard trial, was the passage from a transient trouble to eternal happiness, an escape from the cruelty of earth to the charity of heaven. On his way through the dark valley the martyr believed that there was an invisible hand that would lead him, a friend that would guide him all the more gently and firmly because of the terrors of the flames. For Bruno there was no such support. The philosophical opinions, for the sake of which he surrendered his life, could give him no consolation. He must fight the last fight alone. Is there not something very grand in the attitude of this solitary man, something which human nature cannot help admiring, as he stands in the gloomy hall before his inexorable judges? No accuser, no witness, no advocate is present, but the familiars of the Holy Office, clad in black, are stealthily moving about. The tormentors and the rack are in the vaults below. He is simply told that he has brought upon himself strong suspicions of heresy, since he has said that there are other worlds than ours. He is asked if he will recant and abjure his error. He cannot and will not deny what he knows to be true, and perhaps—for he had often done so before—he tells his judges that they, too, in their hearts are of the same belief. What a contrast between this scene of manly honor, of unshaken firmness, of inflexible adherence to the truth, and that other scene which took place more than fifteen centuries previously by the fireside in the hall of Caiaphas the high-priest, when the cock crew, and "the Lord turned and looked upon Peter"

(Luke xxii. 61)! And yet it is upon Peter that the Church has grounded her right to act as she did to Bruno. But perhaps the day approaches when posterity will offer an expiation for this great ecclesiastical crime, and a statue of Bruno be unveiled under the dome of St. Peter's at Rome.

CHAPTER VII.

CONTROVERSY RESPECTING THE AGE OF THE EARTH.

Scriptural view that the Earth is only six thousand years old, and that it was made in a week.—Patristic chronology founded on the ages of the patriarchs.—Difficulties arising from different estimates in different versions of the Bible.

Legend of the Deluge.—The repeopling.—The Tower of Babel; the confusion of tongues.—The primitive language.

Discovery by Cassini of the oblateness of the planet Jupiter.—Discovery by Newton of the oblateness of the Earth.—Deduction that she has been modeled by mechanical causes.—Confirmation of this by geological discoveries respecting aqueous rocks; corroboration by organic remains.—The necessity of admitting enormously long periods of time.—Displacement of the doctrine of Creation by that of Evolution—Discoveries respecting the Antiquity of Man.

The time-scale and space-scale of the world are infinite.—Moderation with which the discussion of the Age of the World has been conducted.

THE true position of the earth in the universe was established only after a long and severe conflict. The Church used whatever power she had, even to the infliction of death, for sustaining her ideas. But it was in vain. The evidence in behalf of the Copernican theory became irresistible. It was at length universally admitted that the sun is the central, the ruling body of our system; the earth only one, and by no means the largest, of a family of encircling planets. Taught by the issue of that dispute, when the question of the age of the world presented itself for consideration, the Church did not exhibit the active resistance she had displayed on the former occasion. For, though her traditions were again put in jeopardy, they were not, in her judgment, so vitally assailed. To dethrone the Earth from her dominating position was, so the spiritual authorities declared, to undermine the very foundation of revealed truth; but discussions respecting the date of creation might within certain limits be permitted. Those limits were, however, very quickly overpassed, and thus the controversy became as dangerous as the former one had been.

It was not possible to adopt the advice given by Plato in his "Timaeus," when treating of this subject—the origin of the universe: "It is proper that both I who speak and you who judge should remember that we are but men, and therefore, receiving the probable mythological tradition, it is meet that we inquire no further into it." Since the time of St. Augustine the Scriptures had been made the great and final authority in all matters of science, and theologians had deduced from them schemes of chronology and cosmogony which had proved to be stumbling-blocks to the advance of real knowledge.

It is not necessary for us to do more than to allude to some of the leading features of these schemes; their peculiarities will be easily discerned with sufficient clearness. Thus, from the six days of creation and the Sabbath-day of rest, since we are told that a day is with the Lord as a thousand years, it was inferred that the duration of the world will be through six thousand years of suffering, and an additional thousand, a millennium of rest. It was generally admitted that the earth was about four thousand years old at the birth of Christ, but, so careless had Europe been in the study of its annals, that not Until A.D. 627 had it a proper chronology of its own. A Roman abbot, Dionysius Exiguus, or Dennis the Less, then fixed the vulgar era, and gave Europe its present Christian chronology.

The method followed in obtaining the earliest chronological dates was by computations, mainly founded on the lives of the patriarchs. Much difficulty was encountered in reconciling numerical discrepancies. Even if, as was taken for granted in those uncritical ages, Moses was the author of the books imputed to him, due weight was not given to the fact that he related events, many of which took place more than two thousand years before he was born. It scarcely seemed necessary to regard the Pentateuch as of plenary inspiration, since no means had been provided to perpetuate its correctness. The different copies which had escaped the chances of time varied very much; thus the Samaritan made thirteen hundred and seven years from the Creation to the Deluge, the Hebrew sixteen hundred and fifty-six, the Septuagint twenty-two hundred and sixty-three. The Septuagint counted fifteen hundred years more from the Creation to Abraham than the Hebrew. In general, however, there was an inclination to the supposition that the Deluge took place about two thousand years after the Creation, and, after another interval of two thousand years, Christ was born. Persons who had given much attention to the subject affirmed that there were not less than one hundred and thirty-two different opinions as to the year in which the Messiah appeared, and hence they declared that it was inexpedient to press for acceptance the Scriptural numbers too closely, since it was plain, from the great differences in different copies, that there had been no providential intervention to perpetuate a correct reading, nor was there any mark by which men could be guided to the only authentic version. Even those held in the highest esteem contained undeniable errors. Thus the Septuagint made Methuselah live until after the Deluge.

It was thought that, in the antediluvian world, the year consisted of three hundred and sixty days. Some even affirmed that this was the origin of the division of the circle into three hundred and sixty degrees. At the time of the Deluge, so many theologians declared, the motion of the sun was altered, and the year became five days and six hours longer. There was a prevalent opinion that that stupendous event occurred on November 2d, in the year of the world 1656. Dr. Whiston, however, disposed to greater precision, inclined to postpone it to November 28th. Some thought that the rainbow was not seen until after the flood; others, apparently with better reason, inferred that it was then first established as a sign. On coming forth from the ark, men received permission to use flesh as food, the antediluvians having been herbivorous! It would seem that the Deluge had not occasioned any great geographical changes, for Noah, relying on his antediluvian knowledge, proceeded to divide the earth among his three sons, giving to Japhet Europe, to Shem Asia, to Ham Africa. No provision was made for

America, as he did not know of its existence. These patriarchs, undeterred by the terrible solitudes to which they were going, by the undrained swamps and untracked forests, journeyed to their allotted possessions, and commenced the settlement of the continents.

In seventy years the Asiatic family had increased to several hundred. They had found their way to the plains of Mesopotamia, and there, for some motive that we cannot divine, began building a tower "whose top might reach to heaven." Eusebius informs us that the work continued for forty years. They did not abandon it until a miraculous confusion of their language took place and dispersed them all over the earth. St. Ambrose shows that this confusion could not have been brought about by men. Origen believes that not even the angels accomplished it.

The confusion of tongues has given rise to many curious speculations among divines as to the primitive speech of man. Some have thought that the language of Adam consisted altogether of nouns, that they were monosyllables, and that the confusion was occasioned by the introduction of polysyllables. But these learned men must surely have overlooked the numerous conversations reported in Genesis, such as those between the Almighty and Adam, the serpent and Eve, etc. In these all the various parts of speech occur. There was, however, a coincidence of opinion that the primitive language was Hebrew. On the general principles of patristicism, it was fitting that this should be the case.

The Greek Fathers computed that, at the time of the dispersion, seventy-two nations were formed, and in this conclusion St. Augustine coincides. But difficulties seem to have been recognized in these computations; thus the learned Dr. Shuckford, who has treated very elaborately on all the foregoing points in his excellent work "On the Sacred and Profane History of the World connected," demonstrates that there could not have been more than twenty-one or twenty-two men, women, and children, in each of those kingdoms.

A very vital point in this system of chronological computation, based upon the ages of the patriarchs, was the great length of life to which those worthies attained. It was generally supposed that before the Flood "there was a perpetual equinox," and no vicissitudes in Nature. After that event the standard of life diminished one-half, and in the time of the Psalmist it had sunk to seventy years, at which it still remains. Austerities of climate were affirmed to have arisen through the shifting of the earth's axis at the Flood, and to this ill effect were added the noxious influences of that universal catastrophe, which, "converting the surface of the earth into a vast swamp, gave rise to fermentations of the blood and a weakening of the fibres."

With a view of avoiding difficulties arising from the extraordinary length of the patriarchal lives, certain divines suggested that the years spoken of by the sacred penman were not ordinary but lunar years. This, though it might bring the age of those venerable men within the recent term of life, introduced, however, another insuperable difficulty, since it made them have children when only five or six years old.

Sacred science, as interpreted by the Fathers of the Church, demonstrated these facts: 1. That the date of Creation was comparatively recent, not more than four or five thousand years before Christ; 2. That the act of Creation occupied the space of six ordinary days; 3. That the Deluge was universal, and that the animals which survived it were preserved in an ark; 4. That Adam was created perfect in morality and intelligence, that he fell, and that his descendants have shared in his sin and his fall.

Of these points and others that might be mentioned there were two on which ecclesiastical authority felt that it must insist. These were: 1. The recent date of Creation; for, the remoter that event, the more urgent the necessity of vindicating the justice of God, who apparently had left the majority of our race to its fate, and had reserved salvation for the few who were living in the closing ages of the world; 2. The perfect condition of Adam at his creation, since this was necessary to the theory of the fall, and the plan of salvation.

Theological authorities were therefore constrained to look with disfavor on any attempt to carry back the origin of the earth, to an epoch indefinitely remote, and on the Mohammedan theory of the evolution of man from lower forms, or his gradual development to his present condition in the long lapse of time.

From the puerilities, absurdities, and contradictions of the foregoing statement, we may gather how very unsatisfactory this so-called sacred science was. And perhaps we may be brought to the conclusion to which Dr. Shuckford, above quoted, was constrained to come, after his wearisome and unavailing attempt to coordinate its various parts: "As to the Fathers of the first ages of the Church, they were good men, but not men of universal learning."

Sacred cosmogony regards the formation and modeling of the earth as the direct act of God; it rejects the intervention of secondary causes in those events.

Scientific cosmogony dates from the telescopic discovery made by Cassini—an Italian astronomer, under whose care Louis XIV. placed the Observatory of Paris—that the planet Jupiter is not a sphere, but an oblate spheroid, flattened at the poles. Mechanical philosophy demonstrated that such a figure is the necessary result of the rotation of a yielding mass, and that the more rapid the rotation the greater the flattening, or, what comes to the same thing, the greater the equatorial bulging must be.

From considerations—purely of a mechanical kind—Newton had foreseen that such likewise, though to a less striking extent, must be the figure of the earth. To the protuberant mass is due the precession of the equinoxes, which requires twenty-five thousand eight hundred and sixty-eight years for its completion, and also the nutation of the earth's axis, discovered by Bradley. We have already had occasion to remark that the earth's equatorial diameter exceeds the polar by about twenty-six miles.

Two facts are revealed by the oblateness of the earth: 1. That she has formerly been in a yielding or plastic condition; 2. That she has been modeled by a mechanical and therefore a secondary cause.

But this influence of mechanical causes is manifested not only in the exterior configuration of the globe of the earth as a spheroid of revolution, it also plainly appears on an examination of the arrangement of her substance.

If we consider the aqueous rocks, their aggregate is many miles in thickness; yet they undeniably have been of slow deposit. The material of which they consist has been obtained by the disintegration of ancient lands; it has found its way into the water-courses, and by them been distributed anew. Effects of this kind, taking place before our eyes, require a very considerable lapse of time to produce a well-marked result—a water deposit may in this manner measure in thickness a few inches in a century—what, then, shall we say as to the time consumed in the formation of deposits of many thousand yards?

The position of the coast-line of Egypt has been known for much more than two thousand years. In that time it has made, by reason of the detritus brought down by the Nile, a distinctly-marked encroachment on the Mediterranean. But all Lower Egypt has had a similar origin. The coast-line near the mouth of the Mississippi has been well known for three hundred years, and during that time has scarcely made a perceptible advance on the Gulf of Mexico; but there was a time when the delta of that river was at St. Louis, more than seven hundred miles from its present position. In Egypt and in America—in fact, in all countries—the rivers have been inch by inch prolonging the land into the sea; the slowness of their work and the vastness of its extent satisfy us that we must concede for the operation enormous periods of time.

To the same conclusion we are brought if we consider the filling of lakes, the deposit of travertines, the denudation of hills, the cutting action of the sea on its shores, the undermining of cliffs, the weathering of rocks by atmospheric water and carbonic acid.

Sedimentary strata must have been originally deposited in planes nearly horizontal. Vast numbers of them have been forced, either by paroxysms at intervals or by gradual movement, into all manner of angular inclinations. Whatever explanations we may offer of these innumerable and immense tilts and fractures, they would seem to demand for their completion an inconceivable length of time.

The coal-bearing strata in Wales, by their gradual submergence, have attained a thickness of 12,000 feet; in Nova Scotia of 14,570 feet. So slow and so steady was this submergence, that erect trees stand one above another on successive levels; seventeen such repetitions may be counted in a thickness of 4,515 feet. The age of the trees is proved by their size, some being four feet in diameter. Round them, as they gradually went down with the subsiding soil, calamites grew, at one level after another. In the Sydney coal-field fifty-nine fossil forests occur in superposition.

Marine shells, found on mountain-tops far in the interior of continents, were regarded by theological writers as an indisputable illustration of the Deluge. But when, as geological studies became more exact, it was proved that in the crust of the earth vast fresh-water formations are repeatedly intercalated with vast marine ones, like the leaves of a book, it became evident that no single cataclysm was sufficient to account for such results; that the same region, through gradual variations of its level and changes in its topographical surroundings, had sometimes been dry land, sometimes covered with fresh and sometimes with sea water. It became evident also that, for the completion of these changes, tens of thousands of years were required.

To this evidence of a remote origin of the earth, derived from the vast superficial extent, the enormous thickness, and the varied characters of its strata, was added an imposing body of proof depending on its fossil remains. The relative ages of formations having been ascertained, it was shown that there has been an advancing physiological progression of organic forms, both vegetable and animal, from the oldest to the most recent; that those which inhabit the surface in our times are but an insignificant fraction of the prodigious multitude that have inhabited it heretofore; that for each species now living there are thousands that have become extinct. Though special formations are so strikingly characterized by some predominating type of life as to justify such expressions as the age of mollusks, the age of reptiles, the age of mammals, the introduction of the new-comers did not take place abruptly. as by sudden creation. They gradually emerged in an antecedent age, reached their culmination in the one which they characterize, and then gradually died out in a succeeding. There is no such thing as a sudden creation, a sudden strange appearance—but there is a slow metamorphosis, a slow development from a preexisting form. Here again we encounter the necessity of admitting for such results long periods of time. Within the range of history no well-marked instance of such development has been witnessed, and we speak with hesitation of doubtful instances of extinction. Yet in geological times myriads of evolutions and extinctions have occurred.

Since thus, within the experience of man, no case of metamorphosis or development has been observed, some have been disposed to deny its possibility altogether, affirming that all the different species have come into existence by separate creative acts. But surely it is less unphilosophical to suppose that each species has been evolved from a predecessor by a modification of its parts, than that it has suddenly started into existence out of nothing. Nor is there much weight in the remark that no man has ever witnessed such a transformation taking place. Let it be remembered that no man has ever witnessed an act of creation, the sudden appearance of an organic form, without any progenitor.

Abrupt, arbitrary, disconnected creative acts may serve to illustrate the Divine power; but that continuous unbroken chain of organisms which extends from palaeozoic formations to the formations of recent times, a chain in which each link hangs on a preceding and sustains a succeeding one, demonstrates to us not only that the production of animated beings is governed by law, but that it is by law that has undergone no change. In its operation, through myriads of ages, there has been no variation, no suspension.

The foregoing paragraphs may serve to indicate the character of a portion of the evidence with which we must deal in considering the problem of the age of the earth. Through the unintermitting labors of geologists, so immense a mass has been accumulated, that many volumes would be required to contain the details. It is drawn from the phenomena presented by all kinds of rocks, aqueous, igneous, metamorphic. Of aqueous rocks it investigates the thickness, the inclined positions, and how they rest unconformably on one another; how those that are of fresh-water origin are intercalated with those that are marine; how vast masses of material have been removed by slow-acting causes of denudation, and extensive geographical surfaces have been remodeled; how continents have undergone movements of elevation and depression, their shores sunk under the ocean, or sea-beaches and sea-cliffs carried far into the interior. It considers the zoological and botanical facts, the fauna and flora of the successive ages, and how in an orderly manner the chain of organic forms, plants, and animals, has been extended, from its dim and doubtful beginnings to our own times. From facts presented by the deposits of coal-coal which, in all its varieties, has originated from the decay of plants—it not only demon strates the changes that have taken place in the earth's atmosphere, but also universal changes of climate. From other facts it proves that there have been oscillations of temperature, periods in which the mean heat has risen, and periods in which the polar ices and snows have covered large portions of the existing continents—glacial periods, as they are termed.

One school of geologists, resting its argument on very imposing evidence, teaches that the whole mass of the earth, from being in a molten, or perhaps a vaporous condition, has cooled by radiation in the lapse of millions of ages, until it has reached its present equilibrium of temperature. Astronomical observations give great weight to this interpretation, especially so far as the planetary bodies of the solar system are concerned. It is also supported by such facts as the small mean density of the earth, the increasing temperature at increasing depths, the phenomena of volcanoes and injected veins, and those of igneous and metamorphic rocks. To satisfy the physical changes which this school of geologists contemplates, myriads of centuries are required.

But, with the views that the adoption of the Copernican system has given us, it is plain that we cannot consider the origin and biography of the earth in an isolated way; we must include with her all the other members of the system or family to which she belongs. Nay, more, we cannot restrict ourselves to the solar system; we must embrace in our discussions the starry worlds. And, since we have become familiarized with their almost immeasurable distances from one another, we are prepared to accept for their origin an immeasurably remote time. There are stars so far off that their light, fast as it travels, has taken thousands of years to reach us, and hence they must have been in existence many thousands of years ago.

Geologists having unanimously agreed—for perhaps there is not a single dissenting voice—that the chronology of the earth must be greatly extended, attempts have been made to give precision to it. Some of these have been based on astronomical, some on physical principles. Thus calculations founded on the known changes of the eccentricity of the earth's orbit, with a view of determining the lapse of time since the beginning of the last glacial period, have given two hundred and forty thousand years. Though the general postulate of the immensity of geological times may be conceded, such calculations are on too uncertain a theoretical basis to furnish incontestable results.

But, considering the whole subject from the present scientific stand-point, it is very clear that the views presented by theological writers, as derived from the Mosaic record, cannot be admitted. Attempts have been repeatedly made to reconcile the revealed with the discovered facts, but they have proved to be unsatisfactory. The Mosaic time is too short, the order of creation incorrect, the divine interventions too anthropomorphic; and, though the presentment of the subject is in harmony with the ideas that men have entertained, when first their minds were turned to the acquisition of natural knowledge, it is not in accordance with their present conceptions of the insignificance of the earth and the grandeur of the universe.

Among late geological discoveries is one of special interest; it is the detection of human remains and human works in formations which, though geologically recent, are historically very remote.

The fossil remains of men, with rude implements of rough or chipped flint, of polished stone, of bone, of bronze, are found in Europe in caves, in drifts, in peat-beds. They indicate a savage life, spent in hunting and fishing. Recent researches give reason to believe that, under low and base grades, the existence of man can be traced back into the tertiary times. He was contemporary with the southern elephant, the rhinoceros leptorhinus, the great hippopotamus, perhaps even in the miocene contemporary with the mastodon.

At the close of the Tertiary period, from causes not yet determined, the Northern Hemisphere underwent a great depression of temperature. From a torrid it passed to a glacial condition. After a period of prodigious length, the temperature again rose, and the glaciers that had so extensively covered the surface receded. Once more there was a decline in the heat, and the glaciers again advanced, but this time not so far as formerly. This ushered in the Quaternary period, during which very slowly the temperature came to its present degree. The water deposits that were being made required thousands of centuries for their completion. At the beginning of the Quaternary period there were alive the cave-bear, the cave-lion, the amphibious hippopotamus, the rhinoceros with chambered nostrils, the mammoth. In fact, the mammoth swarmed. He delighted in a boreal climate. By degrees the reindeer, the horse, the ox, the bison, multiplied, and disputed with him his food. Partly for this reason, and partly because of the increasing heat, he became extinct. From middle Europe, also, the reindeer retired. His departure marks the end of the Quaternary period.

Since the advent of man on the earth, we have, therefore, to deal with periods of incalculable length. Vast changes in the climate and fauna were produced by the slow operation of causes such as are in action at the present day. Figures cannot enable us to appreciate these enormous lapses of time.

It seems to be satisfactorily established, that a race allied to the Basques may be traced back to the Neolithic age. At that time the British Islands were undergoing a change of level, like that at present occurring in the Scandinavian Peninsula. Scotland was rising, England was sinking. In the Pleistocene age there existed in Central Europe a rude race of hunters and fishers closely allied to the Esquimaux.

In the old glacial drift of Scotland the relics of man are found along with those of the fossil elephant. This carries us back to that time above referred to, when a large portion of Europe was covered with ice, which had edged down from the polar regions to southerly latitudes, and, as glaciers, descended from the summits of the mountain-chains into the plains. Countless species of animals perished in this cataclysm of ice and snow, but man survived.

In his primitive savage condition, living for the most part on fruits, roots, shell-fish, man was in possession of a fact which was certain eventually to insure his civilization. He knew how to make a fire. In peat-beds, under the remains of trees that in those localities have long ago become extinct, his relics are still found, the implements that accompany him indicating a distinct chronological order. Near the surface are those of bronze, lower down those of bone or horn, still lower those of polished stone, and beneath all those of chipped or rough stone. The date of the origin of some of these beds cannot be estimated at less than forty or fifty thousand years.

The caves that have been examined in France and elsewhere have furnished for the Stone age axes, knives, lance and arrow points, scrapers, hammers. The change from what may be termed the chipped to the polished stone period is very gradual. It coincides with the domestication of the dog, an epoch in hunting-life. It embraces thousands of centuries. The appearance of arrow-heads indicates the invention of the bow, and the rise of man from a defensive to an offensive mode of life. The introduction of barbed arrows shows how inventive talent was displaying itself; bone and horn tips, that the huntsman was including smaller animals, and perhaps birds, in his chase; bone whistles, his companionship with other huntsmen or with his dog. The scraping-knives of flint indicate the use of skin for clothing, and rude bodkins and needles its manufacture. Shells perforated for bracelets and necklaces prove how soon a taste for personal adornment was acquired; the implements necessary for the preparation of pigments suggest the painting of the body, and perhaps tattooing; and batons of rank bear witness to the beginning of a social organization.

With the utmost interest we look upon the first germs of art among these primitive men. They have left its rude sketches on pieces of ivory and flakes of bone, and carvings, of the animals contemporary with them. In these prehistoric delineations, sometimes not without spirit, we have mammoths, combats of reindeer. One presents us with a man harpooning a fish, another a hunting-scene of naked men armed with the dart. Man is the only animal who has the propensity of depicting external forms, and of availing himself of the use of fire.

Shell-mounds, consisting of bones and shells, some of which may be justly described as of vast extent, and of a date anterior to the Bronze age, and full of stone implements, bear in all their parts indications of the use of fire. These are often adjacent to the existing coasts sometimes, however, they are far inland, in certain instances as far as fifty miles. Their contents and position indicate for them a date posterior to that of the great extinct mammals, but prior to the domesticated. Some of these, it is said, cannot be less than one hundred thousand years old.

The lake-dwellings in Switzerland—huts built on piles or logs, wattled with boughs—were, as may be inferred from the accompanying implements, begun in the Stone age, and continued into that of Bronze. In the latter period the evidences become numerous of the adoption of an agricultural life.

It must not be supposed that the periods into which geologists have found it convenient to divide the progress of man in civilization are abrupt epochs, which hold good simultaneously for the whole human race. Thus the wandering Indians of America are only at the present moment emerging from the Stone age. They are still to be seen in many places armed with arrows, tipped with flakes of flint. It is but as yesterday that some have obtained, from the white man, iron, fire-arms, and the horse.

So far as investigations have gone, they indisputably refer the existence of man to a date remote from us by many hundreds of thousands of years. It must be borne in mind that these investigations are quite recent, and confined to a very limited geographical space. No researches have yet been made in those regions which might reasonably be regarded as the primitive habitat of man.

We are thus carried back immeasurably beyond the six thousand years of Patristic chronology. It is difficult to assign a shorter date for the last glaciation of Europe than a quarter of a million of years, and human existence antedates that. But not only is it this grand fact that confronts us, we have to admit also a primitive animalized state, and a slow, a gradual development. But this forlorn, this savage condition of humanity is in strong contrast to the paradisiacal happiness of the garden of Eden, and, what is far more serious, it is inconsistent with the theory of the Fall.

I have been induced to place the subject of this chapter out of its proper chronological order, for the sake of presenting what I had to say respecting the nature of the world more completely by itself. The discussions that arose as to the age of the earth were long after the conflict as to the criterion of truth—that is, after the Reformation; indeed, they were substantially included in the present century. They have been conducted with so much moderation as to justify the term I have used in the title of this chapter, "Controversy," rather than "Conflict." Geology has not had to encounter the vindictive opposition with which astronomy was assailed, and, though, on her part, she has insisted on a concession of great antiquity for the earth, she has herself pointed out the unreliability of all numerical estimates thus far offered. The attentive reader of this chapter cannot have failed to observe inconsistencies in the numbers quoted. Though wanting the merit of exactness, those numbers, however, justify the claim of vast antiquity, and draw us to the conclusion that the time-scale of the world answers to the space-scale in magnitude.

CHAPTER VIII.

CONFLICT RESPECTING THE CRITERION OF TRUTH.

Ancient philosophy declares that man has no means of ascertaining the truth.

Differences of belief arise among the early Christians—An ineffectual attempt is made to remedy them by Councils.—Miracle and ordeal proof introduced.

The papacy resorts to auricular confession and the Inquisition.—It perpetrates frightful atrocities for the suppression of differences of opinion.

Effect of the discovery of the Pandects of Justinian and development of the canon law on the nature of evidence.—It becomes more scientific.

The Reformation establishes the rights of individual reason.—Catholicism asserts that the criterion of truth is in the Church. It restrains the reading of books by the Index Expurgatorius, and combats dissent by such means as the massacre of St. Bartholomew's Eve.

Examination of the authenticity of the Pentateuch as the Protestant criterion.—Spurious character of those books.

For Science the criterion of truth is to be found in the revelations of Nature: for the Protestant, it is in the Scriptures; for the Catholic, in an infallible Pope.

"WHAT is truth?" was the passionate demand of a Roman procurator on one of the most momentous occasions in history. And the Divine Person who stood before him, to whom the interrogation was addressed, made no reply—unless, indeed, silence contained the reply.

Often and vainly had that demand been made before—often and vainly has it been made since. No one has yet given a satisfactory answer.

When, at the dawn of science in Greece, the ancient religion was disappearing like a mist at sunrise, the pious and thoughtful men of that country were thrown into a condition of intellectual despair. Anaxagoras plaintively exclaims, "Nothing can be known, nothing can be learned, nothing can be certain, sense is limited, intellect is weak, life is short." Xenophanes tells us that it is impossible for us to be certain even when we utter the truth. Parmenides declares that the very constitution of man prevents him from ascertaining absolute truth. Empedocles affirms that all philosophical and religious systems must be unreliable, because we have no criterion by which to test them. Democritus asserts that even things that are true cannot impart certainty to us; that the final result of human inquiry is the discovery that man is incapable of absolute knowledge; that, even if the truth be in his possession, he cannot be certain of it.

Pyrrho bids us reflect on the necessity of suspending our judgment of things, since we have no criterion of truth; so deep a distrust did he impart to his followers, that they were in the habit of saying, "We assert nothing; no, not even that we assert nothing." Epicurus taught his disciples that truth can never be determined by reason. Arcesilaus, denying both intellectual and sensuous knowledge, publicly avowed that he knew nothing, not even his own ignorance! The general conclusion to which Greek philosophy came was this—that, in view of the contradiction of the evidence of the senses, we cannot distinguish the true from the false; and such is the imperfection of reason, that we cannot affirm the correctness of any philosophical deduction.

It might be supposed that a revelation from God to man would come with such force and clearness as to settle all uncertainties and overwhelm all opposition. A Greek philosopher, less despairing than others, had ventured to affirm that the coexistence of two forms of faith, both claiming to be revealed by the omnipotent God, proves that neither of them is true. But let us remember that it is difficult for men to come to the same conclusion as regards even material and visible things, unless they stand at the same point of view. If discord and distrust were the condition of philosophy three hundred years before the birth of Christ, discord and distrust were the condition of religion three hundred years after his death. This is what Hilary, the Bishop of Poictiers, in his well-known passage written about the time of the Nicene Council, says:

"It is a thing equally deplorable and dangerous that there are, as many creeds as opinions among men, as many doctrines as inclinations, and as many sources of blasphemy as there are faults among us, because we make creeds arbitrarily and explain them as arbitrarily. Every year, nay, every moon, we make new creeds to describe invisible mysteries; we repent of what we have done; we defend those who repent; we anathematize those whom we defend; we condemn either the doctrines of others in ourselves, or our own in that of others; and, reciprocally tearing each other to pieces, we have been the cause of each other's ruin."

These are not mere words; but the import of this self-accusation can be realized fully only by such as are familiar with the ecclesiastical history of those times. As soon as the first fervor of Christianity as a system of benevolence had declined, dissensions appeared. Ecclesiastical historians assert that "as early as the second century began the contest between faith and reason, religion and philosophy, piety and genius." To compose these dissensions, to obtain some authoritative expression, some criterion of truth, assemblies for consultation were resorted to, which eventually took the form of councils. For a long time they had nothing more than an advisory authority; but, when, in the fourth century, Christianity had attained to imperial rule, their dictates became compulsory, being enforced by the civil power. By this the whole face of the Church was changed. Oecumenical councils—parliaments of Christianity—consisting of delegates from all the churches in the world, were summoned by the authority of the emperor; he presided either personally or nominally in them—composed all differences, and was, in fact, the Pope of Christendom. Mosheim, the historian, to whom I have more particularly referred above, speaking of these times, remarks that "there was nothing to exclude the ignorant from ecclesiastical preferment; the savage and illiterate party, who looked on all kinds of learning, particularly philosophy, as pernicious to piety, was increasing;" and, accordingly, "the disputes carried on in the Council of Nicea offered a remarkable example of the greatest ignorance and utter confusion of ideas, particularly in the language and explanations of those who approved of the decisions of that council." Vast as its influence has been, "the ancient critics are neither agreed concerning the time nor place in which it was assembled, the number of those who sat in it, nor the bishop who presided. No authentic acts of its famous sentence have been committed to writing, or, at least, none have been transmitted to our times." The Church had now become what, in the language of modern politicians, would be called "a confederated republic." The will of the council was determined by a majority vote, and, to secure that, all manner of intrigues and impositions were resorted to; the influence of court females, bribery, and violence, were not spared. The Council of Nicea had scarcely adjourned,—when it was plain to all impartial men that, as a method of establishing a criterion of truth in religious matters, such councils were a total failure. The minority had no rights which the majority need respect. The protest of many good men, that a mere majority vote given by delegates, whose right to vote had never been examined and authorized, could not be received as ascertaining absolute truth, was passed over with contempt, and the consequence was, that council was assembled against council, and their jarring and contradictory decrees spread perplexity and confusion throughout the Christian world. In the fourth century alone there were thirteen councils adverse to Arius, fifteen in his favor, and seventeen for the semi-Arians—in all, forty-five. Minorities were perpetually attempting to use the weapon which majorities had abused.

The impartial ecclesiastical historian above quoted, moreover, says that "two monstrous and calamitous errors were adopted in this fourth century: 1. That it was an act of virtue to deceive and lie when, by that means, the interests of the Church might be promoted. 2. That errors in religion, when maintained and adhered to after proper admonition, were punishable with civil penalties and corporal tortures."

Not without astonishment can we look back at what, in those times, were popularly regarded as criteria of truth. Doctrines were considered as established by the number of martyrs who had professed them, by miracles, by the confession of demons, of lunatics, or of persons possessed of evil spirits: thus, St. Ambrose, in his disputes with the Arians, produced men possessed by devils, who, on the approach of the relics of certain martyrs, acknowledged, with loud cries, that the Nicean doctrine of the three persons of the Godhead was true. But the Arians charged him with suborning these infernal witnesses with a weighty bribe. Already, ordeal tribunals were making their appearance. During the following six centuries they were held as a final resort for establishing guilt or innocence, under the forms of trial by cold water, by duel, by the fire, by the cross.

What an utter ignorance of the nature of evidence and its laws have we here! An accused man sinks or swims when thrown into a pond of water; he is burnt or escapes unharmed when he holds a piece of red-hot iron in his hand; a champion whom he has hired is vanquished or vanquishes in single fight; he can keep his arms outstretched like a cross, or fails to do so longer than his accuser, and his innocence or guilt of some imputed crime is established! Are these criteria of truth?

Is it surprising that all Europe was filled with imposture miracles during those ages?—miracles that are a disgrace to the common-sense of man!

But the inevitable day came at length. Assertions and doctrines based upon such preposterous evidence were involved in the discredit that fell upon the evidence itself. As the thirteenth century is approached, we find unbelief in all directions setting in. First, it is plainly seen among the monastic orders, then it spreads rapidly among the common people. Books, such as "The Everlasting Gospel," appear among the former; sects, such as the Catharists, Waldenses,

Petrobrussians, arise among the latter. They agreed in this, "that the public and established religion was a motley system of errors and superstitions, and that the dominion which the pope had usurped over Christians was unlawful and tyrannical; that the claim put forth by Rome, that the Bishop of Rome is the supreme lord of the universe, and that neither princes nor bishops, civil governors nor ecclesiastical rulers, have any lawful power in church or state but what they receive from him, is utterly without foundation, and a usurpation of the rights of man."

To withstand this flood of impiety, the papal government established two institutions: 1. The Inquisition; 2. Auricular confession—the latter as a means of detection, the former as a tribunal for punishment.

In general terms, the commission of the Inquisition was, to extirpate religious dissent by terrorism, and surround heresy with the most horrible associations; this necessarily implied the power of determining what constitutes heresy. The criterion of truth was thus in possession of this tribunal, which was charged "to discover and bring to judgment heretics lurking in towns, houses, cellars, woods, caves, and fields." With such savage alacrity did it carry out its object of protecting the interests of religion, that between 1481 and 1808 it had punished three hundred and forty thousand persons, and of these nearly thirty-two thousand had been burnt! In its earlier days, when public opinion could find no means of protesting against its atrocities, "it often put to death, without appeal, on the very day that they were accused, nobles, clerks, monks, hermits, and lay persons of every rank." In whatever direction thoughtful men looked, the air was full of fearful shadows. No one could indulge in freedom of thought without expecting punishment. So dreadful were the proceedings of the Inquisition, that the exclamation of Pagliarici was the exclamation of thousands: "It is hardly possible for a man to be a Christian, and die in his bed."

The Inquisition destroyed the sectaries of Southern France in the thirteenth century. Its unscrupulous atrocities extirpated Protestantism in Italy and Spain. Nor did it confine itself to religious affairs; it engaged in the suppression of political discontent. Nicolas Eymeric, who was inquisitor-general of the kingdom of Aragon for nearly fifty years, and who died in 1399, has left a frightful statement of its conduct and appalling cruelties in his "Directorium Inquisitorum."

This disgrace of Christianity, and indeed of the human race, had different constitutions in different countries. The papal Inquisition continued the tyranny, and eventually superseded the old episcopal inquisitions. The authority of the bishops was unceremoniously put aside by the officers of the pope.

By the action of the fourth Lateran Council, A.D. 1215, the power of the Inquisition was frightfully increased, the necessity of private confession to a priest—auricular confession—being at that time formally established. This, so far as domestic life was concerned, gave omnipresence and omniscience to the Inquisition. Not a man was safe. In the hands of the priest, who, at the confessional, could extract or extort from them their most secret thoughts, his wife and his servants were turned into spies. Summoned before the dread tribunal, he was simply informed that he lay under strong suspicions of heresy. No accuser was named; but the thumb-screw, the stretching-rope, the boot and wedge, or other enginery of torture, soon supplied that defect, and, innocent or guilty, he accused himself!

Notwithstanding all this power, the Inquisition failed of its purpose. When the heretic could no longer confront it, he evaded it. A dismal disbelief stealthily pervaded all Europe,—a denial of Providence, of the immortality of the soul, of human free-will, and that man can possibly resist the absolute necessity, the destiny which envelops him. Ideas such as these were cherished in silence by multitudes of persons driven to them by the tyrannical acts of ecclesiasticism. In spite of persecution, the Waldenses still survived to propagate their declaration that the Roman Church, since Constantine, had degenerated from its purity and sanctity; to protest against the sale of indulgences, which they said had nearly abolished prayer, fasting, alms; to affirm that it was utterly useless to pray for the souls of the dead, since they must already have gone either to heaven or hell. Though it was generally believed that philosophy or science was pernicious to the interests of Christianity or true piety, the Mohammedan literature then prevailing in Spain was making converts among all classes of society. We see very plainly its influence in many of the sects that then arose; thus, "the Brethren and Sisters of the Free. Spirit" held that "the universe came by emanation from God, and would finally return to him by absorption; that rational souls are so many portions of the Supreme Deity; and that the universe, considered as one great whole, is God." These are ideas that can only be entertained in an advanced intellectual condition. Of this sect it is said that many suffered burning with unclouded serenity, with triumphant feelings of cheerfulness and joy. Their orthodox enemies accused them of gratifying their passions at midnight assemblages in darkened rooms, to which both sexes in a condition of nudity repaired. A similar accusation, as is well known, was brought against the primitive Christians by the fashionable society of Rome.

The influences of the Averroistic philosophy were apparent in many of these sects. That Mohammedan system, considered from a Christian point of view, led to the heretical belief that the end of the precepts of Christianity is the union of the soul with the Supreme Being; that God and Nature have the same relations to each other as the soul and the body; that there is but one individual intelligence; and that one soul performs all the spiritual and rational functions in all the human race. When, subsequently, toward the time of the Reformation, the Italian Averroists were required by the Inquisition to give an account of themselves, they attempted to show that there is a wide distinction between philosophical and religious truth; that things may be philosophically true, and yet theologically false—an exculpatory device condemned at length by the Lateran Council in the time of Leo X.

But, in spite of auricular confession, and the Inquisition, these heretical tendencies survived. It has been truly said that, at the epoch of the Reformation, there lay concealed, in many parts of Europe, persons who entertained the most virulent enmity against Christianity. In this pernicious class were many Aristotelians, such as Pomponatius; many philosophers and wits, such as Bodin, Rabelais, Montaigne; many Italians, as Leo X., Bembo, Bruno.

Miracle-evidence began to fall into discredit during the eleventh and twelfth centuries. The sarcasms of the Hispano-Moorish philosophers had forcibly drawn the attention of many of the more enlightened ecclesiastics to its illusory nature. The discovery of the Pandects of Justinian, at Amalfi, in 1130, doubtless exerted a very powerful influence in promoting the study of Roman jurisprudence, and disseminating better notions as to the character of legal or philosophical evidence. Hallam has cast some doubt on the well-known story of this discovery, but he admits that the celebrated copy in the Laurentian library, at Florence, is the only one containing the entire fifty books. Twenty years subsequently, the monk Gratian collected together the various papal edicts, the canons of councils, the declarations of the Fathers and Doctors of the Church, in a volume called "The Decretum," considered as the earliest authority in canon law. In the next century Gregory IX. published five books of Decretals, and Boniface VIII. subsequently added a sixth. To these followed the Clementine Constitutions, a seventh book of Decretals, and "A Book of Institutes," published together, by Gregory XIII., in 1580, under the title of "Corpus Juris Canonici." The canon law had gradually gained enormous power through the control it had obtained over wills, the guardianship of orphans, marriages, and divorces.

The rejection of miracle-evidence, and the substitution of legal evidence in its stead, accelerated the approach of the Reformation. No longer was it possible to admit the requirement which, in former days, Anselm, the Archbishop of Canterbury, in his treatise, "Cur Deus Homo," had enforced, that we must first believe without examination, and may afterward endeavor to understand what we have thus believed. When Cajetan said to Luther, "Thou must believe that one single drop of Christ's blood is sufficient to redeem the whole human race, and the remaining quantity that was shed in the garden and on the cross was left as a legacy to the pope, to be a treasure from which indulgences were to be drawn," the soul of the sturdy German monk revolted against such a monstrous assertion, nor would he have believed it though a thousand miracles had been worked in its support. This shameful practice of selling indulgences for the commission of sin originated among the bishops, who, when they had need of money for their private pleasures, obtained it in that way. Abbots and monks, to whom this gainful commerce was denied, raised funds by carrying about relics in solemn procession, and charging a fee for touching them. The popes, in their pecuniary straits, perceiving how lucrative the practice might become, deprived the bishops of the right of making such sales, and appropriated it to themselves, establishing agencies, chiefly among the mendicant orders, for the traffic. Among these orders there was a sharp competition, each boasting of the superior value of its indulgences through its greater influence at the court of heaven, its familiar connection with the Virgin Mary and the saints in glory. Even against Luther himself, who had been an Augustinian monk, a calumny was circulated that he was first alienated from the Church by a traffic of this kind having been conferred on the Dominicans, instead of on his own order, at the time when Leo X. was raising funds by this means for building St. Peter's, at Rome, A.D. 1517. and there is reason to think that Leo himself, in the earlier stages of the Reformation, attached weight to that allegation.

Indulgences were thus the immediate inciting cause of the Reformation, but very soon there came into light the real principle that was animating the controversy. It lay in the question, Does the Bible owe its authenticity to the Church? or does the Church owe her authenticity to the Bible? Where is the criterion of truth?

It is not necessary for me here to relate the well known particulars of that controversy, the desolating wars and scenes of blood to which it gave rise: how Luther posted on the door of the cathedral of Wittemberg ninety-five theses, and was summoned to Rome to answer for his offense; how he appealed from the pope, ill-informed at the time, to the pope when he should have been better instructed; how he was condemned as a heretic, and thereupon appealed to a general council; how, through the disputes about purgatory, transubstantiation, auricular confession, absolution, the fundamental idea which lay at the bottom of the whole movement came into relief, the right of individual judgment; how Luther was now excommunicated, A.D. 1520, and in defiance burnt the bull of excommunication and the volumes of the canon law, which he denounced as aiming at the subversion of all civil government, and the exaltation of the papacy; how by this skillful manoeuvre he brought over many of the German princes to his views; how, summoned before the Imperial Diet at Worms, he refused to retract, and, while he was bidden in the castle of Wartburg, his doctrines were spreading, and a reformation under

Zwingli broke out in Switzerland; how the principle of sectarian decomposition embedded in the movement gave rise to rivalries and dissensions between the Germans and the Swiss, and even divided the latter among themselves under the leadership of Zwingli and of Calvin; how the Conference of Marburg, the Diet of Spires, and that at Augsburg, failed to compose the troubles, and eventually the German Reformation assumed a political organization at Smalcalde. The quarrels between the Lutherans and the Calvinists gave hopes to Rome that she might recover her losses.

Leo was not slow to discern that the Lutheran Reformation was something more serious than a squabble among some monks about the profits of indulgence-sales, and the papacy set itself seriously at work to overcome the revolters. It instigated the frightful wars that for so many years desolated Europe, and left animosities which neither the Treaty of Westphalia, nor the Council of Trent after eighteen years of debate, could compose. No one can read without a shudder the attempts that were made to extend the Inquisition in foreign countries. All Europe, Catholic and Protestant, was horror-stricken at the Huguenot massacre of St. Bartholomew's Eve (A.D. 1572). For perfidy and atrocity it has no equal in the annals of the world.

The desperate attempt in which the papacy had been engaged to put down its opponents by instigating civil wars, massacres, and assassinations, proved to be altogether abortive. Nor had the Council of Trent any better result. Ostensibly summoned to correct, illustrate, and fix with perspicacity the doctrine of the Church, to restore the vigor of its discipline, and to reform the lives of its ministers, it was so manipulated that a large majority of its members were Italians, and under the influence of the pope. Hence the Protestants could not possibly accept its decisions.

The issue of the Reformation was the acceptance by all the Protestant Churches of the dogma that the Bible is a sufficient guide for every Christian man. Tradition was rejected, and the right of private interpretation assured. It was thought that the criterion of truth had at length been obtained.

The authority thus imputed to the Scriptures was not restricted to matters of a purely religious or moral kind; it extended over philosophical facts and to the interpretation of Nature. Many went as far as in the old times Epiphanius had done: he believed that the Bible contained a complete system of mineralogy! The Reformers would tolerate no science that was not in accordance with Genesis. Among them there were many who maintained that religion and piety could never flourish unless separated from learning and science. The fatal maxim that the Bible contained the sum and substance of all knowledge, useful or possible to man—a maxim employed with such pernicious effect of old by Tertullian and by St. Augustine, and which had so often been enforced by papal authority—was still strictly insisted upon. The leaders of the Reformation, Luther and Melanchthon, were determined to banish philosophy from the Church. Luther declared that the study of Aristotle is wholly useless; his vilification of that Greek philosopher knew no bounds. He is, says Luther, "truly a devil, a horrid calumniator, a wicked sycophant, a prince of darkness, a real Apollyon, a beast, a most horrid impostor on mankind, one in whom there is scarcely any philosophy, a public and professed liar, a goat, a complete epicure, this twice execrable Aristotle." The schoolmen were, so Luther said, "locusts, caterpillars, frogs, lice." He entertained an abhorrence for them. These opinions, though not so emphatically expressed, were entertained by Calvin. So far as science is concerned, nothing is owed to the Reformation. The Procrustean bed of the Pentateuch was still before her.

In the annals of Christianity the most ill-omened day is that in which she separated herself from science. She compelled Origen, at that time (A.D. 231) its chief representative and supporter in the Church, to abandon his charge in Alexandria, and retire to Caesarea. In vain through many subsequent centuries did her leading men spend themselves in—as the phrase then went—"drawing forth the internal juice and marrow of the Scriptures for the explaining of things." Universal history from the third to the sixteenth century shows with what result. The dark ages owe their darkness to this fatal policy. Here and there, it is true, there were great men, such as Frederick II. and Alphonso X., who, standing at a very elevated and general point of view, had detected the value of learning to civilization, and, in the midst of the dreary prospect that ecclesiasticism had created around them, had recognized that science alone can improve the social condition of man.

The infliction of the death-punishment for difference of opinion was still resorted to. When Calvin caused Servetus to be burnt at Geneva, it was obvious to every one that the spirit of persecution was unimpaired. The offense of that philosopher lay in his belief. This was, that the genuine doctrines of Christianity had been lost even before the time of the Council of Nicea; that the Holy Ghost animates the whole system of Nature, like a soul of the world, and that, with the Christ, it will be absorbed, at the end of all things, into the substance of the Deity, from which they had emanated. For this he was roasted to death over a slow fire. Was there any distinction between this Protestant auto-da-fe and the Catholic one of Vanini, who was burnt at Toulouse, by the Inquisition, in 1629, for his "Dialogues concerning Nature?"

The invention of printing, the dissemination of books, had introduced a class of dangers which the persecution of the Inquisition could not reach. In 1559, Pope Paul IV. instituted the Congregation of the Index Expurgatorius. "Its duty is to examine books and manuscripts intended for publication, and to decide whether the people may be permitted to read them; to correct those books of which the errors are not numerous, and which contain certain useful and salutary truths, so as to bring them into harmony with the doctrines of the Church; to condemn those of which the principles are heretical and pernicious; and to grant the peculiar privilege of perusing heretical books to certain persons. This congregation, which is sometimes held in presence of the pope, but generally in the palace of the Cardinal-president, has a more extensive jurisdiction than that of the Inquisition, as it not only takes cognizance of those books that contain doctrines contrary to the Roman Catholic faith, but of those that concern the duties of morality, the discipline of the Church, the interests of society. Its name is derived from the alphabetical tables or indexes of heretical books and authors composed by its appointment."

The Index Expurgatorius of prohibited books at first indicated those works which it was unlawful to read; but, on this being found insufficient, whatever was not permitted was prohibited—an audacious attempt to prevent all knowledge, except such as suited the purposes of the Church, from reaching the people.

The two rival divisions of the Christian Church—Protestant and Catholic—were thus in accord on one point: to tolerate no science except such as they considered to be agreeable to the Scriptures. The Catholic, being in possession of centralized power, could make its decisions respected wherever its sway was acknowledged, and enforce the monitions of the Index Expurgatorius; the Protestant, whose influence was diffused among many foci in different nations, could not act in such a direct and resolute manner. Its mode of procedure was, by raising a theological odium against an offender, to put him under a social ban—a course perhaps not less effectual than the other.

As we have seen in former chapters, an antagonism between religion and science had existed from the earliest days of Christianity. On every occasion permitting its display it may be detected through successive centuries. We witness it in the downfall of the Alexandrian Museum, in the cases of Erigena and Wiclif, in the contemptuous rejection by the heretics of the thirteenth century of the Scriptural account of the Creation; but it was not until the epoch of Copernicus, Kepler, and Galileo, that the efforts of Science to burst from the thraldom in which she was fettered became uncontrollable. In all countries the political power of the Church had greatly declined; her leading men perceived that the cloudy foundation on which she had stood was dissolving away. Repressive measures against her antagonists, in old times resorted to with effect, could be no longer advantageously employed. To her interests the burning of a philosopher here and there did more harm than good. In her great conflict with astronomy, a conflict in which Galileo stands as the central figure, she received an utter overthrow; and, as we have seen, when the immortal work of Newton was printed, she could offer no resistance, though Leibnitz affirmed, in the face of Europe, that "Newton had robbed the Deity of some of his most excellent attributes, and had sapped the foundation of natural religion."

From the time of Newton to our own time, the divergence of science from the dogmas of the Church has continually increased. The Church declared that the earth is the central and most important body in the universe; that the sun and moon and stars are tributary to it. On these points she was worsted by astronomy. She affirmed that a universal deluge had covered the earth; that the only surviving animals were such as had been saved in an ark. In this her error was established by geology. She taught that there was a first man, who, some six or eight thousand years ago, was suddenly created or called into existence in a condition of physical and moral perfection, and from that condition he fell. But anthropology has shown that human beings existed far back in geological time, and in a savage state but little better than that of the brute.

Many good and well-meaning men have attempted to reconcile the statements of Genesis with the discoveries of science, but it is in vain. The divergence has increased so much, that it has become an absolute opposition. One of the antagonists must give way.

May we not, then, be permitted to examine the authenticity of this book, which, since the second century, has been put forth as the criterion of scientific truth? To maintain itself in a position so exalted, it must challenge human criticism.

In the early Christian ages, many of the most eminent Fathers of the Church had serious doubts respecting the authorship of the entire Pentateuch. I have not space, in the limited compass of these pages, to present in detail the facts and arguments that were then and have since been adduced. The literature of the subject is now very extensive. I may, however, refer the reader to the work of the pious and learned Dean Prideaux, on "The Old and New Testament connected," a work which is one of the literary ornaments of the last century. He will also find the subject more recently and exhaustively discussed by Bishop Colenso. The following paragraphs will convey a sufficiently distinct impression of the present state of the controversy:

The Pentateuch is affirmed to have been written by Moses, under the influence of divine inspiration. Considered thus, as a record vouchsafed and dictated by the Almighty, it commands not only scientific but universal consent.

But here, in the first place, it may be demanded, Who or what is it that has put forth this great claim in its behalf?

Not the work itself. It nowhere claims the authorship of one man, or makes the impious declaration that it is the writing of Almighty God.

Not until after the second century was there any such extravagant demand on human credulity. It originated, not among the higher ranks of Christian philosophers, but among the more fervid Fathers of the Church, whose own writings prove them to have been unlearned and uncritical persons.

Every age, from the second century to our times, has offered men of great ability, both Christian and Jewish, who have altogether repudiated these claims. Their decision has been founded upon the intrinsic evidence of the books themselves. These furnish plain indications of at least two distinct authors, who have been respectively termed Elohistic and Jehovistic. Hupfeld maintains that the Jehovistic narrative bears marks of having been a second original record, wholly independent of the Elohistic. The two sources from which the narratives have been derived are, in many respects, contradictory of each other. Moreover, it is asserted that the books of the Pentateuch are never ascribed to Moses in the inscriptions of Hebrew manuscripts, or in printed copies of the Hebrew Bible, nor are they styled "Books of Moses" in the Septuagint or Vulgate, but only in modern translations.

It is clear that they cannot be imputed to the sole authorship of Moses, since they record his death. It is clear that they were not written until many hundred years after that event, since they contain references to facts which did not occur until after the establishment of the government of kings among the Jews.

No man may dare to impute them to the inspiration of Almighty God—their inconsistencies, incongruities, contradictions, and impossibilities, as exposed by many learned and pious moderns, both German and English, are so great. It is the decision of these critics that Genesis is a narrative based upon legends; that Exodus is not historically true; that the whole Pentateuch is unhistoric and non-Mosaic; it contains the most extraordinary contradictions and impossibilities, sufficient to involve the credibility of the whole—imperfections so many and so conspicuous that they would destroy the authenticity of any modern historical work.

Hengstenberg, in his "Dissertations on the Genuineness of the Pentateuch," says: "It is the unavoidable fate of a spurious historical work of any length to be involved in contradictions. This must be the case to a very great extent with the Pentateuch, if it be not genuine. If the Pentateuch is spurious, its histories and laws have been fabricated in successive portions, and were committed to writing in the course of many centuries by different individuals. From such a mode of origination, a mass of contradictions is inseparable, and the improving hand of a later editor could never be capable of entirely obliterating them."

To the above conclusions I may add that we are expressly told by Ezra (Esdras ii. 14) that he himself, aided by five other persons, wrote these books in the space of forty days. He says that at the time of the Babylonian captivity the ancient sacred writings of the Jews were burnt, and gives a particular detail of the circumstances under which these were composed. He sets forth that he undertook to write all that had been done in the world since the beginning. It may be said that the books of Esdras are apocryphal, but in return it may be demanded, Has that conclusion been reached on evidence that will withstand modern criticism? In the early ages of Christianity, when the story of the fall of man was not considered as essential to the Christian system, and the doctrine of the atonement had not attained that precision which Anselm eventually gave it, it was very generally admitted by the Fathers of the Church that Ezra probably did so compose the Pentateuch. Thus St. Jerome says, "Sive Mosem dicere volueris auctorem Pentateuchi, sive Esdram ejusdem instauratorem operis, non recuso." Clemens Alexandrinus says that when these books had been destroyed in the captivity of Nebuchadnezzar, Esdras, having become inspired prophetically, reproduced them. Irenaeus says the same.

The incidents contained in Genesis, from the first to the tenth chapters inclusive (chapters which, in their bearing upon science, are of more importance than other portions of the Pentateuch), have been obviously compiled from short, fragmentary legends of various authorship. To the critical eye they all, however, present peculiarities which demonstrate that they were written on the banks of the Euphrates, and not in the Desert of Arabia. They contain many Chaldaisms. An Egyptian would not speak of the Mediterranean Sea as being west of him, an Assyrian would. Their scenery and machinery, if such expressions may with propriety be used, are altogether Assyrian, not Egyptian. They were such records as one might expect to meet with in the cuneiform impressions of the tile libraries of the Mesopotamian kings. It is affirmed that one such legend, that of the Deluge, has already been exhumed, and it is not beyond the bounds of probability that the remainder may in like manner be obtained.

From such Assyrian sources, the legends of the creation of the earth and heaven, the garden of Eden, the making of man from clay, and of woman from one of his ribs, the temptation by the serpent, the naming of animals, the cherubim and flaming sword, the Deluge and the ark, the drying up of the waters by the wind, the building of the Tower of Babel, and the confusion of tongues, were obtained by Ezra. He commences abruptly the proper history of the Jews in the eleventh chapter. At that point his universal history ceases; he occupies himself with the story of one family, the descendants of Shem.

It is of this restriction that the Duke of Argyll, in his book on "Primeval Man," very graphically says:

In the genealogy of the family of Shem we have a list of names which are names, and nothing more to us. It is a genealogy which neither does, nor pretends to do, more than to trace the order of succession among a few families only, out of the millions then already existing in the world. Nothing but this order of succession is given, nor is it at all certain that this order is consecutive or complete. Nothing is told us of all that lay behind that curtain of thick darkness, in front of which these names are made to pass; and yet there are, as it were, momentary liftings, through which we have glimpses of great movements which were going on, and had been long going on beyond. No shapes are distinctly seen. Even the direction of those movements can only be guessed. But voices are heard which are "as the voices of many waters." I agree in the opinion of Hupfeld, that "the discovery that the Pentateuch is put together out of various sources, or original documents, is beyond all doubt not only one of the most important and most pregnant with consequences for the interpretation of the historical books of the Old Testament, or rather for the whole of theology and history, but it is also one of the most certain discoveries which have been made in the domain of criticism and the history of literature. Whatever the anticritical party may bring forward to the contrary, it will maintain itself, and not retrograde again through any thing, so long as there exists such a thing as criticism; and it will not be easy for a reader upon the stage of culture on which we stand in the present day, if he goes to the examination unprejudiced, and with an uncorrupted power of appreciating the truth, to be able to ward off its influence."

What then? shall we give up these books? Does not the admission that the narrative of the fall in Eden is legendary carry with it the surrender of that most solemn and sacred of Christian doctrines, the atonement?

Let us reflect on this! Christianity, in its earliest days, when it was converting and conquering the world, knew little or nothing about that doctrine. We have seen that, in his "Apology," Tertullian did not think it worth his while to mention it. It originated among the Gnostic heretics. It was not admitted by the Alexandrian theological school. It was never prominently advanced by the Fathers. It was not brought into its present commanding position until the time of Anselm Philo Judaeus speaks of the story of the fall as symbolical; Origen regarded it as an allegory. Perhaps some of the Protestant churches may, with reason, be accused of inconsistency, since in part they consider it as mythical, in part real. But, if, with them, we admit that the serpent is symbolical of Satan, does not that cast an air of allegory over the whole narrative?

It is to be regretted that the Christian Church has burdened itself with the defense of these books, and voluntarily made itself answerable for their manifest contradictions and errors. Their vindication, if it were possible, should have been resigned to the Jews, among whom they originated, and by whom they have been transmitted to us. Still more, it is to be deeply regretted that the Pentateuch, a production so imperfect as to be unable to stand the touch of modern criticism, should be put forth as the arbiter of science. Let it be remembered that the exposure of the true character of these books has been made, not by captious enemies, but by pious and learned churchmen, some of them of the highest dignity.

While thus the Protestant churches have insisted on the acknowledgment of the Scriptures as the criterion of truth, the Catholic has, in our own times, declared the infallibility of the pope. It may be said that this infallibility applies only to moral or religious things; but where shall the line of separation be drawn? Onmiscience cannot be limited to a restricted group of questions; in its very nature it implies the knowledge of all, and infallibility means omniscience.

Doubtless, if the fundamental principles of Italian Christianity be admitted, their logical issue is an infallible pope. There is no need to dwell on the unphilosophical nature of this conception; it is destroyed by an examination of the political history of the papacy, and the biography of the popes. The former exhibits all the errors and mistakes to which institutions of a confessedly human character have been found liable; the latter is only too frequently a story of sin and shame.

It was not possible that the authoritative promulgation of the dogma of papal infallibility should meet among enlightened Catholics universal acceptance. Serious and wide-spread dissent has been produced. A doctrine so revolting to common-sense could not find any other result. There are many who affirm that, if infallibility exists anywhere, it is in oecumenical councils, and yet such councils have not always agreed with each other. There are also many who remember that councils have deposed popes, and have passed judgment on their clamors and contentions. Not without reason do Protestants demand, What proof can be given that infallibility exists in the Church at all? what proof is there that the Church has ever been fairly or justly represented in any council? and why should the truth be ascertained by the vote of a majority rather than by that of a minority? How often it has happened that one man, standing at the right point of view, has descried the truth, and, after having been denounced and persecuted by all others, they have eventually been constrained to adopt his declarations! Of many great discoveries, has not this been the history?

It is not for Science to compose these contesting claims; it is not for her to determine whether the criterion of truth for the religious man shall be found in the Bible, or in the oecumenical council, or in the pope. She only asks the right, which she so willingly accords to others, of adopting a criterion of her own. If she regards unhistorical legends with disdain; if she considers the vote of a majority in the ascertainment of truth with supreme indifference; if she leaves the claim of infallibility in any human being to be vindicated by the stern logic of coming events—the cold impassiveness which in these matters she maintains is what she displays toward her own doctrines. Without hesitation she would give up the theories of gravitation or undulations, if she found that they were irreconcilable with facts. For her the volume of inspiration is the book of Nature, of which the open scroll is ever spread forth before the eyes of every man. Confronting all, it needs no societies for its dissemination. Infinite in extent, eternal in duration, human ambition and human fanaticism have never been able to tamper with it. On the earth it is illustrated by all that is magnificent and beautiful, on the heavens its letters are suns and worlds.

CHAPTER IX.

CONTROVERSY RESPECTING THE GOVERNMENT OF THE UNIVERSE.

There are two conceptions of the government of the world: 1. By Providence; 2. By Law.—The former maintained by the priesthood.—Sketch of the introduction of the latter.

Kepler discovers the laws that preside over the solar system.—His works are denounced by papal authority.—The foundations of mechanical philosophy are laid by Da Vinci.—Galileo discovers the fundamental laws of Dynamics.—Newton applies them to the movements of the celestial bodies, and shows that the solar system is governed by mathematical necessity.—Herschel extends that conclusion to the universe.—The nebular hypothesis.—Theological exceptions to it.

Evidences of the control of law in the construction of the earth, and in the development of the animal and plant series.—They arose by Evolution, not by Creation.

The reign of law is exhibited by the historic career of human societies, and in the case of individual man.

Partial adoption of this view by some of the Reformed Churches.

Two interpretations may be given of the mode of government of the world. It may be by incessant divine interventions, or by the operation of unvarying law.

To the adoption of the former a priesthood will always incline, since it must desire to be considered as standing between the prayer of the votary and the providential act. Its importance is magnified by the power it claims of determining what that act shall be. In the pre Christian (Roman) religion, the grand office of the priesthood was the discovery of future events by oracles, omens, or an inspection of the entrails of animals, and by the offering of sacrifices to propitiate the gods. In the later, the Christian times, a higher power was claimed; the clergy asserting that, by their intercessions, they could regulate the course of affairs, avert dangers, secure benefits, work miracles, and even change the order of Nature.

Not without reason, therefore, did they look upon the doctrine of government by unvarying law with disfavor. It seemed to depreciate their dignity, to lessen their importance. To them there was something shocking in a God who cannot be swayed by human entreaty, a cold, passionless divinity—something frightful in fatalism, destiny.

But the orderly movement of the heavens could not fail in all ages to make a deep impression on thoughtful observers—the rising and setting of the sun; the increasing or diminishing light of the day; the waxing and waning of the moon; the return of the seasons in their proper courses; the measured march of the wandering planets in the sky—what are all these, and a thousand such, but manifestations of an orderly and unchanging procession of events? The faith of early observers in this interpretation may perhaps have been shaken by the occurrence of such a phenomenon as an eclipse, a sudden and mysterious breach of the ordinary course of natural events; but it would be resumed in tenfold strength as soon as the discovery was made that eclipses themselves recur, and may be predicted.

Astronomical predictions of all kinds depend upon the admission of this fact—that there never has been and never will be any intervention in the operation of natural laws. The scientific philosopher affirms that the condition of the world at any given moment is the direct result of its condition in the preceding moment, and the direct cause of its condition in the subsequent moment. Law and chance are only different names for mechanical necessity.

About fifty years after the death of Copernicus, John Kepler, a native of Wurtemberg, who had adopted the heliocentric theory, and who was deeply impressed with the belief that relationships exist in the revolutions of the planetary bodies round the sun, and that these if correctly examined would reveal the laws under which those movements take place, devoted himself to the study of the distances, times, and velocities of the planets, and the form of their orbits. His method was, to submit the observations to which he had access, such as those of Tycho Brahe, to computations based first on one and then on another hypothesis, rejecting the hypothesis if he found that the calculations did not accord with the observations. The incredible labor he had undergone (he says, "I considered, and I computed, until I almost went mad") was at length rewarded, and in 1609 he published his book, "On the Motions of the Planet Mars." In this he had attempted to reconcile the movements of that planet to the hypothesis of eccentrics and epicycles, but eventually discovered that the orbit of a planet is not a circle but an ellipse, the sun being in one of the foci, and that the areas swept over by a line drawn from the planet to the sun are proportional to the times. These constitute what are now known as the first and second laws of Kepler. Eight years subsequently, he was rewarded by the discovery of a third law, defining the relation between the mean distances of the planets from the sun and the times of their revolutions; "the squares of the periodic times are proportional to the cubes of the distances." In "An Epitome of the Copernican System," published in 1618, he announced this law, and showed that it holds good for the satellites of Jupiter as regards their primary. Hence it was inferred that the laws which preside over the grand movements of the solar system preside also over the less movements of its constituent parts.

The conception of law which is unmistakably conveyed by Kepler's discoveries, and the evidence they gave in support of the heliocentric as against the geocentric theory, could not fail to incur the reprehension of the Roman authorities. The congregation of the Index, therefore, when they denounced the Copernican system as utterly contrary to the Holy Scriptures, prohibited Kepler's "Epitome" of that system. It was on this occasion that Kepler submitted his celebrated remonstrance: "Eighty years have elapsed during which the doctrines of Copernicus regarding the movement of the earth and the immobility of the sun have been promulgated without hinderance, because it was deemed allowable to dispute concerning natural things, and to elucidate the works of God, and now that new testimony is discovered in proof of the truth of those doctrines—testimony which was not known to the spiritual judges—ye would prohibit the promulgation of the true system of the structure of the universe."

None of Kepler's contemporaries believed the law of the areas, nor was it accepted until the publication of the "Principia" of Newton. In fact, no one in those times understood the philosophical meaning of Kepler's laws. He himself did not foresee what they must inevitably lead to. His mistakes showed how far he was from perceiving their result. Thus he thought that each planet is the seat of an intelligent principle, and that there is a relation between the magnitudes of the orbits of the five principal planets and the five regular solids of geometry. At first he inclined to believe that the orbit of Mars is oval, nor was it until after a wearisome study that he detected the grand truth, its elliptical form. An idea of the incorruptibility of the celestial objects had led to the adoption of the Aristotelian doctrine of the perfection of circular motions, and to the belief that there were none but circular motions in the heavens. He bitterly complains of this as having been a fatal "thief of his time." His philosophical daring is illustrated in his breaking through this time-honored tradition.

In some most important particulars Kepler anticipated Newton. He was the first to give clear ideas respecting gravity. He says every particle of matter will rest until it is disturbed by some other particle—that the earth attracts a stone more than the stone attracts the earth, and that bodies move to each other in proportion to their masses; that the earth would ascend to the moon one-fifty-fourth of the distance, and the moon would move toward the earth the other fifty-three. He affirms that the moon's attraction causes the tides, and that the planets must impress irregularities on the moon's motions.

The progress of astronomy is obviously divisible into three periods:

1. The period of observation of the apparent motions of the heavenly bodies.

2. The period of discovery of their real motions, and particularly of the laws of the planetary revolutions; this was signally illustrated by Copernicus and Kepler.

3. The period of the ascertainment of the causes of those laws. It was the epoch of Newton.

The passage of the second into the third period depended on the development of the Dynamical branch of mechanics, which had been in a stagnant condition from the time of Archimedes or the Alexandrian School.

In Christian Europe there had not been a cultivator of mechanical philosophy until Leonardo da Vinci, who was born A.D. 1452. To him, and not to Lord Bacon, must be attributed the renaissance of science. Bacon was not only ignorant of mathematics, but depreciated its application to physical inquiries. He contemptuously rejected the Copernican system, alleging absurd objections to it. While Galileo was on the brink of his great telescopic discoveries, Bacon was publishing doubts as to the utility of instruments in scientific investigations. To ascribe the inductive method to him is to ignore history. His fanciful philosophical suggestions have never been of the slightest practical use. No one has ever thought of employing them. Except among English readers, his name is almost unknown.

To Da Vinci I shall have occasion to allude more particularly on a subsequent page. Of his works still remaining in manuscript, two volumes are at Milan, and one in Paris, carried there by Napoleon. After an interval of about seventy years, Da Vinci was followed by the Dutch engineer, Stevinus, whose work on the principles of equilibrium was published in 1586. Six years afterward appeared Galileo's treatise on mechanics.

To this great Italian is due the establishment of the three fundamental laws of dynamics, known as the Laws of Motion.

The consequences of the establishment of these laws were very important.

It had been supposed that continuous movements, such, for instance, as those of the celestial bodies, could only be maintained by a perpetual consumption and perpetual application of force, but the first of Galileo's laws declared that every body will persevere in its state of rest, or of uniform motion in a right line, until it is compelled to change that state by disturbing forces. A clear perception of this fundamental principle is essential to a comprehension of the elementary facts of physical astronomy. Since all the motions that we witness taking place on the surface of the earth soon come to an end, we are led to infer that rest is the natural condition of things. We have made, then, a very great advance when we have become satisfied that a body is equally indifferent to rest as to motion, and that it equally perseveres in either state until disturbing forces are applied. Such disturbing forces in the case of common movements are friction and the resistance of the air. When no such resistances exist, movement must be perpetual, as is the case with the heavenly bodies, which are moving in a void.

Forces, no matter what their difference of magnitude may be, will exert their full influence conjointly, each as though the other did not exist. Thus, when a ball is suffered to drop from the mouth of a cannon, it falls to the ground in a certain interval of time through the influence of gravity upon it. If, then, it be fired from the cannon, though now it may be projected some thousands of feet in a second, the effect of gravity upon it will be precisely the same as before. In the intermingling of forces there is no deterioration; each produces its own specific effect.

In the latter half of the seventeenth century, through the works of Borelli, Hooke, and Huyghens, it had become plain that circular motions could be accounted for by the laws of Galileo. Borelli, treating of the motions of Jupiter's satellites, shows how a circular movement may arise under the influence of a central force. Hooke exhibited the inflection of a direct motion into a circular by a supervening central attraction.

The year 1687 presents, not only an epoch in European science, but also in the intellectual development of man. It is marked by the publication of the "Principia" of Newton, an incomparable, an immortal work.

On the principle that all bodies attract each other with forces directly as their masses, and inversely as the squares of their distances, Newton showed that all the movements of the celestial bodies may be accounted for, and that Kepler's laws might all have been predicted—the elliptic motions—the described areas the relation of the times and distances. As we have seen, Newton's contemporaries had perceived how circular motions could be explained; that was a special case, but Newton furnished the solution of the general problem, containing all special cases of motion in circles, ellipses, parabolas, hyperbolas—that is, in all the conic sections.

The Alexandrian mathematicians had shown that the direction of movement of falling bodies is toward the centre of the earth. Newton proved that this must necessarily be the case, the general effect of the attraction of all the particles of a sphere being the same as if they were all concentrated in its centre. To this central force, thus determining the fall of bodies, the designation of gravity was given. Up to this time, no one, except Kepler, had considered how far its influence reached. It seemed to Newton possible that it might extend as far as the moon, and be the force that deflects her from a rectilinear path, and makes her revolve in her orbit round the earth. It was easy to compute, on the principle of the law of inverse squares, whether the earth's attraction was sufficient to produce the observed effect. Employing the measures of the size of the earth accessible at the time, Newton found that the moon's deflection was only thirteen feet in a minute; whereas, if his hypothesis of gravitation were true, it should be fifteen feet. But in 1669 Picard, as we have seen, executed the measurement of a degree more carefully than had previously been done; this changed the estimate of the magnitude of the earth, and, therefore, of the distance of the moon; and, Newton's attention having been directed to it by some discussions that took place at the Royal Society in 1679, he obtained Picard's results, went home, took out his old papers, and resumed his calculations. As they drew to a close, he became so much agitated that he was obliged to desire a friend to finish them. The expected coincidence was established. It was proved that the moon is retained in her orbit and made to revolve round the earth by the force of terrestrial gravity. The genii of Kepler had given place to the vortices of Descartes, and these in their turn to the central force of Newton.

In like manner the earth, and each of the planets, are made to move in an elliptic orbit round the sun by his attractive force, and perturbations arise by reason of the disturbing action of the planetary masses on one another. Knowing the masses and the distances, these disturbances may be computed. Later astronomers have even succeeded with the inverse problem, that is, knowing the perturbations or disturbances, to find the place and the mass of the disturbing body. Thus, from the deviations of Uranus from his theoretical position, the discovery of Neptune was accomplished.

Newton's merit consisted in this, that he applied the laws of dynamics to the movements of the celestial bodies, and insisted that scientific theories must be substantiated by the agreement of observations with calculations.

When Kepler announced his three laws, they were received with condemnation by the spiritual authorities, not because of any error they were supposed to present or to contain, but partly because they gave support to the Copernican system, and partly because it was judged inexpedient to admit the prevalence of law of any kind as opposed to providential intervention. The world was regarded as the theatre in which the divine will was daily displayed; it was considered derogatory to the majesty of God that that will should be fettered in any way. The power of the clergy was chiefly manifested in the influence the were alleged to possess in changing his arbitrary determinations. It was thus that they could abate the baleful action of comets, secure fine weather or rain, prevent eclipses, and, arresting the course of Nature, work all manner of miracles; it was thus that the shadow had been made to go back on the dial, and the sun and the moon stopped in mid-career.

In the century preceding the epoch of Newton, a great religious and political revolution had taken place—the Reformation. Though its effect had not been the securing of complete liberty for thought, it had weakened many of the old ecclesiastical bonds. In the reformed countries there was no power to express a condemnation of Newton's works, and among the clergy there was no disposition to give themselves any concern about the matter. At first the attention of the Protestant was engrossed by the movements of his great enemy the Catholic, and when that source of disquietude ceased, and the inevitable partitions of the Reformation arose, that attention was fastened upon the rival and antagonistic Churches. The Lutheran, the Calvinist, the Episcopalian, the Presbyterian, had something more urgent on hand than Newton's mathematical demonstrations.

So, uncondemned, and indeed unobserved, in this clamor of fighting sects, Newton's grand theory solidly established itself. Its philosophical significance was infinitely more momentous than the dogmas that these persons were quarreling about. It not only accepted the heliocentric theory and the laws discovered by Kepler, but it proved that, no matter what might be the weight of opposing ecclesiastical authority, the sun MUST be the centre of our system, and that Kepler's laws are the result of a mathematical necessity. It is impossible that they should be other than they are.

But what is the meaning of all this? Plainly that the solar system is not interrupted by providential interventions, but is under the government of irreversible law—law that is itself the issue of mathematical necessity.

The telescopic observations of Herschel I. satisfied him that there are very many double stars —double not merely because they are accidentally in the same line of view, but because they are connected physically, revolving round each other. These observations were continued and greatly extended by Herschel II. The elements of the elliptic orbit of the double star zeta of the Great Bear were determined by Savary, its period being fifty-eight and one-quarter years; those of another, sigma Coronae, were determined by Hind, its period being more than seven hundred and thirty-six years. The orbital movement of these double suns in ellipses compels us to admit that the law of gravitation holds good far beyond the boundaries of the solar system; indeed, as far as the telescope can reach, it demonstrates the reign of law. D'Alembert, in the Introduction to the Encyclopaedia, says: "The universe is but a single fact; it is only one great truth."

Shall we, then, conclude that the solar and the starry systems have been called into existence by God, and that he has then imposed upon them by his arbitrary will laws under the control of which it was his pleasure that their movements should be made?

Or are there reasons for believing that these several systems came into existence not by such an arbitrary fiat, but through the operation of law?

The following are some peculiarities displayed by the solar system as enumerated by Laplace. All the planets and their satellites move in ellipses of such small eccentricity that they are nearly circles. All the planets move in the same direction and nearly in the same plane. The movements of the satellites are in the same direction as those of the planets. The movements of rotation of the sun, of the planets, and the satellites, are in the same direction as their orbital motions, and in planes little different.

It is impossible that so many coincidences could be the result of chance! Is it not plain that there must have been a common tie among all these bodies, that they are only parts of what must once have been a single mass?

But if we admit that the substance of which the solar system consists once existed in a nebulous condition, and was in rotation, all the above peculiarities follow as necessary mechanical consequences. Nay, more, the formation of planets, the formation of satellites and of asteroids, is accounted for. We see why the outer planets and satellites are larger than the interior ones; why the larger planets rotate rapidly, and the small ones slowly; why of the satellites the outer planets have more, the inner fewer. We are furnished with indications of the time of revolution of the planets in their orbits, and of the satellites in theirs; we perceive the mode of formation of Saturn's rings. We find an explanation of the physical condition of the sun, and the transitions of condition through which the earth and moon have passed, as indicated by their geology.

But two exceptions to the above peculiarities have been noted; they are in the cases of Uranus and Neptune.

The existence of such a nebulous mass once admitted, all the rest follows as a matter of necessity. Is there not, however, a most serious objection in the way? Is not this to exclude Almighty God from the worlds he has made?

First, we must be satisfied whether there is any solid evidence for admitting the existence of such a nebulous mass.

The nebular hypothesis rests primarily on the telescopic discovery made by Herschel I., that there are scattered here and there in the heavens pale, gleaming patches of light, a few of which are large enough to be visible to the naked eye. Of these, many may be resolved by a sufficient telescopic power into a congeries of stars, but some, such as the great nebula in Orion, have resisted the best instruments hitherto made.

It was asserted by those who were indisposed to accept the nebular hypothesis, that the non-resolution was due to imperfection in the telescopes used. In these instruments two distinct functions may be observed: their light-gathering power depends on the diameter of their object mirror or lens, their defining power depends on the exquisite correctness of their optical surfaces. Grand instruments may possess the former quality in perfection by reason of their size, but the latter very imperfectly, either through want of original configuration, or distortion arising from flexure through their own weight. But, unless an instrument be perfect in this respect, as well as adequate in the other, it may fail to decompose a nebula into discrete points.

Fortunately, however, other means for the settlement of this question are available. In 1846, it was discovered by the author of this book that the spectrum of an ignited solid is continuous—that is, has neither dark nor bright lines. Fraunhofer had previously made known that the spectrum of ignited gases is discontinuous. Here, then, is the means of determining whether the light emitted by a given nebula comes from an incandescent gas, or from a congeries of ignited solids, stars, or suns. If its spectrum be discontinuous, it is a true nebula or gas; if continuous, a congeries of stars.

In 1864, Mr. Huggins made this examination in the case of a nebula in the constellation Draco. It proved to be gaseous.

Subsequent observations have shown that, of sixty nebulae examined, nineteen give discontinuous or gaseous spectra—the remainder continuous ones.

It may, therefore, be admitted that physical evidence has at length been obtained, demonstrating the existence of vast masses of matter in a gaseous condition, and at a temperature of incandescence. The hypothesis of Laplace has thus a firm basis. In such a nebular mass, cooling by radiation is a necessary incident, and condensation and rotation the inevitable results. There must be a separation of rings all lying in one plane, a generation of planets and satellites all rotating alike, a central sun and engirdling globes. From a chaotic mass, through the operation of natural laws, an organized system has been produced. An integration of matter into worlds has taken place through a decline of heat.

If such be the cosmogony of the solar system, such the genesis of the planetary worlds, we are constrained to extend our views of the dominion of law, and to recognize its agency in the creation as well as in the conservation of the innumerable orbs that throng the universe.

But, again, it may be asked: "Is there not something profoundly impious in this? Are we not excluding Almighty God from the world he has made?"

We have often witnessed the formation of a cloud in a serene sky. A hazy point, barely perceptible—a little wreath of mist—increases in volume, and becomes darker and denser, until it obscures a large portion of the heavens. It throws itself into fantastic shapes, it gathers a glory from the sun, is borne onward by the wind, and, perhaps, as it gradually came, so it gradually disappears, melting away in the untroubled air.

Now, we say that the little vesicles of which this cloud was composed arose from the condensation of water-vapor preexisting in the atmosphere, through reduction of temperature; we show how they assumed the form they present. We assign optical reasons for the brightness or blackness of the cloud; we explain, on mechanical principles, its drifting before the wind; for its disappearance we account on the principles of chemistry. It never occurs to us to invoke the interposition of the Almighty in the production and fashioning of this fugitive form. We explain all the facts connected with it by physical laws, and perhaps should reverentially hesitate to call into operation the finger of God.

But the universe is nothing more than such a cloud—a cloud of suns and worlds. Supremely grand though it may seem to us, to the Infinite and Eternal Intellect it is no more than a fleeting mist. If there be a multiplicity of worlds in infinite space, there is also a succession of worlds in infinite time. As one after another cloud replaces cloud in the skies, so this starry system, the universe, is the successor of countless others that have preceded it—the predecessor of countless others that will follow. There is an unceasing metamorphosis, a sequence of events, without beginning or end.

If, on physical principles, we account for minor meteorological incidents, mists and clouds, is it not permissible for us to appeal to the same principle in the origin of world-systems and universes, which are only clouds on a space-scale somewhat larger, mists on a time-scale somewhat less transient? Can any man place the line which bounds the physical on one side, the supernatural on the other? Do not our estimates of the extent and the duration of things depend altogether on our point of view? Were we set in the midst of the great nebula of Orion, how transcendently magnificent the scene! The vast transformations, the condensations of a fiery mist into worlds, might seem worthy of the immediate presence, the supervision of God; here, at our distant station, where millions of miles are inappreciable to our eyes, and suns seem no bigger than motes in the air, that nebula is more insignificant than the faintest cloud. Galileo, in his description of the constellation of Orion, did not think it worth while so much as to mention it. The most rigorous theologian of those days would have seen nothing to blame in imputing its origin to secondary causes, nothing irreligious in failing to invoke the arbitrary interference of God in its metamorphoses. If such be the conclusion to which we come respecting it, what would be the conclusion to which an Intelligence seated in it might come respecting us? It occupies an extent of space millions of times greater than that of our solar system; we are invisible from it, and therefore absolutely insignificant. Would such an Intelligence think it necessary to require for our origin and maintenance the immediate intervention of God?

From the solar system let us descend to what is still more insignificant—a little portion of it; let us descend to our own earth. In the lapse of time it has experienced great changes. Have these been due to incessant divine interventions, or to the continuous operation of unfailing law? The aspect of Nature perpetually varies under our eyes, still more grandly and strikingly has it altered in geological times. But the laws guiding those changes never exhibit the slightest variation. In the midst of immense vicissitudes they are immutable. The present order of things is only a link in a vast connected chain reaching back to an incalculable past, and forward to an infinite future.

There is evidence, geological and astronomical, that the temperature of the earth and her satellite was in the remote past very much higher than it is now. A decline so slow as to be imperceptible at short intervals, but manifest enough in the course of many ages, has occurred. The heat has been lost by radiation into space.

The cooling of a mass of any kind, no matter whether large or small, is not discontinuous; it does not go on by fits and starts; it takes place under the operation of a mathematical law, though for such mighty changes as are here contemplated neither the formula of Newton, nor that of Dulong and Petit, may apply. It signifies nothing that periods of partial decline, glacial periods, or others of temporary elevation, have been intercalated; it signifies nothing whether these variations may have arisen from topographical variations, as those of level, or from periodicities in the radiation of the sun. A periodical sun would act as a mere perturbation in the gradual decline of heat. The perturbations of the planetary motions are a confirmation, not a disproof, of gravity.

Now, such a decline of temperature must have been attended by innumerable changes of a physical character in our globe. Her dimensions must have diminished through contraction, the length of her day must have lessened, her surface must have collapsed, and fractures taken place along the lines of least resistance; the density of the sea must have increased, its volume must have become less; the constitution of the atmosphere must have varied, especially in the amount of water-vapor and carbonic acid that it contained; the barometric pressure must have declined.

These changes, and very many more that might be mentioned, must have taken place not in a discontinuous but in an orderly manner, since the master-fact, the decline of heat, that was causing them, was itself following a mathematical law.

But not alone did lifeless Nature submit to these inevitable mutations; living Nature was also simultaneously affected.

An organic form of any kind, vegetable or animal, will remain unchanged only so long as the environment in which it is placed remains unchanged. Should an alteration in the environment occur, the organism will either be modified or destroyed.

Destruction is more likely to happen as the change in the environment is more sudden; modification or transformation is more possible as that change is more gradual.

Since it is demonstrably certain that lifeless Nature has in the lapse of ages undergone vast modifications; since the crust of the earth, and the sea, and the atmosphere, are no longer such as they once were; since the distribution of the land and the ocean and all manner of physical conditions have varied; since there have been such grand changes in the environment of living things on the surface of our planet—it necessarily follows that organic Nature must have passed through destructions and transformations in correspondence thereto.

That such extinctions, such modifications, have taken place, how copious, how convincing, is the evidence!

Here, again, we must observe that, since the disturbing agency was itself following a mathematical law, these its results must be considered as following that law too.

Such considerations, then, plainly force upon us the conclusion that the organic progress of the world has been guided by the operation of immutable law—not determined by discontinuous, disconnected, arbitrary interventions of God. They incline us to view favorably the idea of transmutations of one form into another, rather than that of sudden creations.

Creation implies an abrupt appearance, transformation a gradual change.

In this manner is presented to our contemplation the great theory of Evolution. Every organic being has a place in a chain of events. It is not an isolated, a capricious fact, but an unavoidable phenomenon. It has its place in that vast, orderly concourse which has successively risen in the past, has introduced the present, and is preparing the way for a predestined future. From point to point in this vast progression there has been a gradual, a definite, a continuous unfolding, a resistless order of evolution. But in the midst of these mighty changes stand forth immutable the laws that are dominating over all.

If we examine the introduction of any type of life in the animal series, we find that it is in accordance with transformation, not with creation. Its beginning is under an imperfect form in the midst of other forms, of which the time is nearly complete, and which are passing into extinction. By degrees, one species after another in succession more and more perfect arises, until, after many ages, a culmination is reached. From that there is, in like manner, a long, a gradual decline.

Thus, though the mammal type of life is the characteristic of the Tertiary and post-Tertiary periods, it does not suddenly make its appearance without premonition in those periods. Far back, in the Secondary, we find it under imperfect forms, struggling, as it were, to make good a foothold. At length it gains a predominance under higher and better models.

So, too, of reptiles, the characteristic type of life of the Secondary period. As we see in a dissolving view, out of the fading outlines of a scene that is passing away, the dim form of a new one emerging, which gradually gains strength, reaches its culmination, and then melts away in some other that is displacing it, so reptile-life doubtfully, appears, reaches its culmination, and gradually declines. In all this there is nothing abrupt; the changes shade into each other by insensible degrees.

How could it be otherwise? The hot-blooded animals could not exist in an atmosphere so laden with carbonic acid as was that of the primitive times. But the removal of that noxious ingredient from the air by the leaves of plants under the influence of sunlight, the enveloping of its carbon in the earth under the form of coal, the disengagement of its oxygen, permitted their life. As the atmosphere was thus modified, the sea was involved in the change; it surrendered a large part of its carbonic acid, and the limestone hitherto held in solution by it was deposited in the solid form. For every equivalent of carbon buried in the earth, there was an equivalent of carbonate of lime separated from the sea—not necessarily in an amorphous condition, most frequently under an organic form. The sunshine kept up its work day by day, but there were demanded myriads of days for the work to be completed. It was a slow passage from a noxious to a purified atmosphere, and an equally slow passage from a cold-blooded to a hot-blooded type of life. But the physical changes were taking place under the control of law, and the organic transformations were not sudden or arbitrary providential acts. They were the immediate, the inevitable consequences of the physical changes, and therefore, like them, the necessary issue of law.

For a more detailed consideration of this subject, I may refer the reader to Chapters I, II.,

VII, of the second book of my "Treatise on Human Physiology," published in 1856.

Is the world, then, governed by law or by providential interventions, abruptly breaking the proper sequence of events?

To complete our view of this question, we turn finally to what, in one sense, is the most insignificant, in another the most important, case that can be considered. Do human societies, in their historic career, exhibit the marks of a predetermined progress in an unavoidable track? Is there any evidence that the life of nations is under the control of immutable law?

May we conclude that, in society, as in the individual man, parts never spring from nothing, but are evolved or developed from parts that are already in existence?

If any one should object to or deride the doctrine of the evolution or successive development of the animated forms which constitute that unbroken organic chain reaching from the beginning of life on the globe to the present times, let him reflect that he has himself passed through modifications the counterpart of those he disputes. For nine months his type of life was aquatic, and during that time he assumed, in succession, many distinct but correlated forms. At birth his type of life became aerial; he began respiring the atmospheric air; new elements of food were supplied to him; the mode of his nutrition changed; but as yet he could see nothing, hear nothing, notice nothing. By degrees conscious existence was assumed; he became aware that there is an external world. In due time organs adapted to another change of food, the teeth, appeared, and a change of food ensued. He then passed through the stages of childhood and youth, his bodily form developing, and with it his intellectual powers. At about fifteen years, in consequence of the evolution which special parts of his system had attained, his moral character changed. New ideas, new passions, influenced him. And that that was the cause, and this the effect, is demonstrated when, by the skill of the surgeon, those parts have been interfered with. Nor does the development, the metamorphosis, end here; it requires many years for the body to reach its full perfection, many years for the mind. A culmination is at length reached, and then there is a decline. I need not picture its mournful incidents—the corporeal, the intellectual enfeeblement. Perhaps there is little exaggeration in saying that in less than a century every human being on the face of the globe, if not cut off in an untimely manner, has passed through all these changes.

Is there for each of us a providential intervention as we thus pass from stage to stage of life? or shall we not rather believe that the countless myriads of human beings who have peopled the earth have been under the guidance of an unchanging, a universal law?

But individuals are the elementary constituents of communities—nations. They maintain therein a relation like that which the particles of the body maintain to the body itself. These, introduced into it, commence and complete their function; they die, and are dismissed.

Like the individual, the nation comes into existence without its own knowledge, and dies without its own consent, often against its own will. National life differs in no particular from individual, except in this, that it is spread over a longer span, but no nation can escape its inevitable term. Each, if its history be well considered, shows its time of infancy, its time of youth, its time of maturity, its time of decline, if its phases of life be completed.

In the phases of existence of all, so far as those phases are completed, there are common characteristics, and, as like accordances in individuals point out that all are living under a reign of law, we are justified in inferring that the course of nations, and indeed the progress of humanity, does not take place in a chance or random way, that supernatural interventions never break the chain of historic acts, that every historic event has its warrant in some preceding event, and gives warrant to others that are to follow..

But this conclusion is the essential principle of Stoicism—that Grecian philosophical system which, as I have already said, offered a support in their hour of trial and an unwavering guide in the vicissitudes of life, not only to many illustrious Greeks, but also to some of the great philosophers, statesmen, generals, and emperors of Rome; a system which excluded chance from every thing, and asserted the direction of all events by irresistible necessity, to the promotion of perfect good; a system of earnestness, sternness, austerity, virtue—a protest in favor of the common-sense of mankind. And perhaps we shall not dissent from the remark of Montesquieu, who affirms that the destruction of the Stoics was a great calamity to the human race; for they alone made great citizens, great men.

To the principle of government by law, Latin Christianity, in its papal form, is in absolute contradiction. The history of this branch of the Christian Church is almost a diary of miracles and supernatural interventions. These show that the supplications of holy men have often arrested the course of Nature—if, indeed, there be any such course; that images and pictures have worked wonders; that bones, hairs, and other sacred relics, have wrought miracles. The criterion or proof of the authenticity of many of these objects is, not an unchallengeable record of their origin and history, but an exhibition of their miracle-working powers.

Is not that a strange logic which finds proof of an asserted fact in an inexplicable illustration of something else?

Even in the darkest ages intelligent Christian men must have had misgivings as to these alleged providential or miraculous interventions. There is a solemn grandeur in the orderly progress of Nature which profoundly impresses us; and such is the character of continuity in the events of our individual life that we instinctively doubt the occurrence of the supernatural in that of our neighbor. The intelligent man knows well that, for his personal behoof, the course of Nature has never been checked; for him no miracle has ever been worked; he attributes justly every event of his life to some antecedent event; this he looks upon as the cause, that as the consequence. When it is affirmed that, in his neighbor's behalf, such grand interventions have been vouchsafed, he cannot do otherwise than believe that his neighbor is either deceived, or practising deception.

As might, then, have been anticipated, the Catholic doctrine of miraculous intervention received a rude shock at the time of the Reformation, when predestination and election were upheld by some of the greatest theologians, and accepted by some of the greatest Protestant Churches. With stoical austerity Calvin declares: "We were elected from eternity, before the foundation of the world, from no merit of our own, but according to the purpose of the divine pleasure." In affirming this, Calvin was resting on the belief that God has from all eternity decreed whatever comes to pass. Thus, after the lapse of many ages, were again emerging into prominence the ideas of the Basilidians wad Valentinians, Christian sects of the second century, whose Gnostical views led to the engraftment of the great doctrine of the Trinity upon Christianity. They asserted that all the actions of men are necessary, that even faith is a natural gift, to which men are forcibly determined, and must therefore be saved, though their lives be ever so irregular. From the Supreme God all things proceeded. Thus, also, came into prominence the views which were developed by Augustine in his work, "De dono perseverantiae." These were: that God, by his arbitrary will, has selected certain persons without respect to foreseen faith or good works, and has infallibly ordained to bestow upon them eternal happiness; other persons, in like manner, he has condemned to eternal reprobation. The

Sublapsarians believed that "God permitted the fall of Adam;" the Supralapsarians that "he predestinated it, with all its pernicious consequences, from all eternity, and that our first parents had no liberty from the beginning." In this, these sectarians disregarded the remark of St. Augustine: "Nefas est dicere Deum aliquid nisi bonum predestinare."

Is it true, then, that "predestination to eternal happiness is the everlasting purpose of God, whereby, before the foundations of the world were laid, he hath constantly decreed by his council, secret to us, to deliver from curse and damnation those whom he hath chosen out of mankind?" Is it true that of the human family there are some who, in view of no fault of their own, Almighty God has condemned to unending torture, eternal misery?

In 1595 the Lambeth Articles asserted that "God from eternity hath predestinated certain men unto life; certain he hath reprobated." In 1618 the Synod of Dort decided in favor of this view. It condemned the remonstrants against it, and treated them with such severity, that many of them had to flee to foreign countries. Even in the Church of England, as is manifested by its seventeenth Article of Faith, these doctrines have found favor.

Probably there was no point which brought down from the Catholics on the Protestants severer condemnation than this, their partial acceptance of the government of the world by law. In all Reformed Europe miracles ceased. But, with the cessation of shrine-cure, relic-cure, great pecuniary profits ended. Indeed, as is well known, it was the sale of indulgences that provoked the Reformation—indulgences which are essentially a permit from God for the practice of sin, conditioned on the payment of a certain sum of money to the priest.

Philosophically, the Reformation implied a protest against the Catholic doctrine of incessant divine intervention in human affairs, invoked by sacerdotal agency; but this protest was far from being fully made by all the Reforming Churches. The evidence in behalf of government by law, which has of late years been offered by science, is received by many of them with suspicion, perhaps with dislike; sentiments which, however, must eventually give way before the hourly-increasing weight of evidence.

Shall we not, then, conclude with Cicero, who, quoted by Lactantius, says: "One eternal and immutable law embraces all things and all times?"

CHAPTER X.

LATIN CHRISTIANITY IN RELATION TO MODERN CIVILIZATION.

For more than a thousand years Latin Christianity controlled the intelligence of Europe, and is responsible for the result.

That result is manifested by the condition of the city of Rome at the Reformation, and by the condition of the Continent of Europe in domestic and social life.—European nations suffered under the coexistence of a dual government, a spiritual and a temporal.—They were immersed in ignorance, superstition, discomfort.—Explanation of the failure of Catholicism—Political history of the papacy: it was transmuted from a spiritual confederacy into an absolute monarchy.—Action of the College of Cardinals and the Curia—Demoralization that ensued from the necessity of raising large revenues.

The advantages accruing to Europe during the Catholic rule arose not from direct intention, but were incidental.

The general result is, that the political influence of Catholicism was prejudicial to modern civilization.

LATIN Christianity is responsible for the condition and progress of Europe from the fourth to the sixteenth century. We have now to examine how it discharged its trust.

It will be convenient to limit to the case of Europe what has here to be presented, though, from the claim of the papacy to superhuman origin, and its demand for universal obedience, it should strictly be held to account for the condition of all mankind. Its inefficacy against the great and venerable religions of Southern and Eastern Asia would furnish an important and instructive theme for consideration, and lead us to the conclusion that it has impressed itself only where Roman imperial influences have prevailed; a political conclusion which, however, it contemptuously rejects.

Doubtless at the inception of the Reformation there were many persons who compared the existing social condition with what it had been in ancient times. Morals had not changed, intelligence had not advanced, society had little improved. From the Eternal City itself its splendors had vanished. The marble streets, of which Augustus had once boasted, had disappeared. Temples, broken columns, and the long, arcaded vistas of gigantic aqueducts bestriding the desolate Campagna, presented a mournful scene. From the uses to which they had been respectively put, the Capitol had been known as Goats' Hill, and the site of the Roman Forum, whence laws had been issued to the world, as Cows' Field. The palace of the Caesars was hidden by mounds of earth, crested with flowering shrubs. The baths of Caracalla, with their porticoes, gardens, reservoirs, had long ago become useless through the destruction of their supplying aqueducts. On the ruins of that grand edifice, "flowery glades and thickets of odoriferous trees extended in ever-winding labyrinths upon immense platforms, and dizzy arches suspended in the air." Of the Coliseum, the most colossal of Roman ruins, only about one-third remained. Once capable of accommodating nearly ninety thousand spectators, it had, in succession, been turned into a fortress in the middle ages, and then into a stone-quarry to furnish material for the palaces of degenerate Roman princes. Some of the popes had occupied it as a woollen-mill, some as a saltpetre factory; some had planned the conversion of its magnificent arcades into shops for tradesmen. The iron clamps which bound its stones together had been stolen. The walls were fissured and falling. Even in our own times botanical works have been composed on the plants which have made this noble wreck their home. "The Flora of the Coliseum" contains four hundred and twenty species. Among the ruins of classical buildings might be seen broken columns, cypresses, and mouldy frescoes, dropping from the walls. Even the vegetable world participated in the melancholy change: the myrtle, which once flourished on the Aventine, had nearly become extinct; the laurel, which once gave its leaves to encircle the brows of emperors, had been replaced by ivy—the companion of death.

But perhaps it may be said the popes were not responsible for all this. Let it be remembered that in less than one hundred and forty years the city had been successively taken by Alaric, Genseric, Rieimer, Vitiges, Totila; that many of its great edifices had been converted into defensive works. The aqueducts were destroyed by Vitiges, who ruined the Campagna; the palace of the Caesars was ravaged by Totila; then there had been the Lombard sieges; then Robert Guiscard and his Normans had burnt the city from the Antonine Column to the Flaminian Gate, from the Lateran to the Capitol; then it was sacked and mutilated by the Constable Bourbon; again and again it was flooded by inundations of the Tiber and shattered by earthquakes. We must, however, bear in mind the accusation of Machiavelli, who says, in his "History of Florence," that nearly all the barbarian invasions of Italy were by the invitations of the pontiffs, who called in those hordes! It was not the Goth, nor the Vandal, nor the Norman, nor the Saracen, but the popes and their nephews, who produced the dilapidation of Rome! Lime-kilns had been fed from the ruins, classical buildings had become stone-quarries for the palaces of Italian princes, and churches were decorated from the old temples.

Churches decorated from the temples! It is for this and such as this that the popes must be held responsible. Superb Corinthian columns bad been chiseled into images of the saints. Magnificent Egyptian obelisks had been dishonored by papal inscriptions. The Septizonium of Severus had been demolished to furnish materials for the building of St. Peter's; the bronze roof of the Pantheon had been melted into columns to ornament the apostle's tomb.

The great bell of Viterbo, in the tower of the Capitol, had announced the death of many a pope, and still desecration of the buildings and demoralization of the people went on. Papal Rome manifested no consideration, but rather hatred, for classical Rome, The pontiffs had been subordinates of the Byzantine sovereigns, then lieutenants of the Frankish kings, then arbiters of Europe; their government had changed as much as those of any of the surrounding nations; there had been complete metamorphoses in its maxims, objects, claims. In one point only it had never changed—intolerance. Claiming to be the centre of the religious life of Europe, it steadfastly refused to recognize any religious existence outside of itself, yet both in a political and theological sense it was rotten to the core. Erasmus and Luther heard with amazement the blasphemies and witnessed with a shudder the atheism of the city.

The historian Ranke, to whom I am indebted for many of these facts, has depicted in a very graphic manner the demoralization of the great metropolis. The popes were, for the most part, at their election, aged men. Power was, therefore, incessantly passing into new hands. Every election was a revolution in prospects and expectations. In a community where all might rise, where all might aspire to all, it necessarily followed that every man was occupied in thrusting some other into the background. Though the population of the city at the inception of the Reformation had sunk to eighty thousand, there were vast crowds of placemen, and still greater ones of aspirants for place. The successful occupant of the pontificate had thousands of offices to give away—offices from many of which the incumbents had been remorselessly ejected; many had been created for the purpose of sale. The integrity and capacity of an applicant were never inquired into; the points considered were, what services has he rendered or can he render to the party? how much can he pay for the preferment? An American reader can thoroughly realize this state of things. At every presidential election he witnesses similar acts. The election of a pope by the Conclave is not unlike the nomination of an American president by a convention. In both cases there are many offices to give away.

William of Malmesbury says that in his day the Romans made a sale of whatever was righteous and sacred for gold. After his time there was no improvement; the Church degenerated into an instrument for the exploitation of money. Vast sums were collected in Italy; vast sums were drawn under all manner of pretenses from surrounding and reluctant countries. Of these the most nefarious was the sale of indulgences for the perpetration of sin. Italian religion had become the art of plundering the people.

For more than a thousand years the sovereign pontiffs had been rulers of the city. True, it had witnessed many scenes of devastation for which they were not responsible; but they were responsible for this, that they had never made any vigorous, any persistent effort for its material, its moral improvement. Instead of being in these respects an exemplar for the imitation of the world, it became an exemplar of a condition that ought to be shunned. Things steadily went on from bad to worse, until at the epoch of the Reformation no pious stranger could visit it without being shocked.

The papacy, repudiating science as absolutely incompatible with its pretensions, had in later years addressed itself to the encouragement of art. But music and painting, though they may be exquisite adornments of life, contain no living force that can develop a weak nation into a strong one; nothing that can permanently assure the material well-being or happiness of communities; and hence at the time of the Reformation, to one who thoughtfully considered her condition, Rome had lost all living energy. She was no longer the arbiter of the physical or the religious progress of the world. For the progressive maxims of the republic and the empire, she had substituted the stationary maxims of the papacy. She had the appearance of piety and the possession of art. In this she resembled one of those friar-corpses which we still see in their brown cowls in the vaults of the Cappuccini, with a breviary or some withered flowers in its hands.

From this view of the Eternal City, this survey of what Latin Christianity had done for Rome itself, let us turn to the whole European Continent. Let us try to determine the true value of the system that was guiding society; let us judge it by its fruits.

The condition of nations as to their well-being is most precisely represented by the variations of their population. Forms of government have very little influence on population, but policy may control it completely.

It has been very satisfactorily shown by authors who have given attention to the subject, that the variations of population depend upon the interbalancing of the generative force of society and the resistances to life.

By the generative force of society is meant that instinct which manifests itself in the multiplication of the race. To some extent it depends on climate; but, since the climate of Europe did not sensibly change between the fourth and the sixteenth centuries, we may regard this force as having been, on that continent, during the period under consideration, invariable.

By the resistances to life is meant whatever tends to make individual existence more difficult of support. Among such may be enumerated insufficient food, inadequate clothing, imperfect shelter.

It is also known that, if the resistances become inappreciable, the generative force will double a population in twenty-five years.

The resistances operate in two modes: 1. Physically; since they diminish the number of births, and shorten the term of the life of all. 2. Intellectually; since, in a moral, and particularly in a religious community, they postpone marriage, by causing individuals to decline its responsibilities until they feel that they are competent to meet the charges and cares of a family. Hence the explanation of a long-recognized fact, that the number of marriages during a given period has a connection with the price of food.

The increase of population keeps pace with the increase of food; and, indeed, such being the power of the generative force, it overpasses the means of subsistence, establishing a constant pressure upon them. Under these circumstances, it necessarily happens that a certain amount of destitution must occur. Individuals have come into existence who must be starved.

As illustrations of the variations that have occurred in the population of different countries, may be mentioned the immense diminution of that of Italy in consequence of the wars of Justinian; the depopulation of North Africa in consequence of theological quarrels; its restoration through the establishment of Mohammedanism; the increase of that of all Europe through the feudal system, when estates became more valuable in proportion to the number of retainers they could supply. The crusades caused a sensible diminution, not only through the enormous army losses, but also by reason of the withdrawal of so many able-bodied men from marriage-life. Similar variations have occurred on the American Continent. The population of Mexico was very quickly diminished by two million through the rapacity and atrocious cruelty of the Spaniards, who drove the civilized Indians to despair. The same happened in Peru.

The population of England at the Norman conquest was about two million. In five hundred years it had scarcely doubled. It may be supposed that this stationary condition was to some extent induced by the papal policy of the enforcement of celibacy in the clergy. The "legal generative force" was doubtless affected by that policy, the "actual generative force" was not. For those who have made this subject their study have long ago been satisfied that public celibacy is private wickedness. This mainly determined the laity, as well as the government in England, to suppress the monasteries. It was openly asserted that there were one hundred thousand women in England made dissolute by the clergy.

In my history of the "American Civil War," I have presented some reflections on this point, which I will take the liberty of quoting here: "What, then, does this stationary condition of the population mean? It means, food obtained with hardship, insufficient clothing, personal uncleanness, cabins that could not keep out the weather, the destructive effects of cold and heat, miasm, want of sanitary provisions, absence of physicians, uselessness of shrine-cure, the deceptiveness of miracles, in which society was putting its trust; or, to sum up a long catalogue of sorrows, wants, and sufferings, in one term—it means a high death-rate.

"But more; it means deficient births. And what does that point out? Marriage postponed, licentious life, private wickedness, demoralized society.

"To an American, who lives in a country that was yesterday an interminable and impenetrable desert, but which to-day is filling with a population doubling itself every twenty-five years at the prescribed rate, this awful waste of actual and contingent life cannot but be a most surprising fact. His curiosity will lead him to inquire what kind of system that could have been which was pretending to guide and develop society, but which must be held responsible for this prodigious destruction, excelling, in its insidious result, war, pestilence, and famine combined; insidious, for men were actually believing that it secured their highest temporal interests. How different now! In England, the same geographical surface is sustaining ten times the population of that day, and sending forth its emigrating swarms. Let him, who looks back, with veneration on the past, settle in his own mind what such a system could have been worth."

These variations in the population of Europe have been attended with changes in distribution. The centre of population has passed northward since the establishment of Christianity in the Roman Empire. It has since passed westward, in consequence of the development of manufacturing industry.

We may now examine somewhat more minutely the character of the resistances which thus, for a thousand years, kept the population of Europe stationary. The surface of the Continent was for the most part covered with pathless forests; here and there it was dotted with monasteries and towns. In the lowlands and along the river-courses were fens, sometimes hundreds of miles in extent, exhaling their pestiferous miasms, and spreading agues far and wide. In Paris and London, the houses were of wood daubed with clay, and thatched with straw or reeds. They had no windows, and, until the invention of the saw-mill, very few had wooden floors. The luxury of a carpet was unknown; some straw, scattered in the room, supplied its place. There were no chimneys; the smoke of the ill-fed, cheerless fire escaped through a hole in the roof. In such habitations there was scarcely any protection from the weather. No attempt was made at drainage, but the putrefying garbage and rubbish were simply thrown out of the door. Men, women, and children, slept in the same apartment; not unfrequently, domestic animals were their companions; in such a confusion of the family, it was impossible that modesty or morality could be maintained. The bed was usually a bag of straw, a wooden log served as a pillow. Personal cleanliness was utterly unknown; great officers of state, even dignitaries so high as the Archbishop of Canterbury, swarmed with vermin; such, it is related, was the condition of Thomas a Becket, the antagonist of an English king. To conceal personal impurity, perfumes were necessarily and profusely used. The citizen clothed himself in leather, a garment which, with its ever-accumulating impurity, might last for many years. He was considered to be in circumstances of ease, if he could procure fresh meat once a week for his dinner. The streets had no sewers; they were without pavement or lamps. After nightfall, the chamber-shatters were thrown open, and slops unceremoniously emptied down, to the discomfiture of the wayfarer tracking his path through the narrow streets, with his dismal lantern in his hand.

Aeneas Sylvius, who afterward became Pope Pius II., and was therefore a very competent and impartial writer, has left us a graphic account of a journey he made to the British Islands, about 1430. He describes the houses of the peasantry as constructed of stones put together without mortar; the roofs were of turf, a stiffened bull's-hide served for a door. The food consisted of coarse vegetable products, such as peas, and even the bark of trees. In some places they were unacquainted with bread.

Cabins of reeds plastered with mud, houses of wattled stakes, chimneyless peat-fires from which there was scarcely an escape for the smoke, dens of physical and moral pollution swarming with vermin, wisps of straw twisted round the limbs to keep off the cold, the ague-stricken peasant, with no help except shrine-cure! How was it possible that the population could increase? Shall we, then, wonder that, in the famine of 1030, human flesh was cooked and sold; or that, in that of 1258, fifteen thousand persons died of hunger in London? Shall we wonder that, in some of the invasions of the plague, the deaths were so frightfully numerous that the living could hardly bury the dead? By that of 1348, which came from the East along the lines of commercial travel, and spread all over Europe, one-third of the population of France was destroyed.

Such was the condition of the peasantry, and of the common inhabitants of cities. Not much better was that of the nobles. William of Malmesbury, speaking of the degraded manners of the Anglo-Saxons, says: "Their nobles, devoted to gluttony and voluptuousness, never visited the church, but the matins and the mass were read over to them by a hurrying priest in their bedchambers, before they rose, themselves not listening. The common people were a prey to the more powerful; their property was seized, their bodies dragged away to distant countries; their maidens were either thrown into a brothel, or sold for slaves. Drinking day and night was the general pursuit; vices, the companions of inebriety, followed, effeminating the manly mind." The baronial castles were dens of robbers. The Saxon chronicler records how men and women were caught and dragged into those strongholds, hung up by their thumbs or feet, fire applied to them, knotted strings twisted round their heads, and many other torments inflicted to extort ransom.

All over Europe, the great and profitable political offices were filled by ecclesiastics. In every country there was a dual government: 1. That of a local kind, represented by a temporal sovereign; 2. That of a foreign kind, acknowledging the authority of the pope, This Roman influence was, in the nature of things, superior to the local; it expressed the sovereign will of one man over all the nations of the continent conjointly, and gathered overwhelming power from its compactness and unity. The local influence was necessarily of a feeble nature, since it was commonly weakened by the rivalries of conterminous states, and the dissensions dexterously provoked by its competitor. On not a single occasion could the various European states form a coalition against their common antagonist. Whenever a question arose, they were skillfully taken in detail, and commonly mastered. The ostensible object of papal intrusion was to secure for the different peoples moral well-being; the real object was to obtain large revenues, and give support to vast bodies of ecclesiastics. The revenues thus abstracted were not infrequently many times greater than those passing into the treasury of the local power. Thus, on the occasion of Innocent IV. demanding provision to be made for three hundred additional Italian clergy by the Church of England, and that one of his nephews—a mere boy—should have a stall in Lincoln Cathedral, it was found that the sum already annually abstracted by foreign ecclesiastics from England was thrice that which went into the coffers of the king.

While thus the higher clergy secured every political appointment worth having, and abbots vied with counts in the herds of slaves they possessed—some, it is said, owned not fewer than twenty thousand—begging friars pervaded society in all directions, picking up a share of what still remained to the poor. There was a vast body of non-producers, living in idleness and owning a foreign allegiance, who were subsisting on the fruits of the toil of the laborers. It could not be otherwise than that small farms should be unceasingly merged into the larger estates; that the poor should steadily become poorer; that society, far from improving, should exhibit a continually increasing demoralization. Outside the monastic institutions no attempt at intellectual advancement was made; indeed, so far as the laity were concerned, the influence of the Church was directed to an opposite result, for the maxim universally received was, that "ignorance is the mother of devotion."

The settled practice of republican and imperial Rome was to have swift communication with all her outlying provinces, by means of substantial bridges and roads. One of the prime duties of the legions was to construct them and keep them in repair. By this, her military authority was assured. But the dominion of papal Rome, depending upon a different principle, had no exigencies of that kind, and this duty accordingly was left for the local powers to neglect. And so, in all directions, the roads were almost impassable for a large part of the year. A common means of transportation was in clumsy carts drawn by oxen, going at the most but three or four miles an hour. Where boat-conveyance along rivers could not be had, pack-horses and mules were resorted to for the transportation of merchandise, an adequate means for the slender commerce of the times. When large bodies of men had to be moved, the difficulties became almost insuperable. Of this, perhaps, one of the best illustrations may be found in the story of the march of the first Crusaders. These restraints upon intercommunication tended powerfully to promote the general benighted condition. Journeys by individuals could not be undertaken without much risk, for there was scarcely a moor or a forest that had not its highwaymen.

An illiterate condition everywhere prevailing, gave opportunity for the development of superstition. Europe was full of disgraceful miracles. On all the roads pilgrims were wending their way to the shrines of saints, renowned for the cures they had wrought. It had always been the policy of the Church to discourage the physician and his art; he interfered too much with the gifts and profits of the shrines. Time has brought this once lucrative imposture to its proper value. How many shrines are there now in successful operation in Europe?

For patients too sick to move or be moved, there were no remedies except those of a ghostly kind—the Pater-noster or the Ave. For the prevention of diseases, prayers were put up in the churches, but no sanitary measures were resorted to. From cities reeking with putrefying filth it was thought that the plague might be stayed by the prayers of the priests, by them rain and dry weather might be secured, and deliverance obtained from the baleful influences of eclipses and comets. But when Halley's comet came, in 1456, so tremendous was its apparition that it was necessary for the pope himself to interfere. He exorcised and expelled it from the skies. It slunk away into the abysses of space, terror-stricken by the maledictions of Calixtus III., and did not venture back for seventy-five years!

The physical value of shrine-cures and ghostly remedies is measured by the death-rate. In those days it was, probably, about one in twenty-three, under the present more material practice it is about one in forty.

The moral condition of Europe was signally illustrated when syphilis was introduced from the West Indies by the companions of Columbus. It spread with wonderful rapidity; all ranks of persons, from the Holy Father Leo X. to the beggar by the wayside, contracting the shameful disease. Many excused their misfortune by declaring that it was an epidemic proceeding from a certain malignity in the constitution of the air, but in truth its spread was due to a certain infirmity in the constitution of man—an infirmity which had not been removed by the spiritual guidance under which he had been living.

To the medical efficacy of shrines must be added that of special relics. These were sometimes of the most extraordinary kind. There were several abbeys that possessed our Savior's crown of thorns. Eleven had the lance that had pierced his side. If any person was adventurous enough to suggest that these could not all be authentic, he would have been denounced as an atheist. During the holy wars the Templar-Knights had driven a profitable commerce by bringing from Jerusalem to the Crusading armies bottles of the milk of the Blessed Virgin, which they sold for enormous sums; these bottles were preserved with pious care in many of the great religious establishments. But perhaps none of these impostures surpassed in audacity that offered by a monastery in Jerusalem, which presented to the beholder one of the fingers of the Holy Ghost! Modern society has silently rendered its verdict on these scandalous objects. Though they once nourished the piety of thousands of earnest people, they are now considered too vile to have a place in any public museum.

How shall we account for the great failure we thus detect in the guardianship of the Church over Europe? This is not the result that must have occurred had there been in Rome an unremitting care for the spiritual and material prosperity of the continent, had the universal pastor, the successor of Peter, occupied himself with singleness of purpose for the holiness and happiness of his flock.

The explanation is not difficult to find. It is contained in a story of sin and shame. I prefer, therefore, in the following paragraphs, to offer explanatory facts derived from Catholic authors, and, indeed, to present them as nearly as I can in the words of those writers.

The story I am about to relate is a narrative of the transformation of a confederacy into an absolute monarchy.

In the early times every church, without prejudice to its agreement with the Church universal in all essential points, managed its own affairs with perfect freedom and independence, maintaining its own traditional usages and discipline, all questions not concerning the whole Church, or of primary importance, being settled on the spot.

Until the beginning of the ninth century, there was no change in the constitution of the Roman Church. But about 845 the Isidorian Decretals were fabricated in the west of Gaul—a forgery containing about one hundred pretended decrees of the early popes, together with certain spurious writings of other church dignitaries and acts of synods. This forgery produced an immense extension of the papal power, it displaced the old system of church government, divesting it of the republican attributes it had possessed, and transforming it into an absolute monarchy. It brought the bishops into subjection to Rome, and made the pontiff the supreme judge of the clergy of the whole Christian world. It prepared the way for the great attempt, subsequently made by Hildebrand, to convert the states of Europe into a theocratic priest-kingdom, with the pope at its head.

Gregory VII., the author of this great attempt, saw that his plans would be best carried out through the agency of synods. He, therefore, restricted the right of holding them to the popes and their legates. To aid in the matter, a new system of church law was devised by Anselm of Lucca, partly from the old Isidorian forgeries, and partly from new inventions. To establish the supremacy of Rome, not only had a new civil and a new canon law to be produced, a new history had also to be invented. This furnished needful instances of the deposition and excommunication of kings, and proved that they had always been subordinate to the popes. The decretal letters of the popes were put on a par with Scripture. At length it came to be received, throughout the West, that the popes had been, from the beginning of Christianity, legislators for the whole Church. As absolute sovereigns in later times cannot endure representative assemblies, so the papacy, when it wished to become absolute, found that the synods of particular national churches must be put an end to, and those only under the immediate control of the pontiff permitted. This, in itself, constituted a great revolution.

Another fiction concocted in Rome in the eighth century led to important consequences. It feigned that the Emperor Constantine, in gratitude for his cure from leprosy, and baptism by Pope Sylvester, had bestowed Italy and the Western provinces on the pope, and that, in token of his subordination, he had served the pope as his groom, and led his horse some distance. This forgery was intended to work on the Frankish kings, to impress them with a correct idea of their inferiority, and to show that, in the territorial concessions they made to the Church, they were not giving but only restoring what rightfully belonged to it.

The most potent instrument of the new papal system was Gratian's Decretum, which was issued about the middle of the twelfth century. It was a mass of fabrications. It made the whole Christian world, through the papacy, the domain of the Italian clergy. It inculcated that it is lawful to constrain men to goodness, to torture and execute heretics, and to confiscate their property; that to kill an excommunicated person is not murder; that the pope, in his unlimited superiority to all law, stands on an equality with the Son of God!

As the new system of centralization developed, maxims, that in the olden times would have been held to be shocking, were boldly avowed—the whole Church is the property of the pope to do with as he will; what is simony in others is not simony in him; he is above all law, and can be called to account by none; whoever disobeys him must be put to death; every baptized man is his subject, and must for life remain so, whether he will or not. Up to the end of the twelfth century, the popes were the vicars of Peter; after Innocent III. they were the vicars of Christ.

But an absolute sovereign has need of revenues, and to this the popes were no exception. The institution of legates was brought in from Hildebrand's time. Sometimes their duty was to visit churches, sometimes they were sent on special business, but always invested with unlimited powers to bring back money over the Alps. And since the pope could not only make laws, but could suspend their operation, a legislation was introduced in view to the purchase of dispensations. Monasteries were exempted from episcopal jurisdiction on payment of a tribute to Rome. The pope had now become "the universal bishop;" he had a concurrent jurisdiction in all the dioceses, and could bring any cases before his own courts. His relation to the bishops was that of an absolute sovereign to his officials. A bishop could resign only by his permission, and sees vacated by resignation lapsed to him. Appeals to him were encouraged in every way for the sake of the dispensations; thousands of processes came before the Curia, bringing a rich harvest to Rome. Often when there were disputing claimants to benefices, the pope would oust them all, and appoint a creature of his own. Often the candidates had to waste years in Rome, and either died there, or carried back a vivid impression of the dominant corruption. Germany suffered more than other countries from these appeals and processes, and hence of all countries was best prepared for the Reformation. During the thirteenth and fourteenth centuries the popes made gigantic strides in the acquisition of power. Instead of recommending their favorites for benefices, now they issued mandates. Their Italian partisans must be rewarded; nothing could be done to satisfy their clamors, but to provide for them in foreign countries. Shoals of contesting claimants died in Rome; and, when death took place in that city, the Pope claimed the right of giving away the benefices. At length it was affirmed that he had the right of disposing of all church-offices without distinction, and that the oath of obedience of a bishop to him implied political as well as ecclesiastical subjection. In countries having a dual government this increased the power of the spiritual element prodigiously.

Rights of every kind were remorselessly overthrown to complete this centralization. In this the mendicant orders were most efficient aids. It was the pope and those orders on one side, the bishops and the parochial clergy on the other. The Roman court had seized the rights of synods, metropolitans, bishops, national churches. Incessantly interfered with by the legates, the bishops lost all desire to discipline their dioceses; incessantly interfered with by the begging monks, the parish priest had become powerless in his own village; his pastoral influence was utterly destroyed by the papal indulgences and absolutions they sold. The money was carried off to Rome.

Pecuniary necessities urged many of the popes to resort to such petty expedients as to require from a prince, a bishop, or a grand-master, who had a cause pending in the court, a present of a golden cup filled with ducats. Such necessities also gave origin to jubilees. Sixtus IV. established whole colleges, and sold the places at three or four hundred ducats. Innocent VIII. pawned the papal tiara. Of Leo X. it was said that he squandered the revenues of three popes, he wasted the savings of his predecessor, he spent his own income, he anticipated that of his successor, he created twenty-one hundred and fifty new offices and sold them; they were considered to be a good investment, as they produced twelve per cent. The interest was extorted from Catholic countries. Nowhere in Europe could capital be so well invested as at Rome. Large sums were raised by the foreclosing of mortgages, and not only by the sale but the resale of offices. Men were promoted, for the purpose of selling their offices again.

Though against the papal theory, which denounced usurious practices, an immense papal banking system had sprung up, in connection with the Curia, and sums at usurious interest were advanced to prelates, place-hunters, and litigants. The papal bankers were privileged; all others were under the ban. The Curia had discovered that it was for their interest to have ecclesiastics all over Europe in their debt. They could make them pliant, and excommunicate them for non-payment of interest. In 1327 it was reckoned that half the Christian world was under excommunication: bishops were excommunicated because they could not meet the extortions of legates; and persons were excommunicated, under various pretenses, to compel them to purchase absolution at an exorbitant price. The ecclesiastical revenues of all Europe were flowing into Rome, a sink of corruption, simony, usury, bribery, extortion. The popes, since 1066, when the great centralizing movement began, had no time to pay attention to the internal affairs of their own special flock in the city of Rome. There were thousands of foreign cases, each bringing in money. "Whenever," says the Bishop Alvaro Pelayo, "I entered the apartments of the Roman court clergy, I found them occupied in counting up the gold-coin, which lay about the rooms in heaps." Every opportunity of extending the jurisdiction of the Curia was welcome. Exemptions were so managed that fresh grants were constantly necessary. Bishops were privileged against cathedral chapters, chapters against their bishops; bishops, convents, and individuals, against the extortions of legates.

The two pillars on which the papal system now rested were the College of Cardinals and the Curia. The cardinals, in 1059, had become electors of the popes. Up to that time elections were made by the whole body of the Roman clergy, and the concurrence of the magistrates and citizens was necessary. But Nicolas II. restricted elections to the College of Cardinals by a two-thirds vote, and gave to the German emperor the right of confirmation. For almost two centuries there was a struggle for mastery between the cardinal oligarchy and papal absolutism. The cardinals were willing enough that the pope should be absolute in his foreign rule, but they never failed to attempt, before giving him their votes, to bind him to accord to them a recognized share in the government. After his election, and before his consecration, he swore to observe certain capitulations, such as a participation of revenues between himself and the cardinals; an obligation that he would not remove them, but would permit them to assemble twice a year to discuss whether he had kept his oath. Repeatedly the popes broke their oath. On one side, the cardinals wanted a larger share in the church government and emoluments; on the other, the popes refused to surrender revenues or power. The cardinals wanted to be conspicuous in pomp and extravagance, and for this vast sums were requisite. In one instance, not fewer than five hundred benefices were held by one of them; their friends and retainers must be supplied, their families enriched. It was affirmed that the whole revenues of France were insufficient to meet their expenditures. In their rivalries it sometimes happened that no pope was elected for several years. It seemed as if they wanted to show how easily the Church could get on without the Vicar of Christ.

Toward the close of the eleventh century the Roman Church became the Roman court. In place of the Christian sheep gently following their shepherd in the holy precincts of the city, there had arisen a chancery of writers, notaries, tax-gatherers, where transactions about privileges, dispensations, exemptions, were carried on; and suitors went with petitions from door to door. Rome was a rallying-point for place-hunters of every nation. In presence of the enormous mass of business-processes, graces, indulgences, absolutions, commands, and decisions, addressed to all parts of Europe and Asia, the functions of the local church sank into insignificance. Several hundred persons, whose home was the Curia, were required. Their aim was to rise in it by enlarging the profits of the papal treasury. The whole Christian world had become tributary to it. Here every vestige of religion had disappeared; its members were busy with politics, litigations, and processes; not a word could be heard about spiritual concerns. Every stroke of the pen had its price. Benefices, dispensations, licenses, absolutions, indulgences, privileges, were bought and sold like merchandise. The suitor had to bribe every one, from the doorkeeper to the pope, or his case was lost. Poor men could neither attain preferment, nor hope for it; and the result was, that every cleric felt he had a right to follow the example he had seen at Rome, and that he might make profits out of his spiritual ministries and sacraments, having bought the right to do so at Rome, and having no other way to pay off his debt. The transference of power from Italians to Frenchmen, through the removal of the Curia to Avignon, produced no change—only the Italians felt that the enrichment of Italian families had slipped out of their grasp. They had learned to consider the papacy as their appanage, and that they, under the Christian dispensation, were God's chosen people, as the Jews had been under the Mosaic.

At the end of the thirteenth century a new kingdom was discovered, capable of yielding immense revenues. This was Purgatory. It was shown that the pope could empty it by his indulgences. In this there was no need of hypocrisy. Things were done openly. The original germ of the apostolic primacy had now expanded into a colossal monarchy.

NEED OF A GENERAL COUNCIL. The Inquisition had made the papal system irresistible. All opposition must be punished with death by fire. A mere thought, without having betrayed itself by outward sign, was considered as guilt. As time went on, this practice of the Inquisition became more and more atrocious. Torture was resorted to on mere suspicion. The accused was not allowed to know the name of his accuser. He was not permitted to have any legal adviser. There was no appeal. The Inquisition was ordered not to lean to pity. No recantation was of avail. The innocent family of the accused was deprived of its property by confiscation; half went to the papal treasury, half to the inquisitors. Life only, said Innocent III., was to be left to the sons of misbelievers, and that merely as an act of mercy. The consequence was, that popes, such as Nicolas III., enriched their families through plunder acquired by this tribunal. Inquisitors did the same habitually.

The struggle between the French and Italians for the possession of the papacy inevitably led to the schism of the fourteenth century. For more than forty years two rival popes were now anathematizing each other, two rival Curias were squeezing the nations for money. Eventually, there were three obediences, and triple revenues to be extorted. Nobody, now, could guarantee the validity of the sacraments, for nobody could be sure which was the true pope. Men were thus compelled to think for themselves. They could not find who was the legitimate thinker for them. They began to see that the Church must rid herself of the curialistic chains, and resort to a General Council. That attempt was again and again made, the intention being to raise the Council into a Parliament of Christendom, and make the pope its chief executive officer. But the vast interests that had grown out of the corruption of ages could not so easily be overcome; the Curia again recovered its ascendency, and ecclesiastical trading was resumed. The Germans, who had never been permitted to share in the Curia, took the leading part in these attempts at reform. As things went on from bad to worse, even they at last found out that all hope of reforming the Church by means of councils was delusive. Erasmus exclaimed, "If Christ does not deliver his people from this multiform ecclesiastical tyranny, the tyranny of the Turk will become less intolerable." Cardinals' hats were now sold, and under Leo X. ecclesiastical and religious offices were actually put up to auction. The maxim of life had become, interest first, honor afterward. Among the officials, there was not one who could be honest in the dark, and virtuous without a witness. The violet-colored velvet cloaks and white ermine capes of the cardinals were truly a cover for wickedness.

The unity of the Church, and therefore its power, required the use of Latin as a sacred language. Through this, Rome had stood in an attitude strictly European, and was enabled to maintain a general international relation. It gave her far more power than her asserted celestial authority, and, much as she claims to have done, she is open to condemnation that, with such a signal advantage in her hands, never again to be enjoyed by any successor, she did not accomplish much more. Had not the sovereign pontiffs been so completely occupied with maintaining their emoluments and temporalities in Italy, they might have made the whole continent advance like one man. Their officials could pass without difficulty into every nation, and communicate without embarrassment with each other, from Ireland to Bohemia, from Italy to Scotland. The possession of a common tongue gave them the administration of international affairs with intelligent allies everywhere, speaking the same language.

Not without cause was the hatred manifested by Rome to the restoration of Greek and introduction of Hebrew, and the alarm with which she perceived the modern languages forming out of the vulgar dialects. Not without reason did the Faculty of Theology in Paris re-echo the sentiment that, was prevalent in the time of Ximenes, "What will become of religion if the study of Greek and Hebrew be permitted?" The prevalence of Latin was the condition of her power; its deterioration, the measure of her decay; its disuse, the signal of her limitation to a little principality in Italy. In fact, the development of European languages was the instrument of her overthrow. They formed an effectual communication between the mendicant friars and the illiterate populace, and there was not one of them that did not display in its earliest productions a sovereign contempt for her.

The rise of the many-tongued European literature was therefore coincident with the decline of papal Christianity; European literature was impossible under Catholic rule. A grand, a solemn, an imposing religious unity enforced the literary unity which is implied in the use of a single tongue.

While thus the possession of a universal language so signally secured her power, the real secret of much of the influence of the Church lay in the control she had so skillfully obtained over domestic life. Her influence diminished as that declined. Coincident with this was her displacement in the guidance of international relations by diplomacy.

CATHOLICITY AND CIVILIZATION. In the old times of Roman domination the encampments of the legions in the provinces had always proved to be foci of civilization. The industry and order exhibited in them presented an example not lost on the surrounding barbarians of Britain, Gaul, and Germany. And, though it was no part of their duty to occupy themselves actively in the betterment of the conquered tribes, but rather to keep them in a depressed condition that aided in maintaining subjection, a steady improvement both in the individual and social condition took place.

Under the ecclesiastical domination of Rome similar effects occurred. In the open country the monastery replaced the legionary encampment; in the village or town, the church was a centre of light. A powerful effect was produced by the elegant luxury of the former, and by the sacred and solemn monitions of the latter.

In extolling the papal system for what it did in the organization of the family, the definition of civil policy, the construction of the states of Europe, our praise must be limited by the recollection that the chief object of ecclesiastical policy was the aggrandizement of the Church, not the promotion of civilization. The benefit obtained by the laity was not through any special intention, but incidental or collateral.

There was no far-reaching, no persistent plan to ameliorate the physical condition of the nations. Nothing was done to favor their intellectual development; indeed, on the contrary, it was the settled policy to keep them not merely illiterate, but ignorant. Century after century passed away, and left the peasantry but little better than the cattle in the fields. Intercommunication and locomotion, which tend so powerfully to expand the ideas, received no encouragement; the majority of men died without ever having ventured out of the neighborhood in which they were born. For them there was no hope of personal improvement, none of the bettering of their lot; there were no comprehensive schemes for the avoidance of individual want, none for the resistance of famines. Pestilences were permitted to stalk forth unchecked, or at best opposed only by mummeries. Bad food, wretched clothing, inadequate shelter, were suffered to produce their result, and at the end of a thousand years the population of Europe had not doubled.

If policy may be held accountable as much for the births it prevents as for the deaths it occasions, what a great responsibility there is here!

In this investigation of the influence of Catholicism, we must carefully keep separate what it did for the people and what it did for itself. When we think of the stately monastery, an embodiment of luxury, with its closely-mown lawns, its gardens and bowers, its fountains and many murmuring streams, we must connect it not with the ague-stricken peasant dying without help in the fens, but with the abbot, his ambling palfrey, his hawk and hounds, his well-stocked cellar and larder. He is part of a system that has its centre of authority in Italy.. To that his allegiance is due. For its behoof are all his acts. When we survey, as still we may, the magnificent churches and cathedrals of those times, miracles of architectural skill—the only real miracles of Catholicism—when in imagination we restore the transcendently imposing, the noble services of which they were once the scene, the dim, religious-light streaming in through the many-colored windows, the sounds of voices not inferior in their melody to those of heaven, the priests in their sacred vestments, and above all the prostrate worshipers listening to litanies and prayers in a foreign and unknown tongue, shall we not ask ourselves, Was all this for the sake of those worshipers, or for the glory of the great, the overshadowing authority at Rome?

But perhaps some one may say, Are there not limits to human exertion—things which no political system, no human power, no matter how excellent its intention, can accomplish? Men cannot be raised from barbarism, a continent cannot be civilized, in a day!

The Catholic power is not, however, to be tried by any such standard. It scornfully rejected and still rejects a human origin. It claims to be accredited supernaturally. The sovereign pontiff is the Vicar of God upon earth. Infallible in judgment, it is given to him to accomplish all things by miracle if need be. He had exercised an autocratic tyranny over the intellect of Europe for more than a thousand years; and, though on some occasions he had encountered the resistances of disobedient princes, these, in the aggregate, were of so little moment, that the physical, the political power of the continent may be affirmed to have been at his disposal.

Such facts as have been presented in this chapter were, doubtless, well weighed by the Protestant Reformers of the sixteenth century, and brought them to the conclusion that Catholicism had altogether failed in its mission; that it had become a vast system of delusion and imposture, and that a restoration of true Christianity could only be accomplished by returning to the faith and practices of the primitive times. This was no decision suddenly arrived at; it had long been the opinion of many religious and learned men. The pious Fratricelli in the middle ages had loudly expressed their belief that the fatal gift of a Roman emperor had been the doom of true religion. It wanted nothing more than the voice of Luther to bring men throughout the north of Europe to the determination that the worship of the Virgin Mary, the invocation of saints, the working of miracles, supernatural cures of the sick, the purchase of indulgences for the perpetration of sin, and all other evil practices, lucrative to their abettors, which had been fastened on Christianity, but which were no part of it, should come to an end. Catholicism, as a system for promoting the well-being of man, had plainly failed in justifying its alleged origin; its performance had not corresponded to its great pretensions; and, after an opportunity of more than a thousand years' duration, it had left the masses of men submitted to its influences, both as regards physical well-being and intellectual culture, in a condition far lower than what it ought to have been.

CHAPTER XI.

SCIENCE IN RELATION TO MODERN CIVILIZATION.

Illustration of the general influences of Science from the history of America.

THE INTRODUCTION OF SCIENCE INTO EUROPE.—It passed from Moorish Spain to Upper Italy, and was favored by the absence of the popes at Avignon.—The effects of printing, of maritime adventure, and of the Reformation—Establishment of the Italian scientific societies.

THE INTELLECTUAL INFLUENCE OF SCIENCE.—It changed the mode and the direction of thought in Europe.—The transactions of the Royal Society of London, and other scientific societies, furnish an illustration of this.

THE ECONOMICAL INFLUENCE OF SCIENCE is illustrated by the numerous mechanical and physical inventions, made since the fourteenth century.—Their influence on health and domestic life, on the arts of peace and of war.

Answer to the question, What has Science done for humanity?

EUROPE, at the epoch of the Reformation, furnishes us with the result of the influences of Roman Christianity in the promotion of civilization. America, examined in like manner at the present time, furnishes us with an illustration of the influences of science.

SCIENCE AND CIVILIZATION. In the course of the seventeenth century a sparse European population had settled along the western Atlantic coast. Attracted by the cod-fishery of Newfoundland, the French had a little colony north of the St. Lawrence; the English, Dutch, and Swedes, occupied the shore of New England and the Middle States; some Huguenots were living in the Carolinas. Rumors of a spring that could confer perpetual youth—a fountain of life—had brought a few Spaniards into Florida. Behind the fringe of villages which these adventurers had built, lay a vast and unknown country, inhabited by wandering Indians, whose numbers from the Gulf of Mexico to the St. Lawrence did not exceed one hundred and eighty thousand. From them the European strangers had learned that in those solitary regions there were fresh-water seas, and a great river which they called the Mississippi. Some said that it flowed through Virginia into the Atlantic, some that it passed through Florida, some that it emptied into the Pacific, and some that it reached the Gulf of Mexico. Parted from their native countries by the stormy Atlantic, to cross which implied a voyage of many months, these refugees seemed lost to the world.

But before the close of the nineteenth century the descendants of this feeble people had become one of the great powers of the earth. They had established a republic whose sway extended from the Atlantic to the Pacific. With an army of more than a million men, not on paper, but actually in the field, they had overthrown a domestic assailant. They had maintained at sea a war-fleet of nearly seven hundred ships, carrying five thousand guns, some of them the heaviest in the world. The tonnage of this navy amounted to half a million. In the defense of their national life they had expended in less than five years more than four thousand million dollars. Their census, periodically taken, showed that the population was doubling itself every twenty-five years; it justified the expectation that at the close of that century it would number nearly one hundred million souls.

KNOWLEDGE IS POWER. A silent continent had been changed into a scene of industry; it was full of the din of machinery and the restless moving of men. Where there had been an unbroken forest, there were hundreds of cities and towns. To commerce were furnished in profusion some of the most important staples, as cotton, tobacco, breadstuffs. The mines yielded incredible quantities of gold, iron, coal. Countless churches, colleges, and public schools, testified that a moral influence vivified this material activity. Locomotion was effectually provided for. The railways exceeded in aggregate length those of all Europe combined. In 1873 the aggregate length of the European railways was sixty-three thousand three hundred and sixty miles, that of the American was seventy thousand six hundred and fifty miles. One of them, built across the continent, connected the Atlantic and Pacific Oceans.

But not alone are these material results worthy of notice. Others of a moral and social kind force themselves on our attention. Four million negro slaves had been set free. Legislation, if it inclined to the advantage of any class, inclined to that of the poor. Its intention was to raise them from poverty, and better their lot. A career was open to talent, and that without any restraint. Every thing was possible to intelligence and industry. Many of the most important public offices were filled by men who had risen from the humblest walks of life. If there was not social equality, as there never can be in rich and prosperous communities, there was civil equality, rigorously maintained.

It may perhaps be said that much of this material prosperity arose from special conditions, such as had never occurred in the case of any people before, There was a vast, an open theatre of action, a whole continent ready for any who chose to take possession of it. Nothing more than courage and industry was needed to overcome Nature, and to seize the abounding advantages she offered.

===

ILLUSTRATIONS FROM AMERICAN HISTORY. But must not men be animated by a great principle who successfully transform the primeval solitudes into an abode of civilization, who are not dismayed by gloomy forests, or rivers, mountains, or frightful deserts, who push their conquering way in the course of a century across a continent, and hold it in subjection? Let us contrast with this the results of the invasion of Mexico and Peru by the Spaniards, who in those countries overthrew a wonderful civilization, in many respects superior to their own—a civilization that had been accomplished without iron and gunpowder—a civilization resting on an agriculture that had neither horse, nor ox, nor plough. The Spaniards had a clear base to start from, and no obstruction whatever in their advance. They ruined all that the aboriginal children of America had accomplished. Millions of those unfortunates were destroyed by their cruelty. Nations that for many centuries had been living in contentment and prosperity, under institutions shown by their history to be suitable to them, were plunged into anarchy; the people fell into a baneful superstition, and a greater part of their landed and other property found its way into the possession of the Roman Church.

I have selected the foregoing illustration, drawn from American history, in preference to many others that might have been taken from European, because it furnishes an instance of the operation of the acting principle least interfered with by extraneous conditions. European political progress is less simple than American.

QUARREL BETWEEN FRANCE AND THE PAPACY. Before considering its manner of action, and its results, I will briefly relate how the scientific principle found an introduction into Europe.

INTRODUCTION OF SCIENCE INTO EUROPE. Not only had the Crusades, for many years, brought vast sums to Rome, extorted from the fears or the piety of every Christian nation; they had also increased the papal power to a most dangerous extent. In the dual governments everywhere prevailing in Europe, the spiritual had obtained the mastery; the temporal was little better than its servant.

From all quarters, and under all kinds of pretenses, streams of money were steadily flowing into Italy. The temporal princes found that there were left for them inadequate and impoverished revenues. Philip the Fair, King of France (A.D. 1300), not only determined to check this drain from his dominions, by prohibiting the export of gold and silver without his license; he also resolved that the clergy and the ecclesiastical estates should pay their share of taxes to him. This brought on a mortal contest with the papacy. The king was excommunicated, and, in retaliation, he accused the pope, Boniface VIII., of atheism; demanding that he should be tried by a general council. He sent some trusty persons into Italy, who seized Boniface in his palace at Anagni, and treated him with so much severity, that in a few days he died. The succeeding pontiff, Benedict XI., was poisoned.

The French king was determined that the papacy should be purified and reformed; that it should no longer be the appanage of a few Italian families, who were dexterously transmuting the credulity of Europe into coin—that French influence should prevail in it. He Therefore came to an understanding with the cardinals; a French archbishop was elevated to the pontificate; he took the name of Clement V. The papal court was removed to Avignon, in France, and Rome was abandoned as the metropolis of Christianity.

MOORISH SCIENCE INTRODUCED THROUGH FRANCE. Seventy years elapsed before the papacy was restored to the Eternal City (A.D. 1376). The diminution of its influence in the peninsula, that had thus occurred, gave opportunity for the memorable intellectual movement which soon manifested itself in the great commercial cities of Upper Italy. Contemporaneously, also, there were other propitious events. The result of the Crusades had shaken the faith of all Christendom. In an age when the test of the ordeal of battle was universally accepted, those wars had ended in leaving the Holy Land in the hands of the Saracens; the many thousand Christian warriors who had returned from them did not hesitate to declare that they had found their antagonists not such as had been pictured by the Church, but valiant, courteous, just. Through the gay cities of the South of France a love of romantic literature had been spreading; the wandering troubadours had been singing their songs—songs far from being restricted to ladye-love and feats of war; often their burden was the awful atrocities that had been perpetrated by papal authority—the religious massacres of Languedoc; often their burden was the illicit amours of the clergy. From Moorish Spain the gentle and gallant idea of chivalry had been brought, and with it the noble sentiment of "personal honor," destined in the course of time to give a code of its own to Europe.

EFFECT OF THE GREAT SCHISM. The return of the papacy to Rome was far from restoring the influence of the popes over the Italian Peninsula. More than two generations had passed away since their departure, and, had they come back even in their original strength, they could not have resisted the intellectual progress that had been made during their absence. The papacy, however, came back not to rule, but to be divided against itself, to encounter the Great Schism. Out of its dissensions emerged two rival popes; eventually there were three, each pressing his claims upon the religious, each cursing his rival. A sentiment of indignation soon spread all over Europe, a determination that the shameful scenes which were then enacting should be ended. How could the dogma of a Vicar of God upon earth, the dogma of an infallible pope, be sustained in presence of such scandals? Herein lay the cause of that resolution of the ablest ecclesiastics of those times (which, alas for Europe! could not be carried into effect), that a general council should be made the permanent religious parliament of the whole continent, with the pope as its chief executive officer. Had that intention been accomplished, there would have been at this day no conflict between science and religion; the convulsion of the Reformation would have been avoided; there would have been no jarring Protestant sects. But the Councils of Constance and Basle failed to shake off the Italian yoke, failed to attain that noble result.

Catholicism was thus weakening; as its leaden pressure lifted, the intellect of man expanded. The Saracens had invented the method of making paper from linen rags and from cotton. The Venetians had brought from China to Europe the art of printing. The former of these inventions was essential to the latter. Hence forth, without the possibility of a check, there was intellectual intercommunication among all men.

INVENTION OF PRINTING. The invention of printing was a severe blow to Catholicism, which had, previously, enjoyed the inappreciable advantage of a monopoly of intercommunication. From its central seat, orders could be disseminated through all the ecclesiastical ranks, and fulminated through the pulpits. This monopoly and the amazing power it conferred were destroyed by the press. In modern times, the influence of the pulpit has become insignificant. The pulpit has been thoroughly supplanted by the newspaper.

Yet, Catholicism did not yield its ancient advantage without a struggle. As soon as the inevitable tendency of the new art was detected, a restraint upon it, under the form of a censorship, was attempted. It was made necessary to have a permit, in order to print a book. For this, it was needful that the work should have been read, examined, and approved by the clergy. There must be a certificate that it was a godly and orthodox book. A bull of excommunication was issued in 1501, by Alexander VI., against printers who should publish pernicious doctrines. In 1515 the Lateran Council ordered that no books should be printed but such as had been inspected by the ecclesiastical censors, under pain of excommunication and fine; the censors being directed "to take the utmost care that nothing should be printed contrary to the orthodox faith." There was thus a dread of religious discussion; a terror lest truth should emerge.

But these frantic struggles of the powers of ignorance were unavailing. Intellectual intercommunication among men was secured. It culminated in the modern newspaper, which daily gives its contemporaneous intelligence from all parts of the world. Reading became a common occupation. In ancient society that art was possessed by comparatively few persons. Modern society owes some of its most striking characteristics to this change.

EFFECTS OF MARITIME ENTERPRISE. Such was the result of bringing into Europe the manufacture of paper and the printing-press. In like manner the introduction of the mariner's compass was followed by imposing material and moral effects. These were—the discovery of America in consequence of the rivalry of the Venetians and Genoese about the India trade; the doubling of Africa by De Gama; and the circumnavigation of the earth by Magellan. With respect to the last, the grandest of all human undertakings, it is to be remembered that Catholicism had irrevocably committed itself to the dogma of a flat earth, with the sky as the floor of heaven, and hell in the under-world. Some of the Fathers, whose authority was held to be paramount, had, as we have previously said, furnished philosophical and religious arguments against the globular form. The controversy had now suddenly come to an end—the Church was found to be in error.

The correction of that geographical error was by no means the only important result that followed the three great voyages. The spirit of Columbus, De Gama, Magellan, diffused itself among all the enterprising men of Western Europe. Society had been hitherto living under the dogma of "loyalty to the king, obedience to the Church." It had therefore been living for others, not for itself. The political effect of that dogma had culminated in the Crusades. Countless thousands had perished in wars that could bring them no reward, and of which the result had been conspicuous failure. Experience had revealed the fact that the only gainers were the pontiffs, cardinals, and other ecclesiastics in Rome, and the shipmasters of Venice. But, when it became known that the wealth of Mexico, Peru, and India, might be shared by any one who had enterprise and courage, the motives that had animated the restless populations of Europe suddenly changed. The story of Cortez and Pizarro found enthusiastic listeners everywhere. Maritime adventure supplanted religious enthusiasm.

If we attempt to isolate the principle that lay at the basis of the wonderful social changes that now took place, we may recognize it without difficulty. Heretofore each man had dedicated his services to his superior—feudal or ecclesiastical; now he had resolved to gather the fruits of his exertions himself. Individualism was becoming predominant, loyalty was declining into a sentiment. We shall now see how it was with the Church.

INDIVIDUALISM. Individualism rests on the principle that a man shall be his own master, that he shall have liberty to form his own opinions, freedom to carry into effect his resolves. He is, therefore, ever brought into competition with his fellow-men. His life is a display of energy.

To remove the stagnation of centuries front European life, to vivify suddenly what had hitherto been an inert mass, to impart to it individualism, was to bring it into conflict with the influences that had been oppressing it. All through the fourteenth and fifteenth centuries uneasy strugglings gave a premonition of what was coming. In the early part of the sixteenth (1517), the battle was joined. Individualism found its embodiment in a sturdy German monk, and therefore, perhaps necessarily, asserted its rights under theological forms. There were some preliminary skirmishes about indulgences and other minor matters, but very soon the real cause of dispute came plainly into view. Martin Luther refused to think as he was ordered to do by his ecclesiastical superiors at Rome; he asserted that he had an inalienable right to interpret the Bible for himself.

At her first glance, Rome saw nothing in Martin Luther but a vulgar, insubordinate, quarrelsome monk. Could the Inquisition have laid hold of him, it would have speedily disposed of his affair; but, as the conflict went on, it was discovered that Martin was not standing alone. Many thousands of men, as resolute as himself, were coming up to his support; and, while he carried on the combat with writings and words, they made good his propositions with the sword.

THE REFORMATION. The vilification which was poured on Luther and his doings was so bitter as to be ludicrous. It was declared that his father was not his mother's husband, but an impish incubus, who had deluded her; that, after ten years' struggling with his conscience, he had become an atheist; that he denied the immortality of the soul; that he had composed hymns in honor of drunkenness, a vice to which he was unceasingly addicted; that he blasphemed the Holy Scriptures, and particularly Moses; that he did not believe a word of what he preached; that he had called the Epistle of St. James a thing of straw; and, above all, that the Reformation was no work of his, but, in reality, was due to a certain astrological position of the stars. It was, however, a vulgar saying among the Roman ecclesiastics that Erasmus laid the egg of the Reformation, and Luther hatched it.

Rome at first made the mistake of supposing that this was nothing more than a casual outbreak; she failed to discern that it was, in fact, the culmination of an internal movement which for two centuries had been going on in Europe, and which had been hourly gathering force; that, had there been nothing else, the existence of three popes—three obediences—would have compelled men to think, to deliberate, to conclude for themselves. The Councils of Constance and Basle taught them that there was a higher power than the popes. The long and bloody wars that ensued were closed by the Peace of Westphalia; and then it was found that Central and Northern Europe had cast off the intellectual tyranny of Rome, that individualism had carried its point, and had established the right of every man to think for himself.

DECOMPOSITION OF PROTESTANTISM. But it was impossible that the establishment of this right of private judgment should end with the rejection of Catholicism. Early in the movement some of the most distinguished men, such as Erasmus, who had been among its first promoters, abandoned it. They perceived that many of the Reformers entertained a bitter dislike of learning, and they were afraid of being brought under bigoted caprice. The Protestant party, having thus established its existence by dissent and separation, must, in its turn, submit to the operation of the same principles. A decomposition into many subordinate sects was inevitable. And these, now that they had no longer any thing to fear from their great Italian adversary, commenced partisan warfares on each other. As, in different countries, first one and then another sect rose to power, it stained itself with cruelties perpetrated upon its competitors. The mortal retaliations that had ensued, when, in the chances of the times, the oppressed got the better of their oppressors, convinced the contending sectarians that they must concede to their competitors what they claimed for themselves; and thus, from their broils and their crimes, the great principle of toleration extricated itself. But toleration is only an intermediate stage; and, as the intellectual decomposition of Protestantism keeps going on, that transitional condition will lead to a higher and nobler state—the hope of philosophy in all past ages of the world—a social state in which there shall be unfettered freedom for thought. Toleration, except when extorted by fear, can only come from those who are capable of entertaining and respecting other opinions than their own. It can therefore only come from philosophy. History teaches us only too plainly that fanaticism is stimulated by religion, and neutralized or eradicated by philosophy.

TOLERATION. The avowed object of the Reformation was, to remove from Christianity the pagan ideas and pagan rites engrafted upon it by Constantine and his successors, in their attempt to reconcile the Roman Empire to it. The Protestants designed to bring it back to its primitive purity; and hence, while restoring the ancient doctrines, they cast out of it all such practices as the adoration of the Virgin Mary and the invocation of saints. The Virgin Mary, we are assured by the Evangelists, had accepted the duties of married life, and borne to her husband several children. In the prevailing idolatry, she had ceased to be regarded as the carpenter's wife; she had become the queen of heaven, and the mother of God.

DA VINCI. The science of the Arabians followed the invading track of their literature, which had come into Christendom by two routes—the south of France, and Sicily. Favored by the exile of the popes to Avignon, and by the Great Schism, it made good its foothold in Upper Italy. The Aristotelian or Inductive philosophy, clad in the Saracenic costume that Averroes had given it, made many secret and not a few open friends. It found many minds eager to receive and able to appreciate it. Among these were Leonardo da Vinci, who proclaimed the fundamental principle that experiment and observation are the only reliable foundations of reasoning in science, that experiment is the only trustworthy interpreter of Nature, and is essential to the ascertainment of laws. He showed that the action of two perpendicular forces upon a point is the same as that denoted by the diagonal of a rectangle, of which they represent the sides. From this the passage to the proposition of oblique forces was very easy. This proposition was rediscovered by Stevinus, a century later, and applied by him to the explanation of the mechanical powers. Da Vinci gave a clear exposition of the theory of forces applied obliquely on a lever, discovered the laws of friction subsequently demonstrated by Amontons, and understood the principle of virtual velocities. He treated of the conditions of descent of bodies along inclined planes and circular arcs, invented the camera-obscura, discussed correctly several physiological problems, and foreshadowed some of the great conclusions of modern geology, such as the nature of fossil remains, and the elevation of continents. He explained the earth-light reflected by the moon. With surprising versatility of genius he excelled as a sculptor, architect, engineer; was thoroughly versed in the astronomy, anatomy, and chemistry of his times. In painting, he was the rival of Michel Angelo; in a competition between them, he was considered to have established his superiority. His "Last Supper," on the wall of the refectory of the Dominican convent of Sta. Maria delle Grazie, is well known, from the numerous engravings and copies that have been made of it.

ITALIAN SCIENTIFIC SOCIETIES. Once firmly established in the north of Italy, Science soon extended her sway over the entire peninsula. The increasing number of her devotees is indicated by the rise and rapid multiplication of learned societies. These were reproductions of the Moorish ones that had formerly existed in Granada and Cordova. As if to mark by a monument the track through which civilizing influences had come, the Academy of Toulouse, founded in 1345, has survived to our own times. It represented, however, the gay literature of the south of France, and was known under the fanciful title of "the Academy of Floral Games." The first society for the promotion of physical science, the Academia Secretorum Naturae, was founded at Naples, by Baptista Porta. It was, as Tiraboschi relates, dissolved by the ecclesiastical authorities. The Lyncean was founded by Prince Frederic Cesi at Rome; its device plainly indicated its intention: a lynx, with its eyes turned upward toward heaven, tearing a triple-headed Cerberus with its claws. The Accademia del Cimento, established at Florence, 1657, held its meetings in the ducal palace. It lasted ten years, and was then suppressed at the instance of the papal government; as an equivalent, the brother of the grand-duke was made a cardinal. It numbered many great men, such as Torricelli and Castelli, among its members. The condition of admission into it was an abjuration of all faith, and a resolution to inquire into the truth. These societies extricated the cultivators of science from the isolation in which they had hitherto lived, and, by promoting their intercommunication and union, imparted activity and strength to them all.

Returning now from this digression, this historical sketch of the circumstances under which science was introduced into Europe, I pass to the consideration of its manner of action and its results.

INTELLECTUAL INFLUENCE OF SCIENCE. The influence of science on modern civilization has been twofold: 1. Intellectual; 2. Economical. Under these titles we may conveniently consider it.

Intellectually it overthrew the authority of tradition. It refused to accept, unless accompanied by proof, the dicta of any master, no matter how eminent or honored his name. The conditions of admission into the Italian Accademia del Cimento, and the motto adopted by the Royal Society of London, illustrate the position it took in this respect.

It rejected the supernatural and miraculous as evidence in physical discussions. It abandoned sign-proof such as the Jews in old days required, and denied that a demonstration can be given through an illustration of something else, thus casting aside the logic that had been in vogue for many centuries.

In physical inquiries, its mode of procedure was, to test the value of any proposed hypothesis, by executing computations in any special case on the basis or principle of that hypothesis, and then, by performing an experiment or making an observation, to ascertain whether the result of these agreed with the result of the computation. If it did not, the hypothesis was to be rejected.

We may here introduce an illustration or two of this mode of procedure:

THEORIES OF GRAVITATION AND PHLOGISTON. Newton, suspecting that the influence of the earth's attraction, gravity, may extend as far as the moon, and be the force that causes her to revolve in her orbit round the earth, calculated that, by her motion in her orbit, she was deflected from the tangent thirteen feet every minute; but, by ascertaining the space through which bodies would fall in one minute at the earth's surface, and supposing it to be diminished in the ratio of the inverse square, it appeared that the attraction at the moon's orbit would draw a body through more than fifteen feet. He, therefore, for the time, considered his hypothesis as unsustained. But it so happened that Picard shortly afterward executed more correctly a new measurement of a degree; this changed the estimated magnitude of the earth, and the distance of the moon, which was measured in earth-semidiameters. Newton now renewed his computation, and, as I have related on a previous page, as it drew to a close, foreseeing that a coincidence was about to be established, was so much agitated that he was obliged to ask a friend to complete it. The hypothesis was sustained.

A second instance will sufficiently illustrate the method under consideration. It is presented by the chemical theory of phlogiston. Stahl, the author of this theory, asserted that there is a principle of inflammability, to which he gave the name phlogiston, having the quality of uniting with substances. Thus, when what we now term a metallic oxide was united to it, a metal was produced; and, if the phlogiston were withdrawn, the metal passed back into its earthy or oxidized state. On this principle, then, the metals were compound bodies, earths combined with phlogiston.

SCIENCE AND ECCLESIASTICISM. But during the eighteenth century the balance was introduced as an instrument of chemical research. Now, if the phlogistic hypothesis be true, it would follow that a metal should be the heavier, its oxide the lighter body, for the former contains something—phlogiston—that has been added to the latter. But, on weighing a portion of any metal, and also the oxide producible from it, the latter proves to be the heavier, and here the phlogistic hypothesis fails. Still further, on continuing the investigation, it may be shown that the oxide or calx, as it used to be called, has become heavier by combining with one of the ingredients of the air.

To Lavoisier is usually attributed this test experiment; but the fact that the weight of a metal increases by calcination was established by earlier European experimenters, and, indeed, was well known to the Arabian chemists. Lavoisier, however, was the first to recognize its great importance. In his hands it produced a revolution in chemistry.

The abandonment of the phlogistic theory is an illustration of the readiness with which scientific hypotheses are surrendered, when found to be wanting in accordance with facts. Authority and tradition pass for nothing. Every thing is settled by an appeal to Nature. It is assumed that the answers she gives to a practical interrogation will ever be true.

Comparing now the philosophical principles on which science was proceeding, with the principles on which ecclesiasticism rested, we see that, while the former repudiated tradition, to the latter it was the main support while the former insisted on the agreement of calculation and observation, or the correspondence of reasoning and fact, the latter leaned upon mysteries; while the former summarily rejected its own theories, if it saw that they could not be coordinated with Nature, the latter found merit in a faith that blindly accepted the inexplicable, a satisfied contemplation of "things above reason." The alienation between the two continually increased. On one side there was a sentiment of disdain, on the other a sentiment of hatred. Impartial witnesses on all hands perceived that science was rapidly undermining ecclesiasticism.

MATHEMATICS. Mathematics had thus become the great instrument of scientific research, it had become the instrument of scientific reasoning. In one respect it may be said that it reduced the operations of the mind to a mechanical process, for its symbols often saved the labor of thinking. The habit of mental exactness it encouraged extended to other branches of thought, and produced an intellectual revolution. No longer was it possible to be satisfied with miracle-proof, or the logic that had been relied upon throughout the middle ages. Not only did it thus influence the manner of thinking, it also changed the direction of thought. Of this we may be satisfied by comparing the subjects considered in the transactions of the various learned societies with the discussions that had occupied the attention of the middle ages.

But the use of mathematics was not limited to the verification of theories; as above indicated, it also furnished a means of predicting what had hitherto been unobserved. In this it offered a counterpart to the prophecies of ecclesiasticism. The discovery of Neptune is an instance of the kind furnished by astronomy, and that of conical refraction by the optical theory of undulations.

But, while this great instrument led to such a wonderful development in natural science, it was itself undergoing development—improvement. Let us in a few lines recall its progress.

The germ of algebra may be discerned in the works of Diophantus of Alexandria, who is supposed to have lived in the second century of our era. In that Egyptian school Euclid had formerly collected the great truths of geometry, and arranged them in logical sequence. Archimedes, in Syracuse, had attempted the solution of the higher problems by the method of exhaustions. Such was the tendency of things that, had the patronage of science been continued, algebra would inevitably have been invented.

To the Arabians we owe our knowledge of the rudiments of algebra; we owe to them the very name under which this branch of mathematics passes. They had carefully added, to the remains of the Alexandrian School, improvements obtained in India, and had communicated to the subject a certain consistency and form. The knowledge of algebra, as they possessed it, was first brought into Italy about the beginning of the thirteenth century. It attracted so little attention, that nearly three hundred years elapsed before any European work on the subject appeared. In 1496 Paccioli published his book entitled "Arte Maggiore," or "Alghebra." In 1501, Cardan, of Milan, gave a method for the solution of cubic equations; other improvements were contributed by Scipio Ferreo, 1508, by Tartalea, by Vieta. The Germans now took up the subject. At this time the notation was in an imperfect state.

The publication of the Geometry of Descartes, which contains the application of algebra to the definition and investigation of curve lines (1637), constitutes an epoch in the history of the mathematical sciences. Two years previously, Cavalieri's work on Indivisibles had appeared. This method was improved by Torricelli and others. The way was now open, for the development of the Infinitesimal Calculus, the method of Fluxions of Newton, and the Differential and Integral Calculus of Leibnitz. Though in his possession many years previously, Newton published nothing on Fluxions until 1704; the imperfect notation he employed retarded very much the application of his method. Meantime, on the Continent, very largely through the brilliant solutions of some of the higher problems, accomplished by the Bernouillis, the Calculus of Leibnitz was universally accepted, and improved by many mathematicians. An extraordinary development of the science now took place, and continued throughout the century. To the Binomial theorem, previously discovered by Newton, Taylor now added, in his "Method of Increments," the celebrated theorem that bears his name. This was in 1715. The Calculus of Partial Differences was introduced by Euler in 1734. It was extended by D'Alembert, and was followed by that of Variations, by Euler and Lagrange, and by the method of Derivative Functions, by Lagrange, in 1772.

But it was not only in Italy, in Germany, in England, in France, that this great movement in mathematics was witnessed; Scotland had added a new gem to the intellectual diadem with which her brow is encircled, by the grand invention of Logarithms, by Napier of Merchiston. It is impossible to give any adequate conception of the scientific importance of this incomparable invention. The modern physicist and astronomer will most cordially agree with Briggs, the Professor of Mathematics in Gresham College, in his exclamation: "I never saw a book that pleased me better, and that made I me more wonder!" Not without reason did the immortal Kepler regard Napier "to be the greatest man of his age, in the department to which he had applied his abilities." Napier died in 1617. It is no exaggeration to say that this invention, by shortening the labors, doubled the life of the astronomer.

But here I must check myself. I must remember that my present purpose is not to give the history of mathematics, but to consider what science has done for the advancement of human civilization. And now, at once, recurs the question, How is it that the Church produced no geometer in her autocratic reign of twelve hundred years?

With respect to pure mathematics this remark may be made: Its cultivation does not demand appliances that are beyond the reach of most individuals. Astronomy must have its observatory, chemistry its laboratory; but mathematics asks only personal disposition and a few books. No great expenditures are called for, nor the services of assistants. One would think that nothing could be more congenial, nothing more delightful, even in the retirement of monastic life.

Shall we answer with Eusebius, "It is through contempt of such useless labor that we think so little of these matters; we turn our souls to the exercise of better things?" Better things! What can be better than absolute truth? Are mysteries, miracles, lying impostures, better? It was these that stood in the way!

The ecclesiastical authorities had recognized, from the outset of this scientific invasion, that the principles it was disseminating were absolutely irreconcilable with the current theology. Directly and indirectly, they struggled against it. So great was their detestation of experimental science, that they thought they had gained a great advantage when the Accademia del Cimento was suppressed. Nor was the sentiment restricted to Catholicism. When the Royal Society of London was founded, theological odium was directed against it with so much rancor that, doubtless, it would have been extinguished, had not King Charles II. given it his open and avowed support. It was accused of an intention of "destroying the established religion, of injuring the universities, and of upsetting ancient and solid learning."

THE ROYAL SOCIETY OF LONDON. We have only to turn over the pages of its Transactions to discern how much this society has done for the progress of humanity. It was incorporated in 1662, and has interested itself in all the great scientific movements and discoveries that have since been made. It published Newton's "Principia;" it promoted Halley's voyage, the first scientific expedition undertaken by any government; it made experiments on the transfusion of blood, and accepted Harvey's discovery of the circulation. The encouragement it gave to inoculation led Queen Caroline to beg six condemned criminals for experiment, and then to submit her own children to that operation. Through its encouragement Bradley accomplished his great discovery, the aberration of the fixed stars, and that of the nutation of the earth's axis; to these two discoveries, Delambre says, we owe the exactness of modern astronomy. It promoted the improvement of the thermometer, the measure of temperature, and in Harrison's watch, the chronometer, the measure of time. Through it the Gregorian Calendar was introduced into England, in 1752, against a violent religious opposition. Some of its Fellows were pursued through the streets by an ignorant and infuriated mob, who believed it had robbed them of eleven days of their lives; it was found necessary to conceal the name of Father Walmesley, a learned Jesuit, who had taken deep interest in the matter; and, Bradley happening to die during the commotion, it was declared that he had suffered a judgment from Heaven for his crime!

THE ROYAL SOCIETY OF LONDON. If I were to attempt to do justice to the merits of this great society, I should have to devote many pages, to such subjects as the achromatic telescope of Dollond; the dividing engine of Ramsden, which first gave precision to astronomical observations, the measurement of a degree on the earth's surface by Mason and Dixon; the expeditions of Cook in connection with the transit of Venus; his circumnavigation of the earth; his proof that scurvy, the curse of long sea-voyages, may be avoided by the use of vegetable substances; the polar expeditions; the determination of the density of the earth by Maskelyne's experiments at Scheliallion, and by those of Cavendish; the discovery of the planet Uranus by Herschel; the composition of water by Cavendish and Watt; the determination of the difference of longitude between London and Paris; the invention of the voltaic pile; the surveys of the heavens by the Herschels; the development of the principle of interference by Young, and his establishment of the undulatory theory of light; the ventilation of jails and other buildings; the introduction of gas for city illumination; the ascertainment of the length of the seconds-pendulum; the measurement of the variations of gravity in different latitudes; the operations to ascertain the curvature of the earth; the polar expedition of Ross; the invention of the safety-lamp by Davy, and his decomposition of the alkalies and earths; the electro-magnetic discoveries of Oersted and Faraday; the calculating-engines of Babbage; the measures taken at the instance of Humboldt for the establishment of many magnetic observatories; the verification of contemporaneous magnetic disturbances over the earth's surface. But it is impossible, in the limited space at my disposal, to give even so little as a catalogue of its Transactions. Its spirit was identical with that which animated the Accademia del Cimento, and its motto accordingly was "Nullius in Verba." It proscribed superstition, and permitted only calculation, observation, and experiment.

INFLUENCE OF SCIENCE. Not for a moment must it be supposed that in these great attempts, these great Successes, the Royal Society stood alone. In all the capitals of Europe there were Academies, Institutes, or Societies, equal in distinction, and equally successful in promoting human knowledge and modern civilization.

THE ECONOMICAL INFLUENCES OF SCIENCE.

The scientific study of Nature tends not only to correct and ennoble the intellectual conceptions of man; it serves also to ameliorate his physical condition. It perpetually suggests to him the inquiry, how he may make, by their economical application, ascertained facts subservient to his use.

The investigation of principles is quickly followed by practical inventions. This, indeed, is the characteristic feature of our times. It has produced a great revolution in national policy.

In former ages wars were made for the procuring of slaves. A conqueror transported entire populations, and extorted from them forced labor, for it was only by human labor that human labor could be relieved. But when it was discovered that physical agents and mechanical combinations could be employed to incomparably greater advantage, public policy underwent a change; when it was recognized that the application of a new principle, or the invention of a new machine, was better than the acquisition of an additional slave, peace became preferable to war. And not only so, but nations possessing great slave or serf populations, as was the care in America and Russia, found that considerations of humanity were supported by considerations of interest, and set their bondmen free.

SCIENTIFIC INVENTIONS. Thus we live in a period of which a characteristic is the supplanting of human and animal labor by machines. Its mechanical inventions have wrought a social revolution. We appeal to the natural, not to the supernatural, for the accomplishment of our ends. It is with the "modern civilization" thus arising that Catholicism refuses to be reconciled. The papacy loudly proclaims its inflexible repudiation of this state of affairs, and insists on a restoration of the medieval condition of things.

That a piece of amber, when rubbed, will attract and then repel light bodies, was a fact known six hundred years before Christ. It remained an isolated, uncultivated fact, a mere trifle, until sixteen hundred years after Christ. Then dealt with by the scientific methods of mathematical discussion and experiment, and practical application made of the result, it has permitted men to communicate instantaneously with each other across continents and under oceans. It has centralized the world. By enabling the sovereign authority to transmit its mandates without regard to distance or to time, it has revolutionized statesmanship and condensed political power.

In the Museum of Alexandria there was a machine invented by Hero, the mathematician, a little more than one hundred years before Christ. It revolved by the agency of steam, and was of the form that we should now call a reaction-engine. This, the germ of one of the most important inventions ever made, was remembered as a mere curiosity for seventeen hundred years.

Chance had nothing to do with the invention of the modern steam-engine. It was the product of meditation and experiment. In the middle of the seventeenth century several mechanical engineers attempted to utilize the properties of steam; their labors were brought to perfection by Watt in the middle of the eighteenth.

The steam-engine quickly became the drudge of civilization. It performed the work of many millions of men. It gave, to those who would have been condemned to a life of brutal toil, the opportunity of better pursuits. He who formerly labored might now think.

Its earliest application was in such operations as pumping, wherein mere force is required. Soon, however, it vindicated its delicacy of touch in the industrial arts of spinning and weaving. It created vast manufacturing establishments, and supplied clothing for the world. It changed the industry of nations.

In its application, first to the navigation of rivers, and then to the navigation of the ocean, it more than quadrupled the speed that had heretofore been attained. Instead of forty days being requisite for the passage, the Atlantic might now be crossed in eight. But, in land transportation, its power was most strikingly displayed. The admirable invention of the locomotive enabled men to travel farther in less than an hour than they formerly could have done in more than a day.

The locomotive has not only enlarged the field of human activity, but, by diminishing space, it has increased the capabilities of human life. In the swift transportation of manufactured goods and agricultural products, it has become a most efficient incentive to human industry

The perfection of ocean steam-navigation was greatly promoted by the invention of the chronometer, which rendered it possible to find with accuracy the place of a ship at sea. The great drawback on the advancement of science in the Alexandrian School was the want of an instrument for the measurement of time, and one for the measurement of temperature—the chronometer and the thermometer; indeed, the invention of the latter is essential to that of the former. Clepsydras, or water-clocks, had been tried, but they were deficient in accuracy. Of one of them, ornamented with the signs of the zodiac, and destroyed by certain primitive Christians, St. Polycarp significantly remarked, "In all these monstrous demons is seen an art hostile to God." Not until about 1680 did the chronometer begin to approach accuracy. Hooke, the contemporary of Newton, gave it the balance-wheel, with the spiral spring, and various escapements in succession were devised, such as the anchor, the dead-beat, the duplex, the remontoir. Provisions for the variation of temperature were introduced. It was brought to perfection eventually by Harrison and Arnold, in their hands becoming an accurate measure of the flight of time. To the invention of the chronometer must be added that of the reflecting sextant by Godfrey. This permitted astronomical observations to be made, notwithstanding the motion of a ship.

Improvements in ocean navigation are exercising a powerful influence on the distribution of mankind. They are increasing the amount and altering the character of colonization.

DOMESTIC IMPROVEMENT. But not alone have these great discoveries and inventions, the offspring of scientific investigation, changed the lot of the human race; very many minor ones, perhaps individually insignificant, have in their aggregate accomplished surprising effects. The commencing cultivation of science in the fourteenth century gave a wonderful stimulus to inventive talent, directed mainly to useful practical results; and this, subsequently, was greatly encouraged by the system of patents, which secure to the originator a reasonable portion of the benefits of his skill. It is sufficient to refer in the most cursory manner to a few of these improvements; we appreciate at once how much they have done. The introduction of the saw-mill gave wooden floors to houses, banishing those of gypsum, tile, or stone; improvements cheapening the manufacture of glass gave windows, making possible the warming of apartments. However, it was not until the sixteenth century that glazing could be well done. The cutting of glass by the diamond was then introduced. The addition of chimneys purified the atmosphere of dwellings, smoky and sooty as the huts of savages; it gave that indescribable blessing of northern homes—a cheerful fireside. Hitherto a hole in the roof for the escape of the smoke, a pit in the midst of the floor to contain the fuel, and to be covered with a lid when the curfew-bell sounded or night came, such had been the cheerless and inadequate means of warming.

MUNICIPAL IMPROVEMENTS. Though not without a bitter resistance on the part of the clergy, men began to think that pestilences are not punishments inflicted by God on society for its religious shortcomings, but the physical consequences of filth and wretchedness; that the proper mode of avoiding them is not by praying to the saints, but by insuring personal and municipal cleanliness. In the twelfth century it was found necessary to pave the streets of Paris, the stench in them was so dreadful At once dysenteries and spotted fever diminished; a sanitary condition approaching that of the Moorish cities of Spain, which had been paved for centuries, was attained. In that now beautiful metropolis it was forbidden to keep swine, an ordinance resented by the monks of the abbey of St. Anthony, who demanded that the pigs of that saint should go where they chose; the government was obliged to compromise the matter by requiring that bells should be fastened to the animals' necks. King Philip, the son of Louis the Fat, had been killed by his horse stumbling over a sow. Prohibitions were published against throwing slops out of the windows. In 1870 an eye-witness, the author of this book, at the close of the pontifical rule in Rome, found that, in walking the ordure-defiled streets of that city, it was more necessary to inspect the earth than to contemplate the heavens, in order to preserve personal purity. Until the beginning of the seventeenth century, the streets of Berlin were never swept. There was a law that every countryman, who came to market with a cart, should carry back a load of dirt!

Paving was followed by attempts, often of an imperfect kind, at the construction of drains and sewers. It had become obvious to all reflecting men that these were necessary to the preservation of health, not only in towns, but in isolated houses. Then followed the lighting of the public thoroughfares. At first houses facing the streets were compelled to have candles or lamps in their windows; next the system that had been followed with so much advantage in Cordova and Granada—of having public lamps—was tried, but this was not brought to perfection until the present century, when lighting by gas was invented. Contemporaneously with public lamps were improved organizations for night-watchmen and police.

By the sixteenth century, mechanical inventions and manufacturing improvements were exercising a conspicuous influence on domestic and social life. There were looking-glasses and clocks on the walls, mantels over the fireplaces. Though in many districts the kitchen-fire was still supplied with turf, the use of coal began to prevail. The table in the dining-room offered new delicacies; commerce was bringing to it foreign products; the coarse drinks of the North were supplanted by the delicate wines of the South. Ice-houses were constructed. The bolting of flour, introduced at the windmills, had given whiter and finer bread. By degrees things that had been rarities became common—Indian-corn, the potato, the turkey, and, conspicuous in the long list, tobacco. Forks, an Italian invention, displaced the filthy use of the fingers. It may be said that the diet of civilized men now underwent a radical change. Tea came from China, coffee from Arabia, the use of sugar from India, and these to no insignificant degree supplanted fermented liquors. Carpets replaced on the floors the layer of straw; in the chambers there appeared better beds, in the wardrobes cleaner and more frequently-changed clothing. In many towns the aqueduct was substituted for the public fountain and the street-pump. Ceilings which in the old days would have been dingy with soot and dirt, were now decorated with ornamental frescoes. Baths were more commonly resorted to; there was less need to use perfumery for the concealment of personal odors. An increasing taste for the innocent pleasures of horticulture was manifested, by the introduction of many foreign flowers in the gardens—the tuberose, the auricula, the crown imperial, the Persian lily, the ranunculus, and African marigolds. In the streets there appeared sedans, then close carriages, and at length hackney-coaches.

Among the dull rustics mechanical improvements forced their way, and gradually attained, in the implements for ploughing, sowing, mowing, reaping, thrashing, the perfection of our own times.

MERCANTILE INVENTIONS. It began to be recognized, in spite of the preaching of the mendicant orders, that poverty is the source of crime, the obstruction to knowledge; that the pursuit of riches by commerce is far better than the acquisition of power by war. For, though it may be true, as Montesquieu says, that, while commerce unites nations, it antagonizes individuals, and makes a traffic of morality, it alone can give unity to the world; its dream, its hope, is universal peace.

MEDICAL IMPROVEMENTS. Though, instead of a few pages, it would require volumes to record adequately the ameliorations that took place in domestic and social life after science began to exert its beneficent influences, and inventive talent came to the aid of industry, there are some things which cannot be passed in silence. From the port of Barcelona the Spanish khalifs had carried on an enormous commerce, and they with their coadjutors—Jewish merchants—had adopted or originated many commercial inventions, which, with matters of pure science, they had transmitted to the trading communities of Europe. The art of book-keeping by double entry was thus brought into Upper Italy. The different kinds of insurance were adopted, though strenuously resisted by the clergy. They opposed fire and marine insurance, on the ground that it is a tempting of Providence. Life insurance was regarded as an act of interference with the consequences of God's will. Houses for lending money on interest and on pledges, that is, banking and pawnbroking establishments, were bitterly denounced, and especially was indignation excited against the taking of high rates of interest, which was stigmatized as usury—a feeling existing in some backward communities up to the present day. Bills of exchange in the present form and terms were adopted, the office of the public notary established, and protests for dishonored obligations resorted to. Indeed, it may be said, with but little exaggeration, that the commercial machinery now used was thus introduced. I have already remarked that, in consequence of the discovery of America, the front of Europe had been changed. Many rich Italian merchants and many enterprising Jews, had settled in Holland England, France, and brought into those countries various mercantile devices. The Jews, who cared nothing about papal maledictions, were enriched by the pontifical action in relation to the lending of money at high interest; but Pius II., perceiving the mistake that had been made, withdrew his opposition. Pawnbroking establishments were finally authorized by Leo X., who threatened excommunication of those who wrote against them. In their turn the Protestants now exhibited a dislike against establishments thus authorized by Rome. As the theological dogma, that the plague, like the earthquake, is an unavoidable visitation from God for the sins of men, began to be doubted, attempts were made to resist its progress by the establishment of quarantines. When the Mohammedan discovery of inoculation was brought from Constantinople in 1721, by Lady Mary Wortley Montagu, it was so strenuously resisted by the clergy, that nothing short of its adoption by the royal family of England brought it into use. A similar resistance was exhibited when Jenner introduced his great improvement, vaccination; yet a century ago it was the exception to see a face unpitted by smallpox—now it is the exception to see one so disfigured. In like manner, when the great American discovery of anaesthetics was applied in obstetrical cases, it was discouraged, not so much for physiological reasons, as under the pretense that it was an impious attempt to escape from the curse denounced against all women in Genesis iii. 16.

MAGIC AND MIRACLES. Inventive ingenuity did not restrict itself to the production of useful contrivances, it added amusing ones. Soon after the introduction of science into Italy, the houses of the virtuosi began to abound in all kinds of curious mechanical surprises, and, as they were termed, magical effects. In the latter the invention of the magic-lantern greatly assisted. Not without reason did the ecclesiastics detest experimental philosophy, for a result of no little importance ensued—the juggler became a successful rival to the miracle-worker. The pious frauds enacted in the churches lost their wonder when brought into competition with the tricks of the conjurer in the market-place: he breathed flame, walked on burning coals, held red-hot iron in his teeth, drew basketfuls of eggs out of his mouth, worked miracles by marionettes. Yet the old idea of the supernatural was with difficulty destroyed. A horse, whose master had taught him many tricks, was tried at Lisbon in 1601, found guilty of being, possessed by the devil, and was burnt. Still later than that many witches were brought to the stake.

DISCOVERIES IN ASTRONOMY AND CHEMISTRY. Once fairly introduced, discovery and invention have unceasingly advanced at an accelerated pace. Each continually reacted on the other, continually they sapped supernaturalism. De Dominis commenced, and Newton completed, the explanation of the rainbow; they showed that it was not the weapon of warfare of God, but the accident of rays of light in drops of water. De Dominis was decoyed to Rome through the promise of an archbishopric, and the hope of a cardinal's hat. He was lodged in a fine residence, but carefully watched. Accused of having suggested a concord between Rome and England, he was imprisoned in the castle of St Angelo, and there died. He was brought in his coffin before an ecclesiastical tribunal, adjudged guilty of heresy, and his body, with a heap of heretical books, was cast into the flames. Franklin, by demonstrating the identity of lightning and electricity, deprived Jupiter of his thunder-bolt. The marvels of superstition were displaced by the wonders of truth. The two telescopes, the reflector and the achromatic, inventions of the last century, permitted man to penetrate into the infinite grandeurs of the universe, to recognize, as far as such a thing is possible, its illimitable spaces, its measureless times; and a little later the achromatic microscope placed before his eyes the world of the infinitely small. The air-balloon carried him above the clouds, the diving-bell to the bottom of the sea. The thermometer gave him true measures of the variations of heat; the barometer, of the pressure of the air. The introduction of the balance imparted exactness to chemistry, it proved the indestructibility of matter. The discovery of oxygen, hydrogen, and many other gases, the isolation of aluminum, calcium, and other metals, showed that earth and air and water are not elements. With an enterprise that can never be too much commended, advantage was taken of the transits of Venus, and, by sending expeditions to different regions, the distance of the earth from the sun was determined. The step that European intellect had made between 1456 and 1759 was illustrated by Halley's comet. When it appeared in the former year, it was considered as the harbinger of the vengeance of God, the dispenser of the most dreadful of his retributions, war, pestilence, famine. By order of the pope, all the church-bells in Europe were rung to scare it away, the faithful were commanded to add each day another prayer; and, as their prayers had often in so marked a manner been answered in eclipses and droughts and rains, so on this occasion it was declared that a victory over the comet had been vouchsafed to the pope. But, in the mean time, Halley, guided by the revelations of Kepler and Newton, had discovered that its motions, so far from being controlled by the supplications of Christendom, were guided in an elliptic orbit by destiny. Knowing that Nature bad denied to him an opportunity of witnessing the fulfillment of his daring prophecy, he besought the astronomers of the succeeding generation to watch for its return in 1759, and in that year it came.

INVENTIONS AND DISCOVERIES. Whoever will in a spirit of impartiality examine what had been done by Catholicism for the intellectual and material advancement of Europe, during her long reign, and what has been done by science in its brief period of action, can, I am persuaded, come to no other conclusion than this, that, in instituting a comparison, he has established a contrast. And yet, how imperfect, how inadequate is the catalogue of facts I have furnished in the foregoing pages! I have said nothing of the spread of instruction by the diffusion of the arts of reading and writing, through public schools, and the consequent creation of a reading community; the modes of manufacturing public opinion by newspapers and reviews, the power of journalism, the diffusion of information public and private by the post-office and cheap mails, the individual and social advantages of newspaper advertisements. I have said nothing of the establishment of hospitals, the first exemplar of which was the

Invalides of Paris; nothing of the improved prisons, reformatories, penitentiaries, asylums, the treatment of lunatics, paupers, criminals; nothing of the construction of canals, of sanitary engineering, or of census reports; nothing of the invention of stereotyping, bleaching by chlorine, the cotton-gin, or of the marvelous contrivances with which cotton-mills are filled—contrivances which have given us cheap clothing, and therefore added to cleanliness, comfort, health; nothing of the grand advancement of medicine and surgery, or of the discoveries in physiology, the cultivation of the fine arts, the improvement of agriculture and rural economy, the introduction of chemical manures and farm-machinery. I have not referred to the manufacture of iron and its vast affiliated industries; to those of textile fabrics; to the collection of museums of natural history, antiquities, curiosities. I have passed unnoticed the great subject of the manufacture of machinery by itself—the invention of the slide-rest, the planing-machine, and many other contrivances by which engines can be constructed with almost mathematical correctness. I have said nothing adequate about the railway system, or the electric telegraph, nor about the calculus, or lithography, the airpump, or the voltaic battery; the discovery of Uranus or Neptune, and more than a hundred asteroids; the relation of meteoric streams to comets; nothing of the expeditions by land and sea that have been sent forth by various governments for the determination of important astronomical or geographical questions; nothing of the costly and accurate experiments they have caused to be made for the ascertainment of fundamental physical data. I have been so unjust to our own century that I have made no allusion to some of its greatest scientific triumphs: its grand conceptions in natural history; its discoveries in magnetism and electricity; its invention of the beautiful art of photography; its applications of spectrum analysis; its attempts to bring chemistry under the three laws of Avogadro, of Boyle and Mariotte, and of Charles; its artificial production of organic substances from inorganic material, of which the philosophical consequences are of the utmost importance; its reconstruction of physiology by laying the foundation of that science on chemistry; its improvements and advances in topographical surveying and in the correct representation of the surface of the globe. I have said nothing about rifled-guns and armored ships, nor of the revolution that has been made in the art of war; nothing of that gift to women, the sewing-machine; nothing of the noble contentions and triumphs of the arts of peace—the industrial exhibitions and world's fairs.

What a catalogue have we here, and yet how imperfect! It gives merely a random glimpse at an ever-increasing intellectual commotion—a mention of things as they casually present themselves to view. How striking the contrast between this literary, this scientific activity, and the stagnation of the middle ages!

The intellectual enlightenment that surrounds this activity has imparted unnumbered blessings to the human race. In Russia it has emancipated a vast serf-population; in America it has given freedom to four million negro slaves. In place of the sparse dole of the monastery-gate, it has organized charity and directed legislation to the poor. It has shown medicine its true function, to prevent rather than to cure disease. In statesmanship it has introduced scientific methods, displacing random and empirical legislation by a laborious ascertainment of social facts previous to the application of legal remedies. So conspicuous, so impressive is the manner in which it is elevating men, that the hoary nations of Asia seek to participate in the boon. Let us not forget that our action on them must be attended by their reaction on us. If the destruction of paganism was completed when all the gods were brought to Rome and confronted there, now, when by our wonderful facilities of locomotion strange nations and conflicting religions are brought into common presence—the Mohammedan, the Buddhist, the Brahman-modifications of them all must ensue. In that conflict science alone will stand secure; for it has given us grander views of the universe, more awful views of God.

AMERICAN AND FRENCH REVOLUTIONS. The spirit that has imparted life to this movement, that has animated these discoveries and inventions, is Individualism; in some minds the hope of gain, in other and nobler ones the expectation of honor. It is, then, not to be wondered at that this principle found a political embodiment, and that, during the last century, on two occasions, it gave rise to social convulsions—the American and the French Revolutions. The former has ended in the dedication of a continent to Individualism—there, under republican forms, before the close of the present century, one hundred million people, with no more restraint than their common security requires, will be pursuing an unfettered career. The latter, though it has modified the political aspect of all Europe, and though illustrated by surprising military successes, has, thus far, not consummated its intentions; again and again it has brought upon France fearful disasters. Her dual form of government—her allegiance to her two sovereigns, the political and the spiritual—has made her at once the leader and the antagonist of modern progress. With one hand she has enthroned Reason, with the other she has re-established and sustained the pope. Nor will this anomaly in her conduct cease until she bestows a true education on all her children, even on those of the humblest rustic.

SCIENCE AND CIVILIZATION. The intellectual attack made on existing opinions by the French Revolution was not of a scientific, but of a literary character; it was critical and aggressive. But Science has never been an aggressor. She has always acted on the defensive, and left to her antagonist the making of wanton attacks. Nevertheless, literary dissent is not of such ominous import as scientific; for literature is, in its nature, local—science is cosmopolitan.

If, now, we demand, What has science done for the promotion of modern civilization; what has it done for the happiness, the well-being of society? we shall find our answer in the same manner that we reached a just estimate of what Latin Christianity had done. The reader of the foregoing paragraphs would undoubtedly infer that there must have been an amelioration in the lot of our race; but, when we apply the touchstone of statistics, that inference gathers precision. Systems of philosophy and forms of religion find a measure of their influence on humanity in census-returns. Latin Christianity, in a thousand years, could not double the population of Europe; it did not add perceptibly to the term of individual life. But, as Dr. Jarvis, in his report to the Massachusetts Board of Health, has stated, at the epoch of the Reformation "the average longevity in Geneva was 21.21 years, between 1814 and 1833 it was 40.68; as large a number of persons now live to seventy years as lived to forty, three hundred years ago. In 1693 the British Government borrowed money by selling annuities on lives from infancy upward, on the basis of the average longevity. The contract was profitable. Ninety-seven years later another tontine, or scale of annuities, on the basis of the same expectation of life as in the previous century, was issued. These latter annuitants, however, lived so much longer than their predecessors, that it proved to be a very costly loan for the government. It was found that, while ten thousand of each sex in the first tontine died under the age of twenty-eight, only five thousand seven hundred and seventy-two males and six thousand four hundred and sixteen females in the second tontine died at the same age, one hundred years later."

We have been comparing the spiritual with the practical, the imaginary with the real. The maxims that have been followed in the earlier and the later period produced their inevitable result. In the former that maxim was, "Ignorance is the mother of Devotion in the latter,

Knowledge is Power."

CHAPTER XII.

THE IMPENDING CRISIS. INDICATIONS OF THE APPROACH OF A RELIGIOUS CRISIS.—THE PREDOMINATING CHRISTIAN CHURCH, THE ROMAN, PERCEIVES THIS, AND MAKES PREPARATION FOR IT.—PIUS IX CONVOKES AN OECUMENICAL COUNCIL—RELATIONS OF THE DIFFERENT EUROPEAN GOVERNMENTS TO THE PAPACY.—RELATIONS OF THE CHURCH TO SCIENCE, AS INDICATED BY THE ENCYCLICAL LETTER AND THE SYLLABUS.

Acts of the Vatican Council in relation to the infallibility of the pope, and to Science.—Abstract of decisions arrived at.

Controversy between the Prussian Government and the papacy.—It is a contest between the State and the Church for supremacy—Effect of dual government in Europe—Declaration by the Vatican Council of its position as to Science—The dogmatic constitution of the Catholic faith.—Its definitions respecting God, Revelation, Faith, Reason.—The anathemas it pronounces.—Its denunciation of modern civilization.

The Protestant Evangelical Alliance and its acts.

General review of the foregoing definitions, and acts.—Present condition of the controversy, and its future prospects.

PREDOMINANCE OF CATHOLICITY. No one who is acquainted with the present tone of thought in Christendom can hide from himself the fact that an intellectual, a religious crisis is impending.

In all directions we see the lowering skies, we hear the mutterings of the coming storm. In Germany, the national party is arraying itself against the ultramontane; in France, the men of progress are struggling against the unprogressive, and in their contest the political supremacy of that great country is wellnigh neutralized or lost. In Italy, Rome has passed into the hands of an excommunicated king. The sovereign pontiff, feigning that he is a prisoner, is fulminating from the Vatican his anathemas, and, in the midst of the most convincing proofs of his manifold errors, asserting his own infallibility. A Catholic archbishop with truth declares that the whole civil society of Europe seems to be withdrawing itself in its public life from Christianity. In England and America, religious persons perceive with dismay that the intellectual basis of faith has been undermined by the spirit of the age. They prepare for the approaching disaster in the best manner they can.

The most serious trial through which society can pass is encountered in the exuviation of its religious restraints. The history of Greece and the history of Rome exhibit to us in an impressive manner how great are the perils. But it is not given to religions to endure forever. They necessarily undergo transformation with the intellectual development of man. How many countries are there professing the same religion now that they did at the birth of Christ?

It is estimated that the entire population of Europe is about three hundred and one million. Of these, one hundred and eighty-five million are Roman Catholics, thirty-three million are Greek Catholics. Of Protestants there are seventy-one million, separated into many sects. Of Jews, five million; of Mohammedans, seven million.

Of the religious subdivisions of America an accurate numerical statement cannot be given. The whole of Christian South America is Roman Catholic, the same may be said of Central America and of Mexico, as also of the Spanish and French West India possessions. In the United States and Canada the Protestant population predominates. To Australia the same remark applies. In India the sparse Christian population sinks into insignificance in presence of two hundred million Mohammedans and other Oriental denominations. The Roman Catholic Church is the most widely diffused and the most powerfully organized of all modern societies. It is far more a political than a religious combination. Its principle is that all power is in the clergy, and that for laymen there is only the privilege of obedience. The republican forms under which the Churches existed in primitive Christianity have gradually merged into an absolute centralization, with a man as vice-God at its head. This Church asserts that the divine commission under which it acts comprises civil government; that it has a right to use the state for its own purposes, but that the state has no right to intermeddle with it; that even in Protestant countries it is not merely a coordinate government, but the sovereign power. It insists that the state has no rights over any thing which it declares to be in its domain, and that Protestantism, being a mere rebellion, has no rights at all; that even in Protestant communities the Catholic bishop is the only lawful spiritual pastor.

It is plain, therefore, that of professing Christians the vast majority are Catholic; and such is the authoritative demand of the papacy for supremacy, that, in any survey of the present religious condition of Christendom, regard must be mainly had to its acts. Its movements are guided by the highest intelligence and skill. Catholicism obeys the orders of one man, and has therefore a unity, a compactness, a power, which Protestant denominations do not possess. Moreover, it derives inestimable strength from the souvenirs of the great name of Rome.

Unembarrassed by any hesitating sentiment, the papacy has contemplated the coming intellectual crisis. It has pronounced its decision, and occupied what seems to it to be the most advantageous ground.

This definition of position we find in the acts of the late Vatican Council.

THE OECUMENICAL COUNCIL. Pius IX., by a bull dated June 29, 1868, convoked an Oecumenical Council, to meet in Rome, on December 8, 1869. Its sessions ended in July, 1870. Among other matters submitted to its consideration, two stand forth in conspicuous prominence—they are the assertion of the infallibility of the Roman pontiff, and the definition of the relations of religion to science.

But the convocation of the Council was far from meeting with general approval.

The views of the Oriental Churches were, for the most part, unfavorable. They affirmed that they saw a desire in the Roman pontiff to set himself up as the head of Christianity, whereas they recognized the Lord Jesus Christ alone as the head of the Church. They believed that the Council would only lead to new quarrels and scandals. The sentiment of these venerable Churches is well shown by the incident that, when, in 1867, the Nestorian Patriarch Simeon had been invited by the Chaldean Patriarch to return to Roman Catholic unity, he, in his reply, showed that there was no prospect for harmonious action between the East and the West: "You invite me to kiss humbly the slipper of the Bishop of Rome; but is he not, in every respect, a man like yourself—is his dignity superior to yours? We will never permit to be introduced into our holy temples of worship images and statues, which are nothing but abominable and impure idols. What! shall we attribute to Almighty God a mother, as you dare to do? Away from us, such blasphemy!"

EXPECTATIONS OF THE PAPACY. Eventually, the patriarchs, archbishops, and bishops, from all regions of the world, who took part in this Council, were seven hundred and four.

Rome had seen very plainly that Science was not only rapidly undermining the dogmas of the papacy, but was gathering great political power. She recognized that all over Europe there was a fast-spreading secession among persons of education, and that its true focus was North Germany.

She looked, therefore, with deep interest on the Prusso-Austrian War, giving to Austria whatever encouragement she could. The battle of Sadowa was a bitter disappointment to her.

With satisfaction again she looked upon the breaking out of the Franco-Prussian War, not doubting that its issue would be favorable to France, and therefore favorable to her. Here, again, she was doomed to disappointment at Sedan.

Having now no further hope, for many years to come, from external war, she resolved to see what could be done by internal insurrection, and the present movement in the German Empire is the result of her machinations.

Had Austria or had France succeeded, Protestantism would have been overthrown along with Prussia.

But, while these military movements were being carried on, a movement of a different, an intellectual kind, was engaged in. Its principle was, to restore the worn-out mediaeval doctrines and practices, carrying them to an extreme, no matter what the consequences might be.

ENCYCLICAL LETTER AND SYLLABUS. Not only was it asserted that the papacy has a divine right to participate in the government of all countries, coordinately with their temporal authorities, but that the supremacy of Rome in this matter must be recognized; and that in any question between them the temporal authority must conform itself to her order.

And, since the endangering of her position had been mainly brought about by the progress of science, she presumed to define its boundaries, and prescribe limits to its authority. Still more, she undertook to denounce modern civilization.

These measures were contemplated soon after the return of his Holiness from Gaeta in 1848, and were undertaken by the advice of the Jesuits, who, lingering in the hope that God would work the impossible, supposed that the papacy, in its old age, might be reinvigorated. The organ of the Curia proclaimed the absolute independence of the Church as regards the state; the dependence of the bishops on the pope; of the diocesan clergy on the bishops; the obligation of the Protestants to abandon their atheism, and return to the fold; the absolute condemnation of all kinds of toleration. In December, 1854, in an assembly of bishops, the pope had proclaimed the dogma of the immaculate conception. Ten years subsequently he put forth the celebrated Encyclical Letter and the Syllabus.

The Encyclical Letter is dated December 8, 1864. It was drawn up by learned ecclesiastics, and subsequently debated at the Congregation of the Holy Office, then forwarded to prelates, and finally gone over by the pope and cardinals.

ENCYCLICAL LETTER AND SYLLABUS. Many of the clergy objected to its condemnation of modern civilization. Some of the cardinals were reluctant to concur in it. The Catholic press accepted it, not, however, without misgivings and regrets. The Protestant governments put no obstacle in its way; the Catholic were embarrassed by it. France allowed the publication only of that portion proclaiming the jubilee; Austria and Italy permitted its introduction, but withheld their approval. The political press and legislatures of Catholic countries gave it an unfavorable reception. Many deplored it as likely to widen the breach between the Church and modern society. The Italian press regarded it as determining a war, without truce or armistice, between the papacy and modern civilization. Even in Spain there were journals that regretted "the obstinacy and blindness of the court of Rome, in branding and condemning modern civilization."

It denounces that "most pernicious and insane opinion, that liberty of conscience and of worship is the right of every man, and that this right ought, in every well-governed state, to be proclaimed and asserted by law; and that the will of the people, manifested by public opinion (as it is called), or by other means, constitutes a supreme law, independent of all divine and human rights." It denies the right of parents to educate their children outside the Catholic Church. It denounces "the impudence" of those who presume to subordinate the authority of the Church and of the Apostolic See, "conferred upon it by Christ our Lord, to the judgment of the civil authority." His Holiness commends, to the venerable brothers to whom the Encyclical is addressed, incessant prayer, and, "in order that God may accede the more easily to our and your prayers, let us employ in all confidence, as our mediatrix with him, the Virgin Mary, mother of God, who sits as a queen upon the right hand of her only-begotten Son, our Lord Jesus Christ, in a golden vestment, clothed around with various adornments. There is nothing she cannot obtain from him."

CONVOCATION OF THE COUNCIL. Plainly, the principle now avowed by the papacy must bring it into collision even with governments which had heretofore maintained amicable relations with it. Great dissatisfaction was manifested by Russia, and the incidents that ensued drew forth from his Holiness an allocution (November, 1866) condemnatory of the course of that government. To this, Russia replied, by declaring the Concordat of 1867 abrogated.

Undeterred by the result of the battle of Sadowa (July, 1866), though it was plain that the political condition of Europe was now profoundly affected, and especially the relations of the papacy, the pope delivered an allocution (June 27, 1867), confirming the Encyclical and Syllabus. He announced his intention of convoking an Oecumenical Council.

Accordingly, as we have already mentioned, in the following year (June 29, 1868), a bull was issued convoking that Council. Misunderstandings, however, had now sprung up with Austria. The Austrian Reichsrath had adopted laws introducing equality of civil rights for all the inhabitants of the empire, and restricting the influence of the Church. This produced on the part of the papal government an expostulation. Acting as Russia had done, the Austrian Government found it necessary to abrogate the Concordat of 1855.

In France, as above stated, the publication of the entire Syllabus was not permitted; but Prussia, desirous of keeping on good terms with the papacy, did not disallow it. The exacting disposition of the papacy increased. It was openly declared that the faithful must now sacrifice to the Church, property, life, and even their intellectual convictions. The Protestants and the Greeks were invited to tender their submission.

THE VATICAN COUNCIL. On the appointed day, the Council opened. Its objects were, to translate the Syllabus into practice, to establish the dogma of papal infallibility, and define the relations of religion to science. Every preparation had been made that the points determined on should be carried. The bishops were informed that they were coming to Rome not to deliberate, but to sanction decrees previously made by an infallible pope. No idea was entertained of any such thing as free discussion. The minutes of the meetings were not permitted to be inspected; the prelates of the opposition were hardly allowed to speak. On January 22, 1870, a petition, requesting that the infallibility of the pope should be defined, was presented; an opposition petition of the minority was offered. Hereupon, the deliberations of the minority were forbidden, and their publications prohibited. And, though the Curia had provided a compact majority, it was found expedient to issue an order that to carry any proposition it was not necessary that the vote should be near unanimity, a simple majority sufficed. The remonstrances of the minority were altogether unheeded.

As the Council pressed forward to its object, foreign authorities became alarmed at its reckless determination. A petition drawn up by the Archbishop of Vienna, and signed by several cardinals and archbishops, entreated his Holiness not to submit the dogma of infallibility for consideration, "because the Church has to sustain at present a struggle unknown in former times, against men who oppose religion itself as an institution baneful to human nature, and that it is inopportune to impose upon Catholic nations, led into temptation by so many machinations, more dogmas than the Council of Trent proclaimed." It added that "the definition demanded would furnish fresh arms to the enemies of religion, to excite against the Catholic Church the resentment of men avowedly the best." The Austrian prime-minister addressed a protest to the papal government, warning it against any steps that might lead to encroachments on the rights of Austria. The French Government also addressed a note, suggesting that a French bishop should explain to the Council the condition and the rights of France. To this the papal government replied that a bishop could not reconcile the double duties of an ambassador and a Father of the Council. Hereupon, the French Government, in a very respectful note, remarked that, to prevent ultra opinions from becoming dogmas, it reckoned on the moderation of the bishops, and the prudence of the Holy Father; and, to defend its civil and political laws against the encroachments of the theocracy, it had counted on public reason and the patriotism of French Catholics. In these remonstrances the North-German Confederation joined, seriously pressing them on the consideration of the papal government.

On April 23d, Von Arnim, the Prussian embassador, united with Daru, the French minister, in suggesting to the Curia the inexpediency of reviving mediaeval ideas. The minority bishops, thus encouraged, demanded now that the relations of the spiritual to the secular power should be determined before the pope's infallibility was discussed, and that it should be settled whether Christ had conferred on St. Peter and his successors a power over kings and emperors.

INFALLIBILITY OF THE POPE. No regard was paid to this, not even delay was consented to. The Jesuits, who were at the bottom of the movement, carried their measures through the packed assembly with a high hand. The Council omitted no device to screen itself from popular criticism. Its proceedings were conducted with the utmost secrecy; all who took part in them were bound by a solemn oath to observe silence.

On July 13th, the votes were taken. Of 601 votes, 451 were affirmative. Under the majority rule, the measure was pronounced carried, and, five days subsequently, the pope proclaimed the dogma of his infallibility. It has often been remarked that this was the day on which the French declared war against Prussia. Eight days afterward the French troops were withdrawn from Rome. Perhaps both the statesman and the philosopher will admit that an infallible pope would be a great harmonizing element, if only common-sense could acknowledge him.

Hereupon, the King of Italy addressed an autograph letter to the pope, setting forth in very respectful terms the necessity that his troops should advance and occupy positions "indispensable to the security of his Holiness, and the maintenance of order;" that, while satisfying the national aspirations, the chief of Catholicity, surrounded by the devotion of the Italian populations, "might preserve on the banks of the Tiber a glorious seat, independent of all human sovereignty."

To this his Holiness replied in a brief and caustic letter: "I give thanks to God, who has permitted your majesty to fill the last days of my life with bitterness. For the rest, I cannot grant certain requests, nor conform with certain principles contained in your letter. Again, I call upon God, and into his hands commit my cause, which is his cause. I pray God to grant your majesty many graces, to free you from dangers, and to dispense to you his mercy which you so much need."

THE ITALIAN GOVERNMENT. The Italian troops met with but little resistance. They occupied Rome on September 20, 1870. A manifesto was issued, setting forth the details of a plebiscitum, the vote to be by ballot, the question, "the unification of Italy." Its result showed how completely the popular mind in Italy is emancipated from theology. In the Roman provinces the number of votes on the lists was 167,548; the number who voted, 135,291; the number who voted for annexation, 133,681; the number who voted against it, 1,507; votes annulled, 103. The Parliament of Italy ratified the vote of the Roman people for annexation by a vote of 239 to 20. A royal decree now announced the annexation of the Papal States to the kingdom of Italy, and a manifesto was issued indicating the details of the arrangement. It declared that "by these concessions the Italian Government seeks to prove to Europe that Italy respects the sovereignty of the pope in conformity with the principle of a free Church in a free state."

AFFAIRS IN PRUSSIA. In the Prusso-Austrian War it had been the hope of the papacy, to restore the German Empire under Austria, and make Germany a Catholic nation. In the Franco-German War the French expected ultramontane sympathies in Germany. No means were spared to excite Catholic sentiment against the Protestants. No vilification was spared. They were spoken of as atheists; they were declared incapable of being honest men; their sects were pointed out as indicating that their secession was in a state of dissolution. "The followers of Luther are the most abandoned men in all Europe." Even the pope himself, presuming that the whole world had forgotten all history, did not hesitate to say, "Let the German people understand that no other Church but that of Rome is the Church of freedom and progress."

Meantime, among the clergy of Germany a party was organized to remonstrate against, and even resist, the papal usurpation. It protested against "a man being placed on the throne of God," against a vice-God of any kind, nor would it yield its scientific convictions to ecclesiastical authority. Some did not hesitate to accuse the pope himself of being a heretic. Against these insubordinates excommunications began to be fulminated, and at length it was demanded that certain professors and teachers should be removed from their offices, and infallibilists substituted. With this demand the Prussian Government declined to comply.

The Prussian Government had earnestly desired to remain on amicable terms with the papacy; it had no wish to enter on a theological quarrel; but gradually the conviction was forced upon it that the question was not a religious but a political one—whether the power of the state should be used against the state. A teacher in a gymnasium had been excommunicated; the government, on being required to dismiss him, refused. The Church authorities denounced this as an attack upon faith. The emperor sustained his minister. The organ of the infallible party threatened the emperor with the opposition of all good Catholics, and told him that, in a contention with the pope, systems of government can and must change. It was now plain to every one that the question had become, "Who is to be master in the state, the government or the Roman Church? It is plainly impossible for men to live under two governments, one of which declares to be wrong what the other commands. If the government will not submit to the Roman Church, the two are enemies." A conflict was thus forced upon Prussia by Rome—a conflict in which the latter, impelled by her antagonism to modern civilization, is clearly the aggressor.

ACTION OF THE PRUSSIAN GOVERNMENT. The government, now recognizing its antagonist, defended itself by abolishing the Catholic department in the ministry of Public Worship. This was about midsummer, 1871. In the following November the Imperial Parliament passed a law that ecclesiastics abusing their office, to the disturbance of the public peace, should be criminally punished. And, guided by the principle that the future belongs to him to whom the school belongs, a movement arose for the purpose of separating the schools from the Church.

THE CHURCH A POLITICAL POWER. The Jesuit party was extending and strengthening an organization all over Germany, based on the principle that state legislation in ecclesiastical matters is not binding. Here was an act of open insurrection. Could the government allow itself to be intimidated? The Bishop of Ermeland declared that he would not obey the laws of the state if they touched the Church. The government stopped the payment of his salary; and, perceiving that there could be no peace so long as the Jesuits were permitted to remain in the country, their expulsion was resolved on, and carried into effect. At the close of 1872 his Holiness delivered an allocution, in which he touched on the "persecution of the Church in the German Empire," and asserted that the Church alone has a right to fix the limits between its domain and that of the state—a dangerous and inadmissible principle, since under the term morals the Church comprises all the relations of men to each other, and asserts that whatever does not assist her oppresses her. Hereupon, a few days subsequently (January 9, 1873), four laws were brought forward by the government: 1. Regulating the means by which a person might sever his connection with the Church; 2. Restricting the Church in the exercise of ecclesiastical punishments; 3. Regulating the ecclesiastical power of discipline, forbidding bodily chastisement, regulating fines and banishments granting the privilege of an appeal to the Royal Court of Justice for Ecclesiastical Affairs, the decision of which is final; 4. Ordaining the preliminary education and appointment of priests. They must have had a satisfactory education, passed a public examination conducted by the state, and have a knowledge of philosophy, history, and German literature. Institutions refusing to be superintended by the state are to be closed.

These laws demonstrate that Germany is resolved that she will no longer be dictated to nor embarrassed by a few Italian noble families; that she will be master of her own house. She sees in the conflict, not an affair of religion or of conscience, but a struggle between the sovereignty of state legislation and the sovereignty of the Church. She treats the papacy not in the aspect of a religious, but of a political power, and is resolved that the declaration of the Prussian

Constitution shall be maintained, that "the exercise of religious freedom must not interfere with the duties of a citizen toward the community and the state."

DUAL GOVERNMENT IN EUROPE. With truth it is affirmed that the papacy is administered not oecumenically, not as a universal Church, for all the nations, but for the benefit of some Italian families. Look at its composition! It consists of pope, cardinal bishops, cardinal deacons, who at the present moment are all Italians; cardinal priests, nearly all Italians; ministers and secretaries of the Sacred Congregation in Rome, all Italians. France has not given a pope since the middle ages. It is the same with Austria, Portugal, Spain. In spite of all attempts to change this system of exclusion, to open the dignities of the Church to all Catholicism, no foreigner can reach the holy chair. It is recognized that the Church is a domain given by God to the princely Italian families. Of fifty-five members of the present College of Cardinals, forty are Italians—that is, thirty-two beyond their proper share.

The stumbling-block to the progress of Europe has been its dual system of government. So long as every nation had two sovereigns, a temporal one at home and a spiritual one in a foreign land—there being different temporal masters in different nations, but only one foreign master for all, the pontiff at Rome—how was it possible that history should present us with any thing more than a narrative of the strifes of these rival powers? Whoever will reflect on this state of things will see how it is that those nations which have shaken off the dual form of government are those which have made the greatest advance. He will discern what is the cause of the paralysis which has befallen France. On one hand she wishes to be the leader of Europe, on the other she clings to a dead past. For the sake of propitiating her ignorant classes, she enters upon lines of policy which her intelligence must condemn. So evenly balanced are the two sovereignties under which she lives, that sometimes one, sometimes the other, prevails; and not unfrequently the one uses the other as an engine for the accomplishment of its ends.

INTENTIONS OF THE POPE. But this dual system approaches its close. To the northern nations, less imaginative and less superstitious, it had long ago become intolerable; they rejected it summarily at the epoch of the Reformation, notwithstanding the protestations and pretensions of Rome, Russia, happier than the rest, has never acknowledged the influence of any foreign spiritual power. She gloried in her attachment to the ancient Greek rite, and saw in the papacy nothing more than a troublesome dissenter from the primitive faith. In America the temporal and the spiritual have been absolutely divorced—the latter is not permitted to have any thing to do with affairs of state, though in all other respects liberty is conceded to it. The condition of the New World also satisfies us that both forms of Christianity, Catholic and Protestant, have lost their expansive power; neither can pass beyond its long-established boundary-line—the Catholic republics remain Catholic, the Protestant Protestant. And among the latter the disposition to sectarian isolation is disappearing; persons of different denominations consort without hesitation together. They gather their current opinions from newspapers, not from the Church.

Pius IX., in the movements we have been considering, has had two objects in view: 1. The more thorough centralization of the papacy, with a spiritual autocrat assuming the prerogatives of God at its head; 2. Control over the intellectual development of the nations professing Christianity.

The logical consequence of the former of these is political intervention. He insists that in all cases the temporal must subordinate itself to the spiritual power; all laws inconsistent with the interests of the Church must be repealed. They are not binding on the faithful. In the preceding pages I have briefly related some of the complications that have already occurred in the attempt to maintain this policy.

THE SYLLABUS. I now come to the consideration of the manner in which the papacy proposes to establish its intellectual control; how it defines its relation to its antagonist, Science, and, seeking a restoration of the mediaeval condition, opposes modern civilization, and denounces modern society.

The Encyclical and Syllabus present the principles which it was the object of the Vatican Council to carry into practical effect. The Syllabus stigmatizes pantheism, naturalism, and absolute rationalism, denouncing such opinions as that God is the world; that there is no God other than Nature; that theological matters must be treated in the same manner as philosophical ones, that the methods and principles by which the old scholastic doctors cultivated theology are no longer suitable to the demands of the age and the progress of science; that every man is free to embrace and profess the religion he may believe to be true, guided by the light of his reason; that it appertains to the civil power to define what are the rights and limits in which the Church may exercise authority; that the Church has not the right of availing herself of force or any direct or indirect temporal power; that the Church ought to be separated from the state and the state from the Church; that it is no longer expedient that the Catholic religion shall be held as the only religion of the state, to the exclusion of all other modes of worship; that persons coming to reside in Catholic countries have a right to the public exercise of their own worship; that the Roman pontiff can and ought to reconcile himself to, and agree with, the progress of modern civilization. The Syllabus claims the right of the Church to control public schools, and denies the right of the state in that respect; it claims the control over marriage and divorce.

Such of these principles as the Council found expedient at present to formularize, were set forth by it in "The Dogmatic Constitution of the Catholic Faith." The essential points of this constitution, more especially as regards the relations of religion to science, we have now to examine. It will be understood that the following does not present the entire document, but only an abstract of what appear to be its more important parts.

CONSTITUTION OF CATHOLIC FAITH. This definition opens with a severe review of the principles and consequences of the Protestant Reformation:

"The rejection of the divine authority of the Church to teach, and the subjection of all things belonging to religion to the judgment of each individual, have led to the production of many sects, and, as these differed and disputed with each other, all belief in Christ was overthrown in the minds of not a few, and the Holy Scriptures began to be counted as myths and fables. Christianity has been rejected, and the reign of mere Reason as they call it, or Nature, substituted; many falling into the abyss of pantheism, materialism, and atheism, and, repudiating the reasoning nature of man, and every rule of right and wrong, they are laboring to overthrow the very foundations of human society. As this impious heresy is spreading everywhere, not a few Catholics have been inveigled by it. They have confounded human science and divine faith.

"But the Church, the Mother and Mistress of nations, is ever ready to strengthen the weak, to take to her bosom those that return, and carry them on to better things. And, now the bishops of the whole world being gathered together in this Oecumenical Council, and the Holy Ghost sitting therein, and judging with us, we have determined to declare from this chair of St. Peter the saving doctrine of Christ, and proscribe and condemn the opposing errors.

"OF GOD, THE CREATOR OF ALL THINGS.—The Holy Catholic Apostolic Roman

Church believes that there is one true and living God, Creator and Lord of Heaven and Earth, Almighty, Eternal, Immense, Incomprehensible, Infinite in understanding and will, and in all perfection. He is distinct from the world. Of his own most free counsel he made alike out of nothing two created creatures, a spiritual and a temporal, angelic and earthly. Afterward he made the human nature, composed of both. Moreover, God by his providence protects and governs all things, reaching from end to end mightily, and ordering all things harmoniously. Every thing is open to his eyes, even things that come to pass by the free action of his creatures."

"OF REVELATION.—The Holy Mother Church holds that God can be known with certainty by the natural light of human reason, but that it has also pleased him to reveal himself and the eternal decrees of his will in a supernatural way. This supernatural revelation, as declared by the Holy Council of Trent, is contained in the books of the Old and New Testament, as enumerated in the decrees of that Council, and as are to be had in the old Vulgate Latin edition. These are sacred because they were written under the inspiration of the Holy Ghost. They have God for their author, and as such have been delivered to the Church.

"And, in order to restrain restless spirits, who may give erroneous explanations, it is decreed—renewing the decision of the Council of Trent—that no one may interpret the sacred Scriptures contrary to the sense in which they are interpreted by Holy Mother Church, to whom such interpretation belongs."

"OF FAITH.—Inasmuch as man depends on God as his Lord, and created reason is wholly subject to uncreated truth, he is bound when God makes a revelation to obey it by faith. This faith is a supernatural virtue, and the beginning of man's salvation who believes revealed things to be true, not for their intrinsic truth as seen by the natural light of reason, but for the authority of God in revealing them. But, nevertheless that faith might be agreeable to reason, God willed to join miracles and prophecies, which, showing forth his omnipotence and knowledge, are proofs suited to the understanding of all. Such we have in Moses and the prophets, and above all in Christ. Now, all those things are to be believed which are written in the word of God, or handed down by tradition, which the Church by her teaching has proposed for belief.

"No one can be justified without this faith, nor shall any one, unless he persevere therein to the end, attain everlasting life. Hence God, through his only-begotten Son, has established the Church as the guardian and teacher of his revealed word. For only to the Catholic Church do all those signs belong which make evident the credibility of the Christian faith. Nay, more, the very Church herself, in view of her wonderful propagation, her eminent holiness, her exhaustless fruitfulness in all that is good, her Catholic unity, her unshaken stability, offers a great and evident claim to belief, and an undeniable proof of her divine mission. Thus the Church shows to her children that the faith they hold rests on a most solid foundation. Wherefore, totally unlike is the condition of those who, by the heavenly gift of faith, have embraced the Catholic truth, and of those who, led by human opinions, are following, a false religion."

"OF FAITH AND REASON.—Moreover, the Catholic Church has ever held and now holds that there exists a twofold order of knowledge, each of which is distinct from the other, both as to its principle and its object. As to its principle, because in the one we know by natural reason, in the other by divine faith; as to the object, because, besides those things which our natural reason can attain, there are proposed to our belief mysteries hidden in God, which, unless by him revealed, cannot come to our knowledge.

"Reason, indeed, enlightened by faith, and seeking, with diligence and godly sobriety, may, by

God's gift, come to some understanding, limited in degree, but most wholesome in its effects, of mysteries, both from the analogy of things which are naturally known and from the connection of the mysteries themselves with one another and with man's last end. But never can reason be rendered capable of thoroughly understanding mysteries as it does those truths which form its proper object. For God's mysteries, in their very nature, so far surpass the reach of created intellect, that, even when taught by revelation and received by faith, they remain covered by faith itself, as by a veil, and shrouded, as it were, in darkness as long as in this mortal life.

"But, although faith be above reason, there never can be a real disagreement between them, since the same God who reveals mysteries and infuses faith has given man's soul the light of reason, and God cannot deny himself, nor can one truth ever contradict another. Wherefore the empty shadow of such contradiction arises chiefly from this, that either the doctrines of faith are not understood and set forth as the Church really holds them, or that the vain devices and opinions of men are mistaken for the dictates of reason. We therefore pronounce false every assertion which is contrary to the enlightened truth of faith. Moreover, the Church, which, together with her apostolic office of teaching, is charged also with the guardianship of the deposits of faith, holds likewise from God the right and the duty to condemn 'knowledge, falsely so called,' 'lest any man be cheated by philosophy and vain deceit.' Hence all the Christian faithful are not only forbidden to defend, as legitimate conclusions of science, those opinions which are known to be contrary to the doctrine of faith, especially when condemned by the Church, but are rather absolutely bound to hold them for errors wearing the deceitful appearance of truth."

THE VATICAN ANATHEMAS. "Not only is it impossible for faith and reason ever to contradict each other, but they rather afford each other mutual assistance. For right reason establishes the foundation of faith, and, by the aid of its light, cultivates the science of divine things; and faith, on the other hand, frees and preserves reason from errors, and enriches it with knowledge of many kinds. So far, then, is the Church from opposing the culture of human arts and sciences, that she rather aids and promotes it in many ways. For she is not ignorant of nor does she despise the advantages which flow from them to the life of man; on the contrary, she acknowledges that, as they sprang from God, the Lord of knowledge, so, if they be rightly pursued, they will, through the aid of his grace, lead to God. Nor does she forbid any of those sciences the use of its own principles and its own method within its own proper sphere; but, recognizing this reasonable freedom, she takes care that they may not, by contradicting God's teaching, fall into errors, or, overstepping the due limits, invade or throw into confusion the domain of faith.

"For the doctrine of faith revealed by God has not been proposed, like some philosophical discovery, to be made perfect by human ingenuity, but it has been delivered to the spouse of Christ as a divine deposit, to be faithfully guarded and unerringly set forth. Hence, all tenets of holy faith are to be explained always according to the sense and meaning of the Church; nor is it ever lawful to depart therefrom under pretense or color of a more enlightened explanation. Therefore, as generations and centuries roll on, let the understanding, knowledge, and wisdom of each and every one, of individuals and of the whole Church, grow apace and increase exceedingly, yet only in its kind; that is to say retaining pure and inviolate the sense and meaning and belief of the same doctrine."

Among other canons the following were promulgated.

"Let him be anathema—

"Who denies the one true God, Creator and Lord of all things, visible and invisible.

"Who unblushingly affirms that, besides matter, nothing else exists.

"Who says that the substance or essence of God, and of all things, is one and the same.

"Who says that finite things, both corporeal and spiritual, or at least spiritual things, are emanations of the divine substance; or that the divine essence, by manifestation or development of itself, becomes all things.

"Who does not acknowledge that the world and all things which it contains were produced by God out of nothing.

"Who shall say that man can and ought to, of his own efforts, by means of, constant progress, arrive, at last, at the possession of all truth and goodness.

"Who shall refuse to receive, for sacred and canonical, the books of Holy Scripture in their integrity, with all their parts, according as they were enumerated by the holy Council of Trent, or shall deny that they are Inspired by God.

"Who shall say that human reason is in such wise independent, that faith cannot be demanded of it by God.

"Who shall say that divine revelation cannot be rendered credible by external evidences.

"Who shall say that no miracles can be wrought, or that they can never be known with certainty, and that the divine origin of Christianity cannot be proved by them.

"Who shall say that divine revelation includes no mysteries, but that all the dogmas of faith may be understood and demonstrated by reason duly cultivated.

"Who shall say that human sciences ought to be pursued in such a spirit of freedom that one may be allowed to hold as true their assertions, even when opposed to revealed doctrine.

"Who shall say that it may at any time come to pass, in the progress of science, that the doctrines set forth by the Church must be taken in another sense than that in which the Church has ever received and yet receives them."

THE EVANGELICAL ALLIANCE. The extraordinary and, indeed, it may be said, arrogant assumptions contained in these decisions were far from being received with satisfaction by educated Catholics. On the part of the German universities there was resistance; and, when, at the close of the year, the decrees of the Vatican Council were generally acquiesced in, it was not through conviction of their truth, but through a disciplinary sense of obedience.

By many of the most pious Catholics the entire movement and the results to which it had led were looked upon with the sincerest sorrow. Pere Hyacinthe, in a letter to the superior of his order, says: "I protest against the divorce, as impious as it is insensate, sought to be effected between the Church, which is our eternal mother, and the society of the nineteenth century, of which we are the temporal children, and toward which we have also duties and regards. It is my most profound conviction that, if France in particular, and the Latin race in general, are given up to social, moral, and religious anarchy, the principal cause undoubtedly is not Catholicism itself, but the manner in which Catholicism has for a long time been understood and practised."

Notwithstanding his infallibility, which implies omniscience, his Holiness did not foresee the issue of the Franco-Prussian War. Had the prophetical talent been vouchsafed to him, he would have detected the inopportuneness of the acts of his Council. His request to the King of Prussia for military aid to support his temporal power was denied. The excommunicated King of Italy, as we have seen, took possession of Rome. A bitter papal encyclical, strangely contrasting with the courteous politeness of modern state-papers, was issued, November 1,

1870, denouncing the acts of the Piedmontese court, "which had followed the counsel of the sects of perdition." In this his Holiness declares that he is in captivity, and that he will have no agreement with Belial. He pronounces the greater excommunication, with censures and penalties, against his antagonists, and prays for "the intercession of the immaculate Virgin Mary, mother of God, and that of the blessed apostles Peter and Paul."

Of the various Protestant denominations, several had associated themselves, for the purposes of consultation, under the designation of the Evangelical Alliance. Their last meeting was held in New York, in the autumn of 1873. Though, in this meeting, were gathered together many pious representatives of the Reformed Churches, European and American, it had not the prestige nor the authority of the Great Council that had just previously closed its sessions in St. Peters, at Rome. It could not appeal to an unbroken ancestry of far more than a thousand years; it could not speak with the authority of an equal and, indeed, of a superior to emperors and kings. While profound intelligence and a statesmanlike, worldly wisdom gleamed in every thing that the Vatican Council had done, the Evangelical Alliance met without a clear and precise view of its objects, without any definitely-marked intentions. Its wish was to draw into closer union the various Protestant Churches, but it had no well-grounded hope of accomplishing that desirable result. It illustrated the necessary working, of the principle on which those Churches originated. They were founded on dissent and exist by separation.

Yet in the action of the Evangelical Alliance may be discerned certain very impressive facts. It averted its eyes from its ancient antagonist—that antagonist which had so recently loaded the Reformation with contumely and denunciation—it fastened them, as the Vatican Council had done, on Science. Under that dreaded name there stood before it what seemed to be a spectre of uncertain form, of hourly-dilating proportions, of threatening aspect. Sometimes the Alliance addressed this stupendous apparition in words of courtesy, sometimes in tones of denunciation.

THE VATICAN CONSTITUTION CRITICISED. The Alliance failed to perceive that modern Science is the legitimate sister—indeed, it is the twin-sister—of the Reformation. They were begotten together and were born together. It failed to perceive that, though there is an impossibility of bringing into coalition the many conflicting sects, they may all find in science a point of connection; and that, not a distrustful attitude toward it, but a cordial union with it, is their true policy.

It remains now to offer some reflections on this "Constitution of the Catholic Faith," as defined by the Vatican Council.

For objects to present themselves under identical relations to different persons, they must be seen from the same point of view. In the instance we are now considering, the religious man has his own especial station; the scientific man another, a very different one. It is not for either to demand that his co-observer shall admit that the panorama of facts spread before them is actually such as it appears to him to be.

The Dogmatic Constitution insists on the admission of this postulate, that the Roman Church acts under a divine commission, specially and exclusively delivered to it. In virtue of that great authority, it requires of all men the surrender of their intellectual convictions, and of all nations the subordination of their civil power.

But a claim so imposing must be substantiated by the most decisive and unimpeachable credentials; proofs, not only of an implied and indirect kind, but clear, emphatic, and to the point; proofs that it would be impossible to call in question.

The Church, however, declares, that she will not submit her claim to the arbitrament of human reason; she demands that it shall be at once conceded as an article of faith.

If this be admitted, all bar requirements must necessarily be assented to, no matter how exorbitant they may be.

With strange inconsistency the Dogmatic Constitution deprecates reason, affirming that it cannot determine the points under consideration, and yet submits to it arguments for adjudication. In truth, it might be said that the whole composition is a passionate plea to Reason to stultify itself in favor of Roman Christianity.

With points of view so widely asunder, it is impossible that Religion and Science should accord in their representation of things. Nor can any conclusion in common be reached, except by an appeal to Reason as a supreme and final judge.

There are many religions in the world, some of them of more venerable antiquity, some having far more numerous adherents, than the Roman. How can a selection be made among them, except by such an appeal to Reason? Religion and Science must both submit their claims and their dissensions to its arbitrament.

Against this the Vatican Council protests. It exalts faith to a superiority over reason; it says that they constitute two separate orders of knowledge, having respectively for their objects mysteries and facts. Faith deals with mysteries, reason with facts. Asserting the dominating superiority of faith, it tries to satisfy the reluctant mind with miracles and prophecies.

On the other hand, Science turns away from the incomprehensible, and rests herself on the maxim of Wiclif: "God forceth not a man to believe that which he cannot understand." In the absence of an exhibition of satisfactory credentials on the part of her opponent, she considers whether there be in the history of the papacy, and in the biography of the popes, any thing that can adequately sustain a divine commission, any thing that can justify pontifical infallibility, or extort that unhesitating obedience which is due to the vice-God.

One of the most striking and yet contradictory features of the Dogmatic Constitution is, the reluctant homage it pays to the intelligence of man. It presents a definition of the philosophical basis of Catholicism, but it veils from view the repulsive features of the vulgar faith. It sets forth the attributes of God, the Creator of all things, in words fitly designating its sublime conception, but it abstains from affirming that this most awful and eternal Being was born of an earthly mother, the wife of a Jewish carpenter, who has since become the queen of heaven. The God it depicts is not the God of the middle ages, seated on his golden throne, surrounded by choirs of angels, but the God of Philosophy. The Constitution has nothing to say about the Trinity, nothing of the worship due to the Virgin—on the contrary, that is by implication sternly condemned; nothing about transubstantiation, or the making of the flesh and blood of God by the priest; nothing of the invocation of the saints. It bears on its face subordination to the thought of the age, the impress of the intellectual progress of man.

THE PASSAGE OF EUROPE TO LLAMAISM. Such being the exposition rendered to us respecting the attributes of God, it next instructs us as to his mode of government of the world. The Church asserts that she possesses a supernatural control over all material and moral events. The priesthood, in its various grades, can determine issues of the future, either by the exercise of its inherent attributes, or by its influential invocation of the celestial powers. To the sovereign pontiff it has been given to bind or loose at his pleasure. It is unlawful to appeal from his judgments to an Oecumenical Council, as if to an earthly arbiter superior to him. Powers such as these are consistent with arbitrary rule, but they are inconsistent with the government of the world by immutable law. Hence the Dogmatic Constitution plants itself firmly in behalf of incessant providential interventions; it will not for a moment admit that in natural things there is an irresistible sequence of events, or in the affairs of men an unavoidable course of acts.

But has not the order of civilization in all parts of the world been the same? Does not the growth of society resemble individual growth? Do not both exhibit to us phases of youth, of maturity, of decrepitude? To a person who has carefully considered the progressive civilization of groups of men in regions of the earth far apart, who has observed the identical forms under which that advancing civilization has manifested itself, is it not clear that the procedure is determined by law? The religious ideas of the Incas of Peru and the emperors of Mexico, and the ceremonials of their court-life, were the same as those in Europe—the same as those in Asia. The current of thought had been the same. A swarm of bees carried to some distant land will build its combs and regulate its social institutions as other unknown swarms would do, and so with separated and disconnected swarms of men. So invariable is this sequence of thought and act, that there are philosophers who, transferring the past example offered by Asiatic history to the case of Europe, would not hesitate to sustain the proposition—given a bishop of Rome and some centuries, and you will have an infallible pope: given an infallible pope and a little more time, and you will have Llamaism—Llamaism to which Asia has long, ago attained.

As to the origin of corporeal and spiritual things, the Dogmatic Constitution adds a solemn emphasis to its declarations, by anathematizing all those who hold the doctrine of emanation, or who believe that visible Nature is only a manifestation of the Divine Essence. In this its authors had a task of no ordinary difficulty before them. They must encounter those formidable ideas, whether old or new, which in our times are so strongly forcing themselves on thoughtful men. The doctrine of the conservation and correlation of Force yields as its logical issue the time-worn Oriental emanation theory; the doctrines of Evolution and Development strike at that of successive creative acts. The former rests on the fundamental principle that the quantity of force in the universe is invariable. Though that quantity can neither be increased nor diminished, the forms under which Force expresses itself may be transmuted into each other. As yet this doctrine has not received complete scientific demonstration, but so numerous and so cogent are the arguments adduced in its behalf, that it stands in an imposing, almost in an authoritative attitude. Now, the Asiatic theory of emanation and absorption is seen to be in harmony with this grand idea. It does not hold that, at the conception of a human being, a soul is created by God out of nothing and given to it, but that a portion of the already existing, the divine, the universal intelligence, is imparted, and, when life is over, this returns to and is absorbed in the general source from which it originally came. The authors of the Constitution forbid these ideas to be held, under pain of eternal punishment.

In like manner they dispose of the doctrines of Evolution and Development, bluntly insisting that the Church believes in distinct creative acts. The doctrine that every living form is derived from some preceding form is scientifically in a much more advanced position than that concerning Force, and probably may be considered as established, whatever may become of the additions with which it has recently been overlaid.

In her condemnation of the Reformation, the Church carries into effect her ideas of the subordination of reason to faith. In her eyes the Reformation is an impious heresy, leading to the abyss of pantheism, materialism, and atheism, and tending to overthrow the very foundations of human society. She therefore would restrain those "restless spirits" who, following Luther, have upheld the "right of every man to interpret the Scriptures for himself." She asserts that it is a wicked error to admit Protestants to equal political privileges with Catholics, and that to coerce them and suppress them is a sacred duty; that it is abominable to permit them to establish educational institutions. Gregory XVI. denounced freedom of conscience as an insane folly, and the freedom of the press a pestilent error, which cannot be sufficiently detested.

But how is it possible to recognize an inspired and infallible oracle on the Tiber, when it is remembered that again and again successive popes have contradicted each other; that popes have denounced councils, and councils have denounced popes; that the Bible of Sixtus V. had so many admitted errors—nearly two thousand—that its own authors had to recall it? How is it possible for the children of the Church to regard as "delusive errors" the globular form of the earth, her position as a planet in the solar system, her rotation on her axis, her movement round the sun? How can they deny that there are antipodes, and other worlds than ours? How can they believe that the world was made out of nothing, completed in a week, finished just as we see it now; that it has undergone no change, but that its parts have worked so indifferently as to require incessant interventions?

THE ERRORS OF ECCLESIASTICISM. When Science is thus commanded to surrender her intellectual convictions, may she not ask the ecclesiastic to remember the past? The contest respecting the figure of the earth, and the location of heaven and hell, ended adversely to him. He affirmed that the earth is an extended plane, and that the sky is a firmament, the floor of heaven, through which again and again persons have been seen to ascend. The globular form demonstrated beyond any possibility of contradiction by astronomical facts, and by the voyage of Magellan's ship, he then maintained that it is the central body of the universe, all others being in subordination to it, and it the grand object of God's regard. Forced from this position, he next affirmed that it is motionless, the sun and the stars actually revolving, as they apparently do, around it. The invention of the telescope proved that here again he was in error. Then he maintained that all the motions of the solar system are regulated by providential intervention; the "Principia" of Newton demonstrated that they are due to irresistible law. He then affirmed that the earth and all the celestial bodies were created about six thousand years ago, and that in six days the order of Nature was settled, and plants and animals in their various tribes introduced. Constrained by the accumulating mass of adverse evidence, he enlarged his days into periods of indefinite length—only, however, to find that even this device was inadequate. The six ages, with their six special creations, could no longer be maintained, when it was discovered that species, slowly emerged in one age, reached a culmination in a second, and gradually died out in a third: this overlapping from age to age would not only have demanded creations, but re-creations also. He affirmed that there had been a deluge, which covered the whole earth above the tops of the highest mountains, and that the waters of this flood were removed by a wind. Correct ideas respecting the dimensions of the atmosphere, and of the sea, and of the operation of evaporation, proved how untenable these statements are. Of the progenitors of the human race, he declared that they had come from their Maker's hand perfect, both in body and mind, and had subsequently experienced a fall. He is now considering how best to dispose of the evidence continually accumulating respecting the savage condition of prehistoric man.

Is it at all surprising that the number of those who hold the opinions of the Church in light esteem should so rapidly increase? How can that be received as a trustworthy guide in the invisible, which falls into so many errors in the visible? How can that give confidence in the moral, the spiritual, which has so signally failed in the physical? It is not possible to dispose of these conflicting facts as "empty shadows," "vain devices," "fictions coming from knowledge falsely so called," "errors wearing the deceitful appearance of truth," as the Church stigmatizes them. On the contrary, they are stern witnesses, bearing emphatic and unimpeachable testimony against the ecclesiastical claim to infallibility, and fastening a conviction of ignorance and blindness upon her.

Convicted of so many errors, the papacy makes no attempt at explanation. It ignores the whole matter Nay, more, relying on the efficacy of audacity, though confronted by these facts, it lays claim to infallibility.

SEPARATION OF CATHOLICISM AND CIVILIZATION. But, to the pontiff, no other rights can be conceded than those he can establish at the bar of Reason. He cannot claim infallibility in religious affairs, and decline it in scientific. Infallibility embraces all things. It implies omniscience. If it holds good for theology, it necessarily holds good for science. How is it possible to coordinate the infallibility of the papacy with the well-known errors into which it has fallen?

Does it not, then, become needful to reject the claim of the papacy to the employment of coercion in the maintenance of its opinions; to repudiate utterly the declaration that "the Inquisition is an urgent necessity in view of the unbelief of the present age," and in the name of human nature to protest loudly against the ferocity and terrorism of that institution? Has not conscience inalienable rights?

An impassable and hourly-widening gulf intervenes between Catholicism and the spirit of the age. Catholicism insists that blind faith is superior to reason; that mysteries are of more importance than facts. She claims to be the sole interpreter of Nature and revelation, the supreme arbiter of knowledge; she summarily rejects all modern criticism of the Scriptures, and orders the Bible to be accepted in accordance with the views of the theologians of Trent; she openly avows her hatred of free institutions and constitutional systems, and declares that those are in damnable error who regard the reconciliation of the pope with modern civilization as either possible or desirable.

SCIENCE AND PROTESTANTISM. But the spirit of the age demands—is the human intellect to be subordinated to the Tridentine Fathers, or to the fancy of illiterate and uncritical persons who wrote in the earlier ages of the Church? It sees no merit in blind faith, but rather distrusts it. It looks forward to an improvement in the popular canon of credibility for a decision between fact and fiction. It does not consider itself bound to believe fables and falsehoods that have been invented for ecclesiastical ends. It finds no argument in behalf of their truth, that traditions and legends have been long-lived; in this respect, those of the Church are greatly inferior to the fables of paganism. The longevity of the Church itself is not due to divine protection or intervention, but to the skill with which it has adapted its policy to existing circumstances. If antiquity be the criterion of authenticity, the claims of Buddhism must be respected; it has the superior warrant of many centuries. There can be no defense of those deliberate falsifications of history, that concealment of historical facts, of which the Church has so often taken advantage. In these things the end does not justify the means.

Then has it in truth come to this, that Roman Christianity and Science are recognized by their respective adherents as being absolutely incompatible; they cannot exist together; one must yield to the other; mankind must make its choice—it cannot have both.

SCIENCE AND FAITH. While such is, perhaps, the issue as regards Catholicism, a reconciliation of the Reformation with Science is not only possible, but would easily take place, if the Protestant Churches would only live up to the maxim taught by Luther, and established by so many years of war. That maxim is, the right of private interpretation of the Scriptures. It was the foundation of intellectual liberty. But, if a personal interpretation of the book of Revelation is permissible, how can it be denied in the case of the book of Nature? In the misunderstandings that have taken place, we must ever bear in mind the infirmities of men. The generations that immediately followed the Reformation may perhaps be excused for not comprehending the full significance of their cardinal principle, and for not on all occasions carrying it into effect. When Calvin caused Servetus, to be burnt, he was animated, not by the principles of the Reformation, but by those of Catholicism, from which he had not been able to emancipate himself completely. And when the clergy of influential Protestant confessions have stigmatized the investigators of Nature as infidels and atheists, the same may be said. For Catholicism to reconcile itself to Science, there are formidable, perhaps insuperable obstacles in the way. For Protestantism to achieve that great result there are not. In the one case there is a bitter, a mortal animosity to be overcome; in the other, a friendship, that misunderstandings have alienated, to be restored.

CIVILIZATION AND RELIGION. But, whatever may be the preparatory incidents of that great impending intellectual crisis which Christendom must soon inevitably witness, of this we may rest assured, that the silent secession from the public faith, which in so ominous a manner characterizes the present generation, will find at length political expression. It is not without significance that France reenforces the ultramontane tendencies of her lower population, by the promotion of pilgrimages, the perpetration of miracles, the exhibition of celestial apparitions. Constrained to do this by her destiny, she does it with a blush. It is not without significance that Germany resolves to rid herself of the incubus of a dual government, by the exclusion of the Italian element, and to carry to its completion that Reformation which three centuries ago she left unfinished. The time approaches when men must take their choice between quiescent, immobile faith and ever-advancing Science—faith, with its mediaeval consolations, Science, which is incessantly scattering its material blessings in the pathway of life, elevating the lot of man in this world, and unifying the human race. Its triumphs are solid and enduring. But the glory which Catholicism might gain from a conflict with material ideas is at the best only like that of other celestial meteors when they touch the atmosphere of the earth—transitory and useless.

Though Guizot's affirmation that the Church has always sided with despotism is only too true, it must be remembered that in the policy she follows there is much of political necessity. She is urged on by the pressure of nineteen centuries. But, if the irresistible indicates itself in her action, the inevitable manifests itself in her life. For it is with the papacy as with a man. It has passed through the struggles of infancy, it has displayed the energies of maturity, and, its work completed, it must sink into the feebleness and querulousness of old age. Its youth can never be renewed. The influence of its souvenirs alone will remain. As pagan Rome threw her departing shadow over the empire and tinctured all its thoughts, so Christian Rome casts her parting shadow over Europe.

INADMISSIBLE CLAIMS OF CATHOLICISM. Will modern civilization consent to abandon the career of advancement which has given it so much power and happiness? Will it consent to retrace its steps to the semi-barbarian ignorance and superstition of the middle ages?

Will it submit to the dictation of a power, which, claiming divine authority, can present no adequate credentials of its office; a power which kept Europe in a stagnant condition for many centuries, ferociously suppressing by the stake and the sword every attempt at progress; a power that is founded in a cloud of mysteries; that sets itself above reason and common-sense; that loudly proclaims the hatred it entertains against liberty of thought and freedom in civil institutions; that professes its intention of repressing the one and destroying the other whenever it can find the opportunity; that denounces as most pernicious and insane the opinion that liberty of conscience and of worship is the right of every man; that protests against that right being proclaimed and asserted by law in every well-governed state; that contemptuously repudiates the principle that the will of the people, manifested by public opinion (as it is called) or by other means, shall constitute law; that refuses to every man any title to opinion in matters of religion, but holds that it is simply his duty to believe what he is told by the Church, and to obey her commands; that will not permit any temporal government to define the rights and prescribe limits to the authority of the Church; that declares it not only may but will resort to force to discipline disobedient individuals; that invades the sanctify of private life, by making, at the confessional, the wife and daughters and servants of one suspected, spies and informers against him; that tries him without an accuser, and by torture makes him bear witness against himself; that denies the right of parents to educate their children outside of its own Church, and insists that to it alone belongs the supervision of domestic life and the control of marriages and divorces; that denounces "the impudence" of those who presume to subordinate the authority of the Church to the civil authority, or who advocate the separation of the Church from the state; that absolutely repudiates all toleration, and affirms that the Catholic religion is entitled to be held as the only religion in every country, to the exclusion of all other modes of worship; that requires all laws standing in the way of its interests to be repealed, and, if that be refused, orders all its followers to disobey them?

ISSUE OF THE CONFLICT. This power, conscious that it can work no miracle to serve itself, does not hesitate to disturb society by its intrigues against governments, and seeks to accomplish its ends by alliances with despotism.

Claims such as these mean a revolt against modern civilization, an intention of destroying it, no matter at what social cost. To submit to them without resistance, men must be slaves indeed!

As to the issue of the coming conflict, can any one doubt? Whatever is resting on fiction and fraud will be overthrown. Institutions that organize impostures and spread delusions must show what right they have to exist. Faith must render an account of herself to Reason. Mysteries must give place to facts. Religion must relinquish that imperious, that domineering position which she has so long maintained against Science. There must be absolute freedom for thought. The ecclesiastic must learn to keep himself within the domain he has chosen, and cease to tyrannize over the philosopher, who, conscious of his own strength and the purity of his motives, will bear such interference no longer. What was written by Esdras near the willow-fringed rivers of Babylon, more than twenty-three centuries ago, still holds good: "As for Truth it endureth and is always strong; it liveth and conquereth for evermore."

Printed by Amazon Italia Logistica S.r.l.
Torrazza Piemonte (TO), Italy

11646868R00103